UNCEASING STRIFE, UNENDING FEAR

UNCEASING STRIFE, UNENDING FEAR

JACQUES DE THÉRINES AND THE FREEDOM OF THE CHURCH IN THE AGE OF THE LAST CAPETIANS

William Chester Jordan

PRINCETON UNIVERSITY PRESS

PRINCETON AND OXFORD

LIBRARY OF CONGRESS CATALOGING-IN-PUBLICATION DATA
JORDAN, WILLIAM C., 1948–
UNCEASING STRIFE, UNENDING FEAR :
JACQUES DE THÉRINES AND THE FREEDOM OF THE CHURCH
IN THE AGE OF THE LAST
CAPETIANS / WILLIAM CHESTER JORDAN.
P.   CM.
INCLUDES BIBLIOGRAPHICAL REFERENCES AND INDEX.
ISBN: 0-691-12120-6 (ALK. PAPER)
1. DE THÉRINES, JACQUES. 2. FRANCE—CHURCH HISTORY.
3. CHURCH HISTORY—MIDDLE AGES, 600–1500. I. TITLE.

BX4705.D4285J67 2005
282'.44'09022—DC22   2004053455

BRITISH LIBRARY CATALOGING-IN-PUBLICATION DATA IS AVAILABLE

THIS BOOK HAS BEEN COMPOSED IN GALLIARD

PRINTED ON ACID-FREE PAPER. ∞

PUP.PRINCETON.EDU

PRINTED IN THE UNITED STATES OF AMERICA

1 3 5 7 9 10 8 6 4 2

For Mom, . . . , Urban, Vicky, John, Clare, Lorna
and
to the memory of John Bell Henneman and Charles T. Wood,
good friends and fine scholars

CONTENTS

PREFACE

USING THE CAREER of the French churchman Jacques de Thérines, this book retells some of the most dramatic episodes in the history of French ecclesiastical politics in the early fourteenth century. The period experienced the notorious and ultimately violent confrontation of Pope Boniface VIII and King Philip IV the Fair over the limits of royal and papal power, what Brian Tierney in a widely read book called "the Struggle of Church and State." It was also the era when the French crown moved savagely but efficiently in expelling its Jews and, with greater savagery and equal efficiency, in destroying the Order of the Knights Templars. With comparable determination and violence, ecclesiastical princes of the period, especially Pope John XXII, imposed punishments on radical critics of the church's wealth. The age also witnessed the papacy's relocation to Avignon (an act that would later be likened to the Babylonian Captivity of the ancient Jews), revolutionary aristocratic movements in opposition to the French crown's authoritarianism, and the crisis of the Great Famine, when both crown and ecclesiastical resources were stretched to the limit in the attempt to succor the poor and forestall social revolution. Jacques de Thérines played a significant and often critical role in nearly every one of these events, often at considerable personal risk. Yet he died peacefully, having lived, so his epitaph insists, the "model of a pious life."

Despite his importance, very few scholarly studies give much space to Jacques. The best biographical sketch is that of Noël Valois, published in 1914 in the thirty-fourth volume of the *Histoire littéraire de la France*. No one knew as much about Jacques de Thérines as Valois or had more closely studied his works. His masterful summaries of these writings in that publication and his edition of one of the works some years before in the great archival and historical journal *Bibliothèque de l'Ecole de Chartes* have in large part provided the raw material for subsequent scholars, even though two of Jacques de Thérines's treatises were already partly available in early modern editions. One major source, Jacques's scholastic writings—summarized briefly by Valois but at the time still unpublished—received an edition in 1958, a fruit of Palémon Glorieux's extraordinary project to print the works of the medieval faculty of theology at the University of Paris, where Jacques studied and taught for many years. The result was an edition of three hundred pages in closely packed type. At least two more of Jacques's treatises, more polemical than scholastic, remain unpublished. I have been helped by Valois's summaries of these and of all the works (it is frighteningly hard not to mimic his prose, since he usually keeps very close to his subject's *ipsissima verba*), but for the unpublished works in particular I have consulted manuscript versions and quoted them if the language helps give the flavor of the discourse. Where editions or even partial editions exist, I quote from these (reluctantly maintaining early modern editors' classicizing spellings), since I am presuming that the reader will have readier access to them than to the manuscripts themselves or microfilms of them.

Ninety years is a long time in scholarship, but there is still a freshness and vigor to Valois's study, and his clarifications of difficult points, though not invariably persuasive, have an authoritative quality about them. Nonetheless, the *Histoire littéraire*'s format was very constricted, typically a brief essay on the author's life, followed by summaries of his works along with incipits and explicits of the various manuscripts. The emphasis was also narrowly and traditionally literary, as the title implies. In Jacques de Thérines's case, this meant that Valois was obliged to neglect or merely sketch aspects of his life that the commission directing the *Histoire littéraire* regarded as largely irrelevant to his literary output. Yet as a Cistercian monk, Jacques pursued a career that took him to the headship of two major Cistercian monasteries in France, Chaalis and Pontigny, and to a remarkable extent it is possible to reconstruct his role as an administrator and to interweave its story with the story of his intellectual and polemical pursuits.

Noël Valois died suddenly and unexpectedly a few months beyond the publication of the life-and-works biography of Jacques de Thérines in *Histoire littéraire*, so he never returned to the task of rounding out his portrait of Jacques in a different, less constricted forum. Palémon Glorieux had little interest in Jacques per se when he published the scholastic writings. His overarching desire was to provide scholars with still another cache of data for a future assessment of philosophical and theological discourses at the medieval University of Paris. In between these two giants of medieval scholarship, Jean-Berthold Mahn began to publish work on the Cistercians, particularly in France. This led him, through Noël Valois's studies, to Jacques de Thérines. Mahn's knowledge of Cistercian history was deep, and if he had turned his considerable talents to Jacques, he would have produced an impressive study, one whose substance, it seems reasonable to think, must have affected the character of the present book. But nearly all of Mahn's work was published posthumously. The young man, with his still new degree, joined the French army in 1939. After France fell to the Nazis, he returned to writing history briefly but joined the Resistance in the summer of 1943. He escaped France to North Africa, where he enlisted in a Free French unit. He was killed in Italy on 23 April 1944.

Aside from a few specialized students of Cistercian finance and Franco-Jewish history whose work will be cited in the pages to come, no one has paid much attention to Jacques de Thérines in a half century. For a while I was content to count myself among those few specialized students, but over time the references to Jacques de Thérines became so frequent in my research that I decided to look more thoroughly into his career. This book is the result. It seeks to remedy the neglect into which a fascinating man has unjustly fallen while at the same time letting Jacques's story serve as a connecting thread for a narrative of the often tragic, and always compelling, history of the early fourteenth century.

ACKNOWLEDGMENTS

I N DOING THE RESEARCH and writing for this book, I have benefited from being able to call on a number of graduate and undergradu-
ate students, who tracked down sources and helped in many other
ways: James Byrne, Elspeth Carruthers, Tina Enhoffer, Holly Grieco, Lee
Hadbavny, and especially Anne Lester, whose transformation from a student to a no-holds-barred critic took place while I was finishing the book.
The staffs of the Österreichische Nationalbibliothek (Vienna), the Bibliothèque Nationale Française (Paris), the Institut de Recherche et d'Histoire de Textes (Orléans), the Bibliothèque Municipale of Dijon, and the
Archives Départementales of the Yonne (Auxerre) provided microfilms,
when needed, as well as direct access to manuscripts, when this was required. The helpful staff and the ready availability of the magnificent collections of Speer Library of Princeton Theological Seminary and of the
Marquand and Firestone Libraries of Princeton University made the project feasible.

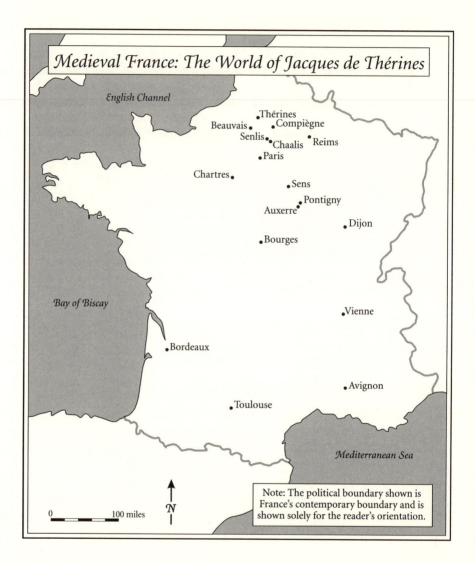

Medieval France: The World of Jacques de Thérines

English Channel

•Thérines
Beauvais• •Compiègne
Senlis• • •Reims
• •Chaalis
•Paris
Chartres•

•Sens
•Pontigny
Auxerre•
•Dijon
•Bourges

Bay of Biscay

•Vienne

•Bordeaux

•Avignon

•Toulouse

Mediterranean Sea

Note: The political boundary shown is
France's contemporary boundary and is
shown solely for the reader's orientation.

0 ———— 100 miles

N

1

ENCROACHMENTS ON ECCLESIASTICAL

AUTHORITY: TAXATION, CLERICAL IMMUNITY,

AND THE JEWS

T HE LITTLE FRENCH VILLAGE of Thérines, population 155, is located in the *département* of the Oise, the *arrondissement* of Beauvais, and the *canton* of Songeons. Its *code postal* is 60380. Despite its diminutive size, the village has a mayor (in the year 2000, it was M. Roland Vasseur), and his *mairie* has an official municipal telephone and fax machine. By the characteristic and exacting French bureaucratic standards that are the administrative legacy of the nation's history, Thérines has all it needs for its communal identity. What it does not have, however, is a history. Numerous Web sites exist for the French communes, designed largely for potential tourists and also for history buffs. The sites typically list a selection of published histories of the villages and cities they survey. There is no such history referenced for Thérines, and the Web site's invitation to browsers to help redress the lack has so far gone unanswered.

Unfortunately, the village's most illustrious son, a churchman named Jacques who flourished in the early fourteenth century, was effectively deracinated by early modern humanists, who misread the subscription, *Jacobus de Therinis*, on one of his Latin treatises as *Jacobus de Thermis*, a common enough kind of error.[1] Jacques was thereby transmogrified into Jacopo, an otherwise unattested scion of a prestigious Sicilian family with roots in Palermo and the nearby port of Termini (Latin, *Thermae*).[2] Not until the great early twentieth-century medievalist Noël Valois corrected the reading was Jacques recovered for France, although the good news has been slow in reaching his childhood home of Thérines.

The relocation of Jacques makes some aspects of his career far more commonplace than if a Sicilian lineage had been confirmed. No more the adventurous youth from the port of Termini determined on seeking his fortune in the alien north and abandoning forever the sea, the sunshine, and the fig trees of his homeland, Jacques emerges instead as a deeply rooted individual, geographically circumscribed all his life. Born in the second half of the thirteenth century, he spent most of his career in Paris and the territory bounded by the modern limits of the *département* of the Oise, which borders the Paris region, with only a few more distant trips, necessitated by the business of the church to whose service he gave his life.

If his family and neighbors were typical of the region's minor nobility from which monastic communities were very largely recruited, they attached themselves intimately to a small number of local ecclesiastical institutions.[3] To this extent, the episcopal city of Beauvais, from which Thérines is twenty or so miles distant, was a magnet for young men from aspiring village families.[4] The Cistercian monastery of Chaalis (*Karoli Locus*), founded in 1136, was one among several prestigious and attractive centers of monastic life in the region, too, and an unsurprising place as Jacques's choice for entering upon a clerical career. In turn, he became an example. It was at the monastery of Chaalis that another Thérines native, Jean, a bachelor in theology, served as a monk toward the end of Jacques's life; like Jacques he studied and entered upon a teaching career at Paris.[5] That such a tiny village produced similar careers in the same narrow geographical orbit in so brief an interval matches nicely the pattern in families and among neighbors observable elsewhere in northern France.[6]

Either with a privately hired tutor or under the care of the local parish priest or schoolmaster, Jacques learned the rudiments of reading and writing Latin. With his intellectual gifts, he was an obvious candidate to encourage toward further study, probably in the cathedral school of Beauvais with its fine library.[7] After professing as a monk in the Cistercian house of Chaalis, he spent considerable time at the Cistercian College of Saint-Bernard in Paris in order to complete his higher education and be accorded the title master (*magister*).[8] The college was the center of Cistercian learning in France and Christendom. The monks sent there and the scholars at other colleges of the university experienced a bubbling cauldron of rigorous learning, distracting activity, bitter rivalries, and intellectual arrogance. The experience had the potential to seduce many into a permanent desire for the academic life. It turned many others off to the posturing. And it provoked ambivalent feelings, comprising both repulsion and attraction, among still others. Among those at the university who heard bishops and papal legates denounce the excessive cleverness and intellectual daring of its leading scholars, not everyone responded negatively.[9]

No firm date can be given as to when Jacques came into this remarkable environment, where he was as likely to observe the king in procession to Notre Dame as he was to see a company of miserable beggars on the cathedral porch. He was in the city by 1293, the date of the death of Jean de Weerde, one of his likely teachers, and probably by 1290, for he seems to have been there at about the time of reports of a famous miracle that occurred that year on the Place Saint-Jean-en-Grève.[10] The erstwhile student had risen already to a professorship in the Faculty of Theology at the University of Paris when we first encounter him by name in an institutional record dated 1305–1306.[11] He subscribes as "Jacobus, monacus de

Caroliloco Ordinis Cisterciencis" and is one of several "regent masters" or professors who subscribe.

The record is a fairly typical, flowery request to the king of France imploring him to give aid to an acquaintance of the masters, a physician, one Raoul de Vémars, with respect to a benefice in the royal gift.[12] Jacques's knowledge of Raoul depended in part simply on the latter's long association with the university's theological faculty. Raoul had been a scholar in theology (*scolaris in theologia*), the request to the king explained, for approximately fourteen years and had developed a reputation as an eloquent preacher. He was of mature years and a man of great "probity," his backers also informed the king. But Vémars is another one of those small villages slightly north of Paris and very near Chaalis. It is at least possible that Jacques's inclusion on the list of Raoul's patrons reflects an acquaintance that predated their university years. Raoul, like Jacques, was an intensely local man. The benefice at issue was near *Taverniacum*, modern Taverny, hardly (with a little exaggeration) a stone's throw from Vémars and Chaalis.[13]

Despite the conventionally flattering tone taken with the king in their request to him to help Raoul de Vémars ("Let your most high majesty flourish in the Lord that he may magnify your prosperity and increase your days"), Jacques, like many Cistercian monks, had strong reason to be suspicious of this particular king, Philip IV the Fair (1285–1314). The difficulties went back at least to 1294–1297 when England and France were at war over their rulers' authority and power in the duchy of Aquitaine, the region in southwestern France that Edward I, the English king (1272–1307), held as a fief from Philip IV.[14] Both sides in the war, of course, argued the justness of their cause. Both kings expected their subjects to contribute financially to the war effort. And both taxed the clergy to this end. Neither, however, received the prior papal permission formally required, at least since the Fourth Lateran Council (1215), to do so. The Cistercian Order, which was technically an exempt order, not even obligated to contribute funds to crusader princes, was nonetheless targeted along with other clergy and exempt orders, in part no doubt because of its tradition of giving voluntary or gracious grants to crusader princes despite the exemption.[15]

In fact, the granting of gracious aids in the decades before the war with England had already laid bare to its abbots some of the financial problems of the Cistercian Order.[16] Many abbeys, not least the nunneries, found it impossible to pay the portions levied on them by the abbot fathers (from Cîteaux and her first four daughter houses, La Ferté, Pontigny, Clairvaux, and Morimond) in conjunction with the order's annual collective meetings, the General Chapters. Many houses' incapacity or reluctance to contribute perhaps also pointed to a broader financial crisis, as older orders, like theirs, suffered a relative loss of popularity with donors. It was the mendicant friars, Franciscans and Dominicans, who attracted more and more largesse in the course of the thirteenth century.

The principal abbots of the Cistercian Order in France met at Philip IV's command at Dijon in Burgundy in late 1294 or early 1295 and agreed, perhaps in a mood of "war fever," to contribute to the expenses of the war with England, but they carefully worded their response in an effort to limit the grant if a truce were to be reached between the two kingdoms.[17] They insisted that their own people would make the collections and then transfer the tax to the secular authorities.[18] Even so, there was grassroots opposition to the capitulation, for the king's agents in the southeastern district of Beaucaire were obliged to seize some of the order's goods for failure to pay up in a timely manner in June 1295.[19] Opposition to the king really mounted, however, after Pope Boniface VIII (1294–1303) reacted vigorously to Philip's policy and to Edward's as well and issued the bull *Clericis laicos* (February 1296), forbidding clergy to pay such levies to princes and threatening those churchmen who did so anyway with the spiritual censure of excommunication.[20] As a result of this declaration the Cistercians gained an excuse for resistance, and as a further consequence, as Jeffrey Denton remarks, "impressive evidence of the determination of the Cistercians to defend traditional clerical rights in the face of the king's policies" emerges from the surviving documents.[21]

The situation continued to deteriorate, with the enraged French king prohibiting the export of precious metals to Rome.[22] Given the papacy's extraordinary dependence on the contribution of the church in Gaul to its financial well-being, the pope was under pressure to compromise. He nevertheless continued to take a hard-line stance in defense of the freedom of the church, at least until ambassadors led by Philip's closest adviser, Pierre Flote, reached Boniface and threatened to offer support to those Italian cardinals hostile to him and his family, and to victims of his wrath who wanted to appeal to a general council against his authority. Then and only then did Boniface agree to relent.[23] The bull *Clericis laicos* was now creatively reinterpreted at the papal curia as a very general statement of the customary principles governing the relations between the church and secular princes.[24] In the new reading the bull was not understood as censuring any particular king, let alone Philip IV. Boniface also explained, in the bull *Etsi de statu* (July 1297), that however appropriate it was for princes to obtain papal permission before taxing the church, there were times, times of "dangerous emergency," when they could not wait for permission while also fulfilling their God-given duty to defend their realms. It was up to them, the wielders of the temporal sword, to determine when circumstances constituted urgent necessity and required access to ecclesiastical revenues, "notwithstanding any kind of privilege or exemption obtained from the apostolic see." So much for matters of principle and the Cistercian Order's perhaps hesitant and belated but ultimately vigorous resistance to Philip's demands.

At the time Boniface issued *Clericis laicos*, he made an angry pointed allusion to the possible role of universities in Philip the Fair's formulation of his taxation policy: "Universities, too, which may have been to blame in these matters, we subject," the pope declaimed, "to ecclesiastical interdict." The entire faculty and student body of the University of Paris, one of the universities to which he was referring, was clerical; so an interdict, a ban on ecclesiastical services, was no empty threat. Nor was Boniface misguided in assuming a role for university masters, for it was traditional for rulers, and in particular the French crown, to seek advice and support from the learned masters at the University of Paris.[25] The university could speak "corporately" in a single voice. But the formal corporate status of the university notwithstanding, there was a cacophony of voices and had been for decades within the institution. The residents of the Cistercian College of Saint-Bernard, like Jacques de Thérines, were pulled among several loyalties—to the university itself, to the crown, and to the pope. This pattern and the torment it provoked would soon repeat themselves, despite the evident reconciliation of pope and king in 1297.[26]

For Pope Boniface VIII was deeply afflicted by his humiliation. Partly to recoup his prestige but more immediately to respond to an exceptional manifestation of popular devotion in Rome at Christmas in 1299, he designated the year 1300 a jubilee year.[27] It was an unprecedented declaration. Pilgrims who visited the prescribed holy sites in Rome were to receive extraordinary spiritual indulgences. The year-long outpouring of devotion reflected in the hundreds of thousands of pilgrims who made the trip delighted the pope, as it delighted innumerable municipal officials, merchants, innkeepers, and entrepreneurs of the Eternal City, and it was great fun for local clergy to have an opportunity to meet and count the myriad of foreign pilgrims who flocked to the woefully underpopulated city.[28] A pope whose reputation had so recently suffered appeared to have recovered both his popular support and his dignity.

The recovery, however, was short-lived, and once more the Cistercians' situation in France was closely tied to the pope's difficulties. Again, the story, told as a clash of church and state, is a dramatic one.[29] Reports reached the crown in 1301 that a southern French bishop, Bernard Saisset of Pamiers, had maligned the king. Philip was like an owl, he said, handsome, fair, "Bel," but he just stared. Someday he would be deprived of his realm. He was a useless "bastard" who did not deserve his throne, a particularly unseemly though utterly baseless slur on a "holy lineage" descended from Louis IX, whom Boniface VIII canonized in 1297.[30] Philip, according to the recklessly outspoken southern bishop, was also more like an immaterial wraith than a human being or even a brute animal. Saisset did not desist from impugning the French ("northerners") in general; he even expressed his willingness to make common cause with the rebellious count of Foix, if he had a chance, against the French king.

When the prelate's probably drunken words were repeated to Philip, he quite unsurprisingly regarded them as a treasonous affront to the royal dignity. He was capable, on rare occasions, of forgiving insults. A preacher once recalled with admiration his refusal to punish a provincial noblewoman who said the usually taciturn monarch was a born dummy (*mutum*).[31] But he considered Bernard Saisset's words particularly dangerous, because they came from a bishop whose loyalty he needed in Pamiers. The city was in the heartland of a region in which many of the inhabitants resented northern French domination, a legacy of the early thirteenth-century conquest of the south in the Crusade against the so-called Cathar or Albigensian heretics and the subsequent transfer of territorial authority to northerners working for the French crown.

The Inquisition's establishment in 1234, a critical development in this story, came five years after the treaty of capitulation that ended the twenty-year Crusade. The inquisitors' efforts were quite effective in inducing natives to repudiate the kinds of behavior and suppress their public adherence to opinions that churchmen deemed heretical and imagined as constituting a separate church.[32] But their success came at a cost, namely, deep resentment over the interference of the inquisitorial commissions in local life and over the imposition of penalties like penitential pilgrimages, imprisonment, confiscation of property, and relaxation of "contumacious heretics" to the secular arm for execution.[33] This undermined loyalty to the crown. Despite occasionally manifesting a certain sympathy with southerners' complaints about the inquisitors, the king always returned to supporting the heretic hunters.[34] How serious a threat the dismay in Languedoc was to political peace may be doubted, but Philip was certainly primed to regard utterances like those attributed to the bishop of Pamiers as incendiary.

The arrest and judicial process against the bishop, put in train with more ardor than soberness of thought, violated canon law in some of its particulars (the bishop, for instance, was at first put in a secular prison), and also, as Pope Boniface VIII was not slow in pointing out, they challenged the freedom of the church.[35] Under different circumstances, pacific and diplomatic parties might have mollified the king's anger and the pope's displeasure. But in the event, both men, despite one or two early conciliatory gestures on the king's part and later ones on the pope's, stood their ground. In the bull *Ausculta fili* ("Listen, son") of December 1301, Boniface reprimanded Philip.[36] The tone was sharp and offended those at the French court, who circulated an even harsher paraphrase of it with the intention of eliciting sympathy from influential groups.

The situation quickly worsened.[37] Nobles, churchmen, and townsmen were called together in assemblies often regarded by historians, a little anachronistically, as the first summoning of the Estates General of France.[38] The king's men explained the situation to them and asked the nobles and townsmen to send letters of protest to the cardinals; they permitted the clergy to write the pope directly. All were subsequently requested to adhere to a list of charges against the pope, whose final enumeration was extremely vicious. On 23 June 1303, for example, the adhesion of the University of Paris referred to Boniface VIII's "diverse, enormous and horrible and detestable crimes, certain of which manifestly stink of heresy."[39] Boniface prepared to depose the king but was kidnapped from his residence at Anagni by French agents on 7 September 1303 and humiliated before he could issue a bull of deposition.[40] Though he was rescued soon after, he did not live long. Steadily after Boniface's death on 11 October 1303 in Rome, to which the pontiff had returned from Anagni, the king brought the situation under his own control.[41] The new pope, Benedict XI, elected on 22 October 1303—a mere eleven days after his predecessor's death—tried to reach an agreement with Philip's ambassadors without conceding too much, particularly with regard to the dignity of his predecessor on the papal throne and the culpability of those who carried out the kidnapping.[42] But Benedict himself had scarcely more than eight months to live.[43] On 7 July 1304 began a papal interregnum that lasted almost a year until the election, on 5 June 1305, of a southern Frenchman as Pope Clement V, a man with whom the French king worked more comfortably. Clement eventually absolved the kidnappers, who had acted, he accepted, with commendable if perhaps excessive zeal for the love of Holy Church, but he managed to forestall the posthumous deposition of Boniface VIII that the French crown craved.[44]

In 1301 and 1302 and even into early 1303 many French churchmen were more than willing to believe that Boniface had overstepped his authority and transgressed good sense by reprimanding the French king and by his evident unwillingness to avoid a scandal in the church that would inevitably hurt them.[45] They remembered his humiliating turnabout in the struggle over clerical taxation a few years before, which at the time undermined their own opposition to Philip, and they probably expected that after some posturing he would abandon his position again. Cistercians in France do not seem to have differed much from others in this regard early in the crisis.[46] As the propaganda war heated up, however, the king's polemicists dredged up the canard that Boniface had engineered the (illicit) resignation of his predecessor, Celestine V, in 1294 and kept this angelic pope under lock and key until he withered away two years later through the harsh imprisonment.[47] Other allegations—that Boniface endorsed sodomy and that he denied the soul's immortality—joined this slur.[48] In response to the king's angry refusal to allow his bishops to attend a council that the pope called for 1302 to deal with the dispute, many churchmen began to have misgivings about their own positions. Some, but by no means the bulk of the French hierarchy, made known their intent to defy the king and went to the council, which met in Rome at the end of October 1302.[49] One of these was the abbot of Cîteaux, the titular head of the entire Cistercian Order.[50] Philip threatened to seize all the goods of these men that his agents could get their hands on.[51]

Cistercians, indeed, were prominent among those who now began actively to resist.[52] Not all Cistercians stood firm or even believed in the rightness of the pope's position. The royal treasurer, the Cistercian abbot of Jouy, continued loyally in his post during Philip's struggle with Boniface.[53] And Cistercians at the University of Paris, like Jacques de Thérines, were again divided by their mixed loyalties. The corporate voice of the university, to recall an earlier observation, was raised unequivocally in the king's favor. Did the Cistercian scholars and masters share this point of view? Given the weight of evidence on the University of Paris indicating conflicts of opinion as to the extent of papal authority, it is possible to doubt it.[54] Historians of these events, however, originally opposed to the opinions of Catholic apologists but now more or less as a mere conventional reflex, constantly remind readers that only a minority of churchmen and of Cistercians publicly defied the king, and that their deeds should not be taken as an indication of a major failure of the French crown to command the church's loyalty in the realm. Unfortunately, even the greatest of these historians fails to take into account the fear that potential resisters felt.[55] That any churchmen at all chose openly to refuse to adhere to the crown's indictment of Boniface is perhaps more remarkable than that the majority were unwilling to make an open stand. Undoubtedly some were hoping against hope even deep into the crisis that a compromise would render open resistance unnecessary. The line between rationality and self-deceit or even cowardice is fine.

The fact is that many Cistercian houses did refuse to adhere in 1303, and many monks (though how many is unknown) retreated into exile rather than endure the situation.[56] Jean de Pontoise, the defiant abbot of Cîteaux, was virtually put under house arrest, as Tilmann Schmidt's research shows, for his outspoken opposition to the king's violation of ecclesiastical privilege, the freedom of the church.[57] After Boniface died and the first signs of the church's capitulation began to manifest themselves, Abbot Jean resigned, succeeded by the Cistercian abbot of Jouy, the royal treasurer, and he died soon after.[58] The fiercely royalist scholar Pierre Dupuy, who in the mid–seventeenth century collected and edited the documents relating to the disputes between Boniface VIII and Philip IV, threw doubt on the cause of the abbot's resignation, in a backhanded sort of way, almost certainly to belittle the extent and longevity of the opposition to Philip.[59] But Jean's integrity rings truer than Dupuy's doubt. He was long remembered for his stalwart opposition to the king, even as one standing nearly alone—refusing to assent to the royal measures and openly scornful and contemptuous both of the king and of those prelates who supported the crown.[60] This heroic figure attracted many Cistercians and inspired not a few to resist the crown.

Thus it seems a little jarring to find Jacques de Thérines, a Cistercian at the University of Paris, a few months after Abbot Jean's death using conventional flatteries to ask Philip the Fair for a favor for an old friend. Perhaps it would be a little less jarring if the date of the letter the professor subscribed to were 1306, as is possible.[61] A year or two would go a long way toward softening animosities, even if the Chaalis monk went briefly into voluntary exile from the University of Paris in 1303. But time and again as we pursue Jacques's story we will see that he, like Abbot Jean of Cîteaux before him, was anything but a timid man or one whose loyalty to the see of Saint Peter was less than absolute.

In any case, what follows almost immediately after this first appearance of Jacques's name in a university document is a torrent of his academic writing and publications, one of the earliest of which is a quodlibetal question on the expulsion of Jews from Christian principalities, potentially a very dangerous subject in the France of the time.[62] Quodlibets, as they have come down to us, are the summaries of disputed questions (varying from what look like attempted but highly abbreviated transcripts or talking notes to fully revised literary renditions) that professors discussed before learned audiences of the University of Paris. These disputes or debates regularly occurred during Advent/Christmas and Lent, and as the word implies (*quodlibet* means "whatever"), any question—serious or not—could be set for debate or even broached from the floor. The quodlibets of an extraordinary number of both famous and obscure professors have survived because they were collected and circulated. The genre flourished from the 1230s to the 1320s, and it constituted very popular reading in the academy.[63] For example, an astounding 137 manuscripts survive of Thomas Aquinas's carefully edited quodlibetal questions.[64]

It was always informative and sometimes great fun to hear or read quodlibets. The subjects could be risqué. (It does not take an overheated modern cultural sensitivity to regard them sometimes as tasteless.) Who was better in bed, black women or white women?[65] How, one is tempted to ask, could professorial celibates who had never seen an African woman even claim to know? The answer is that they extrapolated from ancient and earlier medieval texts on women, physiognomy, biology, and ethnic customs.[66] The quodlibets, to a modern psychological sensibility, also at times seem to reveal some of the feelings of inadequacy and uncertainty in the university professoriat. Why would professional pacifists who rarely, if ever, risked their lives in battle agree to dispute in public about who were more courageous in war, black men or white men?[67] How could theologians who admitted, as a dogmatic article of the faith, the thoroughly transformative power of baptism argue that the sacrament was insufficient for Jews?[68] Even if the preferred answers were obvious in the cultural context—white knights were bolder than black; of course Jews could become Christians through baptism—simply to raise the issues and hear or read the strong counterarguments might provoke at least mild, if not disabling, cognitive dissonance.

Jacques de Thérines's quodlibets typically if not unrelievedly address graver rather than lighter issues, as is the case with the collections of many other professors who used the debating forum and the genre to think aloud and on parchment about still unsettled questions of philosophy, temporal authority, the economy, theology, and canon law.[69] But Palémon Glorieux, the learned editor of Jacques's quodlibets and a great admirer of the giants of medieval scholasticism, like Thomas Aquinas, Duns Scotus, and William of Ockham, was hard on the *érudit* from Thérines, whose "conscientious and reasonable" thought, he felt, did not rise to the "transcendent" quality of theirs.[70] This judgment seems misplaced, however, if only because the basis of comparison is unfair. For Jacques's surviving contributions to specifically theological and philosophical genres, unlike his controversial works, take up less than a single volume in its modern printing, trivial in quantity compared, say, to Aquinas's academic and related writings, which fill approximately fifty tomes in one modern edition.[71] Such voluminous levels of production and survival are fairly common among the most famous scholastic theologians and philosophers and include of course their great summas as well as their quodlibetal questions.

Transcendent or not, Jacques's oeuvre addressed difficult issues in intelligent ways.[72] The twenty-two questions discussed in his first quodlibetal collection and the nineteen in the second focus mostly on highly rarefied issues of theology and philosophy. The following list hardly exhausts the matters he takes on: existence, essence, potentiality, the scientific status of theology, the beatific vision, the hypostatic union, the passion, angelic intelligence, nature, motion, infinity and eternity, and the varieties of reason and rationality. "Does the enlightenment [*lumen*] of faith differ from the enlightenment of prophecy *secundum speciem*?" is a typical sort of phrasing.[73] But occasionally, droll or gritty questions occupy a place in the collection. If a monk had the gift of foreknowledge from God and knew he was damned, was there any reason for him to remain a monk? The Cistercian offers six good reasons for the affirmative, including that it was good to serve God without hope of reward.[74] If a woman married a man, thereby saving him from capital punishment (presumably in a rape case, since marriage after the fact quashed the charge at law), was the marriage/ pardon licit if the man, unbeknownst to everyone at the time, was already married and his first wife petitioned the judge for her husband? A firm no: saving one's soul (exiting from an adulterous relationship with the second "wife" and ceding the pardon) trumps saving one's body.[75]

The best guide to the place of Jacques's views in the philosophical and theological world of which he was a part is his editor, Glorieux, who divides the master's oeuvre into five categories: metaphysics, cosmology, theodicy, psychology, and morality.[76] Like all such categorizations of the jumbles of questions in quodlibetal collections, this one is somewhat arbitrary, and it is difficult to fit all of Jacques's answers into the assigned boxes. In particular Glorieux's categories of morality and psychology function rather as catchalls.

What Glorieux classifies as moral questions do deal with terms that evoke moral sentiments and actions (virtues and vices), but Jacques's approach was not to query whether such-and-such a virtue was possible or to establish why it was necessary, which is how some modern moral philosophers might engage the philosophical problematic of virtue (or vice). Rather Jacques was usually content to argue the origin of virtue (whether in the intellect or in the will), to discuss the relationship of specific virtues to others, and to assess the relative importance of the virtues. In other words, his interests were broadly and typically taxonomic. How did a particular virtue, like prudence or justice, stand in relation to other virtues?[77] Was happiness an act of the intellect or of the will; were the moral virtues situated in the will or in the "sensitive appetite"?[78] Occasionally, however, Jacques dealt with practical questions, such as whether a person known to be in mortal sin should be permitted to receive the body of Christ in communion.[79] In this case, the master made a distinction as to whether the sin was manifest or known simply to the priest, and he marshaled texts in support of denying the sacrament to the manifest mortal sinner, while offering four arguments in favor of administering it to the sinner whose sin remains unknown to the community at large. While there is obvious moral content in the discussion, Glorieux apparently did not feel that it fitted well with the other quodlibetal questions he identified as moral, and so he left it unclassified.

The rubric of psychology that Glorieux employs, following medieval usage, is not what present-day people, in the long wake of Freudianism, would recognize as appropriate. Medieval psychology treated the soul and the intellect and how they achieved knowledge and translated knowledge, through the will, into action. Scholastic psychologists were as fascinated with rational creatures (human beings) as with superrational or intuitive ones (angels). In most cases, the quodlibetal questions Glorieux considers as falling into the category of psychology conform to medieval sensibilities. It seems particularly arbitrary, therefore, for Glorieux to regard quodlibetal question 1.14, that on the expulsion of Jews, as an exercise in scholastic psychology.[80]

Indeed, though one of the shorter of Jacques's quodlibetal questions, 1.14 is the most politically charged of them all. One can almost see the distinguished master before his Christmas holiday audience in 1306, the date of the debate, ready to put his views on the line in the fraught atmosphere of Paris that winter. The atmosphere was fraught for good reason.

On 21 June 1306 secret policy discussions between Philip IV and his closest advisers culminated in a decision (also kept secret) to arrest and expel all the Jews from the kingdom of France.[81] Orchestrating arrangements extremely subtly over the next month (with word of their plans not leaking out at all), the crown achieved a stunning surprise attack, the rounding up, seizure, and formal arrest of approximately one hundred thousand human beings—men, women, and children—in a single day (*in una die*), Friday, 22 July 1306, in a kingdom of about ten million people distributed, within its medieval borders, over nearly two hundred thousand square miles.[82]

The Jews, whose neighborhoods were easy to identify and isolate because of the availability of information from tax documents that had accumulated in local royal bureaus over the years, were kept in the few formal jails and in communal buildings until such time as thorough searches were made of their homes for account books (records of their outstanding loans, now payable to the crown) and for their cash and goods.[83] This phase of the undertaking came to an end at different times over the next several months, depending in part on how many men could be put to the work of confiscation (*captio*). It also depended perhaps on whether local crown agents thought it was useful to keep Jews in captivity longer to induce some of them to convert. (A few did convert.) Negotiations between the crown and those barons who had direct lordship over Jews in France occasioned still other delays. All Jews were being expelled, both the crown's and the barons', but it was difficult to coordinate efforts.

The overall result was that expulsion dates differed markedly around the kingdom.[84] Some Jews were on the road, allowed only a little traveling money and the clothes on their backs, already in August, others only in September. The last Jews to leave the kingdom did so in October. But at whatever date they were expelled, they left under the same condition, "on pain of death." Also, many suffered indignities and even death from "exhaustion and suffering" as they traveled into exile. No evidence survives that either sick people or women in advanced pregnancy were allowed to postpone their journeys. Some border princes refused to let them settle in their lands—in a sense, they reexpelled them. Others, persuaded by the financial contributions of native Jews, let the refugees settle, but word must rapidly have disseminated in France that the Christian inhabitants of these lands often reacted hostilely to the newcomers, precipitating new expulsions.

Scarcely two months after the last Jews left the realm of France on royal orders from Paris, Jacques de Thérines, in the same city and in the shadow of the king's palace, chose to address the question of the appropriateness of expelling Jews. Given the regular dates for quodlibetal performances, this was his earliest opportunity to do so.[85] He could and did treat the matter as a hypothetical question, but depending on what he said and wrote in resolving the question, his answer would be regarded as either an endorsement or a denunciation of the particular policies of Philip the Fair.[86] There is no doubt that it would have been regarded as a denunciation, and, as Valois pointed out long ago, it took courage for the professor to say what he said.[87]

Jacques framed the question in this way: "Should Jews expelled from one region be expelled from another" (*Vtrum Iudei expulsi de una regione debeant expelli de alia*). Jews had been expelled from England in 1290.[88] Nearly all, about two thousand, took up residence in France, from which, along with all native French Jews, they had just been expelled in the late summer and autumn of 1306. And many of these exiles suffered expulsion from lands where they subsequently tried to settle. Jacques assumed for the sake of argument that the cause of the initial expulsion was just, since the Jews' activity as "usurers" was a manifest sin.[89] The question, then, that he addressed was whether the Jewish habit of usurious activity created a legitimate presumption against them: would they not reengage in illicit moneylending in—and, therefore, transgress the laws of—any other region (*sic nec in alia*) in which they resettled? Should they be expelled even in the absence of proof of their guilt?[90] Implicit, here, is the more fundamental question as to whether presently law-abiding people, despite a long history of breaking the law, should be subjected to arbitrary power. Jacques did not question whether the power exercised was legitimate, only whether it conformed to the higher precepts that he affirmed and defended.

The contrary view, indeed, which he associated with the Fathers of the church and which modern historians typically associate with one in particular, Saint Augustine, was that Jews should be permitted to live among Christians.[91] This is the view he then emphatically and repeatedly endorsed, and he offered six reasons for doing so, of which the first was that the Jews' very presence in Christendom helped confirm the validity of the Christian faith. The Jews preserved the Old Testament and constantly attested to its antiquity and integrity. Christians argued from the Old to the truth of the New. Christians who were weak in the faith could take heart from the Old Testament prophecies, their authenticity being guaranteed by the Jews, who also saw these texts as pointing to a messiah. While Jews balked, as Jacques acknowledged, at regarding Jesus as the promised messiah, Christians, properly instructed, would see the truth of the Catholic position and be strengthened in their faith.[92]

Second, said Jacques, the very sight of Jews reminded Christians of Jesus's passion, for contemporary Jews were his betrayers' descendants. Christians ought not to take the presence of Jews in their communities as license to kill them for failing to repudiate the actions of their forebears. "Slay them not, lest my people forget" (Ps. 58 [59].11). Quite the contrary, Christians should pray for them to be brought to the true faith, as Jesus himself prayed for his tormentors: "Father, forgive them; for they know not what they do" (Luke 23.34).[93]

Jacques was not a modern liberal, born out of due time. He was defending the church's traditional teaching, whatever his personal feelings about Jews. Perhaps he was moved by their arrest and brutal expulsion, and this sympathy occasioned his decision to discuss the question of exile. Some fine historians have certainly thought so.[94] But it is equally possible that he was wholly indifferent to their fate, and what really galled him was the king's indifference to traditional ecclesiastical teaching. In the long history of Philip the Fair's disputes with the church, after all, it was the king's alleged violation of norms of behavior established by the church that was his enemies' chief charge against him.

At any rate, Jacques went on to say, in offering his third reason not to expel Jews, faith actually grew stronger when it was in danger, in this case from the continuing presence of nonbelievers. Faith that survived in such circumstances was sometimes even further fortified with miracles. Here Jacques made reference to a relatively recent event (1290), the first fully documented accusation of host desecration, in which a Parisian Jew was alleged to have secured the sacrament from a poor Christian woman and tried to destroy it—unsuccessfully. Boiling it did not work, and when he stabbed it, it bled. In the end the Jew was discovered and the miracles revealed. The Jew's execution followed, as did, possibly, the conversion of some members of his family to Christianity.[95] Many Christians, Jacques implied, found their faith strengthened by these miracles. Moreover, the church, in the person of Pope Boniface VIII, recognized the validity of the miracles by allowing a chapel to be erected and consecrated on the spot where they occurred, the Place Saint-Jean-en-Grève in Paris.[96] In 1299 King Philip the Fair himself ceded to the religious serving the new sanctuary a house that was adjacent to this "Chapel of Miracles," as it was known.[97] If there were no Jews, there would have been no miracles (*exemplum de eukaristia in sancto Johanne in Grauia*), and no strengthening of the faith among skeptics.[98]

Why else should Jews be allowed to remain? Jacques provided three more reasons. Their dispersal in many regions throughout the Christian world was a constant reproach to them for their infidelity. It testified to their failure to overcome Christ even though they, "vile enemies of his cross" (*inimici cruces eius uiles*), crucified him. "Their continuous desolation and dispersion," he insisted, "contributes to Christ's glory and honor and to their multiple confusion."[99] Or, again, the saints and the Fathers, inflamed and inspired by the Holy Spirit (*Spiritu Sancto inflammati et inspirati*), would not have permitted Jews to live among Christians if it was detrimental to the faith to do so, and the ancient Fathers ought to be imitated by us (*sunt a nobis imitandi*). "Trust in the Lord with all thine heart; and lean not unto thine own understanding" (Prov. 3.5).[100] Finally, how else could Jews be converted to the Catholic faith? The responsibility to convert the Jews, Jacques asserted, was laid as a divine burden on the Christian people, a position he supported by reference to prophetic passages from the Bible and with particular citations to papal letters incorporated into the canon law.[101]

With this Jacques brought his six arguments against expulsion to a close, and to judge by the form of his quodlibetal questions in general, the entire discussion should end at this point. Scribal practice can help explain a remarkable anomaly in this case, namely, the fact that a short coda was added to the discussion. Presumably, when Jacques gave his talking notes to his scribe for the transcription of his quodlibetal questions into a collection a few years later, he also gave him an additional note jotted down soon after the debate—a note that preserved his answer to a (completely unexpected?) question from the floor following his formal presentation.[102] From the tenor and vocabulary of this answer, one can infer that the question was deliberately provocative.

One can also infer that the question went something like this: But what if the numbers and concentration of Jews become so great that they constitute a danger to the Christian "kingdom"? Should they be expelled then? The word kingdom (*regnum*), used in what I have called the coda, was new to the discussion. Jacques's preferred usage was "region" (*regio*), a general word that could be marshaled as record evidence, when the quodlibets were circulated, that his discussion was hypothetical or abstract. It is relevant in this regard that he also never used the word "king" (*rex*) in the formal discussion, except in a quotation from the Bible about the messiah-king. Power *is exercised* against the Jews, always in the passive voice; Jacques never accused a king directly of exercising the power to expel. The scholastic convention of abstraction actually cast its protective cloak over the Cistercian master's speech. Now, however, the matter of the kingdom was raised openly.

Jacques's response is arresting. How could he say no? From Philip II Augustus's time in the late twelfth century the charge was being made that the Jews were increasing in such numbers—in Paris, in particular—that they constituted an implicit threat to the Christian people.[103] He therefore conceded that a dangerous confederation of large numbers of Jews might appropriately be expelled from a (the)—indeed, any—kingdom (*de aliquo regno*), but only temporarily (*ad tempus*), as it were, and as a way to break up the confederation.[104] This kind of expulsion one might call instrumental in that it reenacted the dispersion of the Jews, which was the punishment that God, in medieval Christian understanding, justly meant them to suffer. According to Jacques, however, no such expulsion should be undertaken except after long hard thought (*maturo consilio mediante*), and, most important, no such expulsion should be permanent, a point, he insisted, that his six reasons established firmly.[105] Were eyebrows raised in the audience? Contemporary commentators, after all, make plain that everyone knew what the king intended: the Jews were "never again to return."[106] This was dangerous business.

If word got back to the king that a learned professor, a Cistercian at the University of Paris, spoke "publicly" in a way that could be regarded as open criticism of his expulsion of the Jews, we have no evidence that he did anything about it. Perhaps Philip IV regarded the act as another absurd if irritating eruption from a member of the order, but one that, given the crown's already successful *accomplishment* of the expulsion, was of minimal significance. Or perhaps he knew perfectly well that quodlibets were largely intellectual games that he believed he could afford to ignore. It is possible, too, that Jacques de Thérines took the chance he did precisely because the likelihood of retribution after the fact of the expulsion was low; the Cistercians could hardly be further marginalized than they already were.

And yet there is a coda to the story, not just to the text of the quodlibetal question. In 1306 Philip IV's heir, Louis, like all the other barons of the realm who had direct lordship over Jews, expelled his Jews from the county of Champagne, which he held in vassalage of his father and as an inheritance since 1305 from his mother. But at his mother's death, he also ascended the throne of Navarre, and in Navarre "King" Louis, though a mere seventeen-year-old, was no one's vassal. "Should Jews expelled from one region be expelled from another?"—this was the original question Jacques de Thérines raised. Jewish refugees from the kingdom of France were flooding into the kingdom of Navarre. What did Louis—the son of the man who had made them refugees—do? He permitted them to settle and to get on with their lives.[107] Jacques's quodlibetal discussion may have been occasioned by his self-perceived need to justify the young king's actions and even, by giving him a respectable argument drawn from the tradition of the "Fathers," to shield him from paternal wrath.

There is a coda to the coda. No expulsion of Jews, not even a justifiable one, Jacques de Thérines insisted at Christmas 1306, should be anything more than temporary (*ad tempus*). In 1315, a few months after Louis of Navarre succeeded Philip the Fair as king of France, he annulled his father's expulsion order and readmitted Jews to the realm. He offered several reasons for doing so in the decree he issued.[108] One will sound familiar, because it was the overriding, emphatic, and often repeated one for Jacques de Thérines as well: the Fathers of the church commanded it.[109]

2

THE POPE IN AVIGNON AND

THE CRISIS OF THE TEMPLARS

FOLLOWING BONIFACE VIII'S DEATH IN 1303, the brief pontificate of his successor Benedict XI, and a yearlong papal interregnum, the cardinals elected Bertrand Got, the archbishop of Bordeaux, as Pope Clement V (1305–1314). Clement was remarkably energetic and successful in easing tensions with the French crown, although his relations with Philip the Fair were not immediately cordial.[1] He was, however, remarkably slow in setting out for Rome, the Apostolic See. From his election on 5 June 1305 until 1309, Clement was on the move from one locale to another in Languedoc and Provence.[2] One of his favorite retreats in these years was his old archiepiscopal seat, the Aquitanian capital city of Bordeaux, where he was often in residence from 11 May 1306.[3] Clement was himself an Aquitanian and evidently found the familiarity of his home territory and its speech attractive.[4] In the end, he never traveled to the Eternal City but in 1309 established his chief residence, originally for administrative purposes, in the great fortress city of Avignon on the Rhône River border with medieval France. Although the pope repeatedly—before 1309 and thereafter—signaled his intention to go to Rome, there were always more or less good reasons, chiefly recurrent instability in Italy, that his advisers alleged prevented him from making the journey.[5]

By the autumn of 1306, more than a year into his pontificate, many people were wondering and worrying about why Saint Peter's spiritual heir did not leave Bordeaux and set out for Saint Peter's see. Could a man licitly exercise the papal office, without setting foot in the Apostolic See or at least attempting to? The question seemed like a fair one—a good one to debate—and the annual Christmas quodlibets at the University of Paris in 1306 were an ideal venue for the debate. It may be misleading to see any deep significance in the placement of Jacques de Thérines's quodlibetal question on the expulsion of Jews (1.14), in the collection of his twenty-two Christmas 1306 questions, next to that on the authority of a pope who stays in Bordeaux (1.13). It may not even accurately reflect the order of performance. On the other hand, there is a certain balance achieved by the placement: while the views Jacques expressed on expulsion could only have angered the French king, those on the legitimacy of a pope residing in France, which the Cistercian defended, would have been somewhat more congenial to him.[6]

In this case, distinctly unlike that of the expulsion of Jews, Jacques did not employ the cloak of scholastic anonymity. Although his answer theoretically applied to any pope who chose not to reside in Italy, he was explicit that the case he was addressing was Clement's (*casus pertinens ad dominum papam Clementem*).[7] He commenced by tackling one of the justifications that people around the pope were giving for his delay, namely, the disturbed religious situation in Italy. Clement's defenders maintained that Italy was infected with heresy through the doctrines of Fra Dolcino (d'Ossula or di Novara), known to modern audiences through the telling of a version of his story in Umberto Eco's detective novel *The Name of the Rose*.[8] The pope's counselors advised him to distance himself spiritually, of course, but also geographically from the taint of the heresy. So the question became, "There being such heresy in Italy, whether the pope should remain in Bordeaux or go to Italy."[9]

Jacques de Thérines chose what appears to be an idiosyncratic approach to this question. He parsed it as if part of the argument hinged on whether the views attributed to Dolcino were as extreme as his detractors alleged. In other words, the Cistercian declined to treat the question as hypothetical or abstract. He did not formulate the issue, as he might have, thus: Whenever there is serious heresy in Italy, can the pope legitimately avoid Rome? He was responding to critics who were suggesting that the specific danger from Dolcino's followers, against whom Clement endorsed the use of military force, was being overblown. As Sophia Menache points out, chroniclers differed in their estimates of Dolcino's adherents by a factor of fifteen, from as few as two hundred to as many as three thousand.[10] Jacques's first order of business, then, was to reiterate the papal position that Dolcino's views seriously deviated from orthodox opinion yet were somehow still appealing to simple Christians, in which case their *potential* for disturbing the general peace of the church throughout Christendom had to be acknowledged. By looking at his response, we begin also to uncover Jacques's more general attitude toward the prerogatives of the pope, the threat of heresy, and the preservation of the church's purity. The delineation of these views will enhance our understanding of his later contributions to discussions about the accusations against the Templar Order, Marguerite Porete, and the Spiritual Franciscans—three of the most celebrated accusations of heresy in his time and also among the most celebrated in the entire Middle Ages.

Dolcino's enemies regarded him and his followers as notorious heretics.[11] At this stage in his career the apostate, according to Jacques, preached three errors.[12] The first was that the pope had neither the keys nor the power of the keys to heaven, but only asserted he had them. Second, Dolcino is supposed to have taught that there were three stages (he seems actually to have taught that there were four) in the salvational history of the world since the Incarnation.[13] The original stage, according to Jacques, Dolcino associated with the apostles, who were both poor and good; the next, with the confessors, saintly men, who were both rich in spiritual gifts and good; and the last with present-day prelates, who combined material wealth with their wickedness. Third, Jacques alleged that Dolcino, drawing on the Epistle of James in the New Testament, taught literally that every falling into temptation was a joy, and that the blessed were those men who tested themselves successfully through temptation and thereby achieved the crown of everlasting life: no man could really be virtuous and chaste or deserve the reward of eternal life unless he tested his virtue by sleeping unclothed with a naked woman (*nec meretur remunerationem nisi uirtutem suam probauerit nudus cum nuda*).

The seriousness of the deviation from orthodox teaching, at least as Jacques represented these propositions, hardly needs comment. The belief that the pope was the successor of Saint Peter to whom Jesus gave the "keys of the kingdom of heaven" (Matt. 16.19) was the cornerstone of papal authority in spiritual matters. Dissenters from the papal interpretation, like Dolcino, argued either that the authority was Peter's alone or, more typically, that the church through its bishops inherited and exercised the power of the keys and, therefore, salvation collectively.[14] The assertions about the three stages (*status* was the word Jacques used) marked Dolcino as a Joachite, a follower or adapter of the views of Abbot Joachim of Fiore (d. 1202).[15] Radical Franciscans had taken up the abbot's mystical teachings in the mid–thirteenth century. To these men if not quite to Dolcino the life and ministry of Francis of Assisi (1182–1226) signified the beginning of the church's purification in a new Age of the Spirit.[16] These views about Francis and the procession of the *status* were repeatedly condemned as heretical.[17]

Lastly, orthodox theologians regarded Dolcino's alleged interpretation of the Epistle of James (1.2 and 1.12) on the joy and utility of temptation as a perverse reading of the apostle's words. The apostle was not urging men to seek out temptation, such as by sleeping nude with a potential lover. Saint James was recognizing that temptation was strong—indeed, as medieval interpretation had it, that the tribulation that tempted men and women to abandon the Christian life was terrifyingly powerful—and he was urging men to resist, knowing that their successful resistance betokened the all-encompassing joy of eternal salvation.[18] The underlying issue here, besides the heresy, to use my own words rather than Jacques's, was that Dolcino's fetishizing of temptation was actually quite attractive to those he preached to. Men wanted to be tempted; there was something titillating about it. Even if Fra Dolcino wished them to enter into temptation only in order to be disgusted with themselves and remain chaste, and thus contribute to their chances of salvation, many would fail the test and be lost either by the sin of the thought (lust) or by that of the act itself (fornication). Fra Dolcino, in Jacques's reckoning, was therefore all the more to be stopped. On all these matters—the papal claim to the keys, the *status* of salvational history, and the interpretation of the Epistle of James—the Cistercian master quoted texts from the Fathers, Aristotle, and more contemporary philosophers and theologians in defense of orthodoxy.[19]

Having made clear at considerable length that Fra Dolcino's preaching was profoundly dangerous and potentially a threat to the whole Christian church, Jacques concluded that it made perfect sense for the pontiff to reside temporarily (*ad tempus*) in Bordeaux or, for that matter, anywhere else rather than Rome, since it was expedient that the secular arm (*brachium seculare*) be given full license to root out and destroy the Italian heresy by force (*per uirtutem armorum*). The implication is that the requisite authorities were carrying out this operation more efficiently (*et hoc bene posset fieri*) because the papal court and petitioners to it were absent in Bordeaux (*Burdegalis remanendo*). Jacques conceded that Rome as the Apostolic See had a genuine claim on the pope's presence, but the claim of the universal church exceeded that of the Roman see, understood as a geographical entity.[20]

The Cistercian also had no patience with the argument that because Italy was the "head" of Christendom, the pope needed to be in Rome to act the physician for the sick (that is, heretic-infested) head. He silently acknowledged the validity of the organic argument that if the head was infected, all the members of the body were at risk. But in this case the physician, the pope, had assigned the medicine in the form of the secular arm, holy war, as it was his prerogative to do. Accepting the plausibility of the argument that this medicine could be better administered with Clement in France, Jacques had no difficulty with the pontiff's delaying his departure for Rome.[21]

Jacques's assumption, as the phrase *ad tempus* suggests, was that the pope would not prolong his absence. A year and a half into Clement V's pontificate, and reassured by statements emanating from the papal court that the pontiff contemplated an imminent return to Rome, conditional only on the eradication of the Dolcino threat, Jacques had no reason at Christmastime 1306 to feel anything but confident about the pope's intentions. In the event, of course, the papacy remained at Bordeaux even after Fra Dolcino's arrest on 13 March 1307, the burning before his eyes of his dear companion, Margareta, and his own execution on 1 June.[22] Indeed, because from 1309 the papacy settled at Avignon for the remainder of Clement V's pontificate, calls for a return to Rome did not abate.[23] But as far as Jacques was concerned, the pope could do as he saw fit.

On a broader point, Jacques was a realist: the pope's temporarily staying away from Italy in order to give secular powers and local religious authorities full sway in eradicating the heresy was no assurance that only good or that any other good measures, like controlling the arrogance of rich Gallic prelates, were going to come from the decisions made by the absentee papal court in France.[24] Good things as well as bad happened in Rome and Bordeaux, whether the pope was present or not. People behaved virtuously and maliciously whether they were in Bordeaux or Rome: *Vnde et Rome et Burdegalis existente eo, possunt bona et mala fieri, et potest aliquis utrobique agere bene uel male.* "Enough said": *Et hoc sufficiat de illo.*[25] This cynical aside was the first written salvo in Jacques de Thérines's career-long contempt for the highest ranks of the secular clergy, whom he regarded as tainted by their worldliness and jealous of the privileges and covetous of the wealth that had accrued over the centuries to the monks and their monasteries.[26] Even the heretic Dolcino, Jacques would undoubtedly have conceded, identified the malice of the prelates correctly, despite his heterodox assigning of it to a formal *status* of salvational history.

• • • • •

There were a great many people besides prelates who, many came to believe, behaved with particular malice in a series of acts in the kingdom of France commencing on Friday, 13 October 1307. In what was a virtual reenactment of his lightning strike against the Jews of his kingdom the year before, Philip and his advisers, again after very careful secret planning, had every member of the Order of the Temple in France, along with those associated with or employed by them, arrested—some fifteen thousand individuals on that one day.[27] In the wake of the sweep, given the French king's determination, came the widespread recognition that the order and its members would never enjoy the same honor they had once enjoyed in France (and Christendom). All that was in doubt were the details as to what fate held in store for them.

The Order of the Temple of Solomon in Jerusalem, or the Templars, as they were known for short, constituted the first military order in the history of the church.[28] Although the Order of the Hospital of Saint John of Jerusalem institutionally predates the Order of the Temple, it took on a military character only after the latter's establishment. The Templars' origin is encrusted with legends; yet scholars agree on a few basic facts. After the conquest of Jerusalem in 1099 during the First Crusade and the subsequent consolidation of territorial gains in the Holy Land, a small group of men in 1119–1120 formalized a brotherhood devoted to protecting Christian pilgrims. Despite some misgivings among conservative clerics over the propriety of warrior-monks, this brotherhood came to be recognized as a quasi-monastic order within the church. The Knights took vows of celibacy and absolute obedience, as other monks did. They had restricted diets, though not quite so restricted—since they were warriors—as those of typical monks. On many matters they had to answer not to local religious authorities, but solely to the pope. And they received the enthusiastic imprimatur of no less a figure than Bernard of Clairvaux, the most influential Cistercian and one of the most influential churchmen in general of the twelfth century.

The Order of the Temple expanded far beyond the Holy Land.[29] Its commanderies dotted the landscape of Catholic Europe, providing centers for recruitment and sites for experienced warriors' initial training of the younger noblemen who joined, and for that of their social inferiors, who served in the lower ranks.[30] The commanderies were also nuclei for the accumulation of income-producing estates for the order's activities in the East and refuges for sick, maimed, and retired brothers.[31] The houses, so widely dispersed across the map, served as points in an efficient network for the dissemination of information to and from the Holy Land as well as for the transfer of funds across long distances.[32] The monk-knights' reputation for bravery, efficiency, and honesty and the fortified strength of their commandery in Paris inspired the French king, Philip II Augustus (1179/80–1223), to employ them as royal treasurers, a policy that remained in effect deep into the reign of Philip the Fair.[33]

From the point of view of the Catholic faithful the picture sketched is a bright one. There were shadows, too. In 1291 the last continental outpost in the Crusader States, the port of Acre, fell to Muslim forces. A large part of the blame for the fall of Acre, as for the loss of the Holy Land in general, was placed on the military orders, in that they had developed a disabling rivalry among themselves and with secular princes.[34] It had long since been proposed that all the military orders operating in the Crusader States, including the Templars, the Hospitallers, and the Teutonic Knights, either combine their resources or be supplanted by an entirely new and unified order. These suggestions became more insistent in papal and French discussions after 1291 about how to recover the Holy Land.[35] Moreover, there was widespread resentment among bishops and their staffs and to some extent among lay princes, too, at the relative independence of the Templars with respect to episcopal and secular jurisdiction. None of these criticisms was uniquely aimed at the Templars. Critics, for example, lumped the Templars with all the other military orders as being overprivileged, and, much more problematically, with the so-called pacifist cloistered exempt orders (Cistercians, Premonstratensians, and Carthusians), which enjoyed a much higher level of immunity from episcopal authority and lived under far more weighty disciplinary structures.[36]

When Jacques de Thérines took up the issue of the relative rank of justice as a virtue, in a quodlibetal question on the taxonomy of the virtues, and, as a subsidiary problem, addressed whether justice required that everyone (lay and clerical) be treated in the same way, he chose as his exemplary case the privileges that set the exempt orders apart from nonexempt orders (Benedictines) as well as from the secular clergy and from the laity.[37] His reference to the Templars is laconic.[38] (This was, once more, at the annual Christmas debates of 1306.) Jacques would return to the question of the legitimacy and appropriateness of clerical exemptions and ecclesiastical immunities many times later in his life.[39] Here he had a singular reason to pull the Templar example out of his hat. He wanted to counter what he regarded as a scurrilous charge, one that was being repeated with increasing frequency, namely, that the military orders' immunities disempowered the princes who tried to get them to mount a coherent defense of the Crusader States, and that their wealth, partly a consequence of their privileges, made them soft, unwilling to fight. Their failure to hold on to the Holy Land therefore endangered the faith (*per hoc fides periclitatur*).[40] It abandoned believing Christians to Muslim power and thereby, on account of their fear, to the temptations of conversion. It is not surprising that a Cistercian, like Jacques—who would sometimes refer to his Cistercian predecessor Bernard of Clairvaux simply as "the blessed one" (*beatus*), the model of holiness—chose the saint's beloved Templars rather than, say, the Hospitallers to make his case.[41]

The regent master from Thérines was sorely exercised by the relentless and ever shriller criticism of the Templars, although he probably felt that they were a good deal less praiseworthy than in Bernard's time. He concentrated on that part of the critique that focused on exemptions. He did not regard the Templars as exempt, or perhaps one should say that he did not regard them as exempt in the pure sense of the word, in part because they were warriors, heroic but soiled by blood, and not inmates of a cloistered monastic order. Criticism of the Knights, therefore—even valid criticism (although this spiritual son of Saint Bernard did not concede that all the grounds were necessarily valid)—was irrelevant to any discussion of exemptions. And he would feel the same way later, indeed even more so, when lurid crimes, like blasphemy, apostasy, idolatry, and coerced sodomy, would be formally alleged against the Templars soon after their arrest.[42] Exemption did not foster these crimes any more than it had led to the loss of the Holy Land, because, as far as Jacques was concerned, the Knights were not exempt in any proper meaning of the term.[43]

The critique of exemption, as if it were relevant to the Templars, thus set the Cistercian master off on a torrent of vituperation at Christmas 1306. To the general point that justice required that everyone be treated alike and that exemptions prevented this, he responded in the negative, simply because everyone was not alike. Justice, indeed, necessitated treating fundamentally and essentially different groups, such as clergy and laypeople, differently. He seems to have thought that this point was self-evident and, therefore, required no defense, although his notes might not fully represent the extent of his engagement with the issue. The text makes it seem as though he was contemptuous and dismissive of the opposing position.[44]

An opinion that Jacques regarded as equally meretricious was that there was an insufficient distinction between exempt and nonexempt clergy in how they functioned and what they did to render exemption compatible with the virtue of justice. Here his contempt virtually drips from the page. How different were the exempt from the nonexempt, that is, from most bishops and secular priests? The exempt clergy in the here and now (*hiis diebus*) "do more for strengthening and exalting the faith than the nonexempt." It was the exempt orders that produced the greater number of learned teachers and better churchmen in general. As for the bishops, who so resented the independence of the exempt orders, their opinions seemed hardly worth taking seriously. According to Jacques, the bishops' story, in his time, was one of failure. Contemporary bishops had little or no interest in the salvation of the souls of the Christian people. They sought only wealth. They were given over to extortion. Consummate failures, they lacked, in his bitter words, just about everything worthy of a cleric, and in its place there was nothing but puffery and vanity.[45] These traits were what he elsewhere stigmatized as rich Gallic prelates' arrogance.[46] To the objection that his own vaunted Bernard of Clairvaux cautioned against excessive independence from episcopal authority, Jacques spat fire. Bernard was then—the good old days—when bishops were holy and devout men who showed forth the "zeal of religion," monklike ardor.[47] It was sadly different now. Was the Cistercian thinking of the recent history of episcopal submissiveness to Philip the Fair during the struggles with Boniface VIII, when it was his own exempt order that stood virtually alone against the most powerful ruler in Europe? Who can say? But as theater his performance made a good show.

Jacques's attempt to separate criticism of the Templars from criticism of exemption was not entirely successful. Commentators hostile to the military orders continued to conflate the privileges of these orders with the full status of exemption that Cistercians, Premonstratensians, and Carthusians claimed. What was the difference, after all? The excessive secrecy that distinguished the Templar Order's chapter meetings, where recruits were inducted, gave a form of autonomy that looked like the equivalent of exemption.[48] The vow of secrecy with regard to proceedings in chapter was intended to prevent strategic and tactical information, which would have been useful to Christendom's enemies, from becoming public knowledge. But it was alleged that the secrecy masked rather more sordid activities, sexual and otherwise. Who could know whether the allegations were true, since even if there were brothers who desired to denounce their sinful comrades, they were under an absolute vow not to reveal chapter business and were under an equally absolute vow of obedience to the grand master of the order?[49] How did this functionally differ from exemption? The secrecy and the Templars' refusal to mitigate the secrecy sustained their detractors' suspicions and undergirded the argument that they were exempt, and therefore that exemption was wholly bad. For the moment, however, the question of whether the Templars were or were not exempt faded as other issues gained prominence.

Indeed, a veritable cascade of criticisms began to look like an orchestrated campaign of vilification of the Knights. Where was it leading? Long before his order to arrest them, Philip the Fair and the pope discussed some of the rumors swirling around the Templars. This first took place in a meeting in November 1305, almost immediately following Clement's election. The pontiff explained that from his own inquiries he had learned that the Knights denied all wrongdoing, but he was prepared to launch a more formal inquiry.[50] Philip kept up the pressure. The year 1306 brought with it drastic reforms in the royal coinage and the expulsion of the Jews.[51] Both actions had repercussions that were unexpected. The revaluation of the coinage sent people into the streets in Paris and Laon in protest at a policy that promised to impoverish further the poorest of them.[52] And the poorest of the poor—those in debt to the already impoverished Jews— expressed their discontent also in the wake of the expulsion: without Jews who were they to borrow from? Christian moneylenders, without the competition from Jewish moneylenders, would charge even higher rates of interest than the poor were already paying.[53] But it was the revaluation riot in 1306 that briefly sent the king into hiding at the Templar fortress in Paris.[54]

I have speculated elsewhere that this experience was decisive.[55] Joseph Strayer was certainly correct that Philip did not suddenly become aware of, and immediately covet, Templar wealth during his forced sojourn at the fortress in 1306.[56] But a different factor did come into play. The Paris Templars were treasurers to the crown, and their extensive private banking activities also commanded a large part of their attention. Philip briefly experimented with a fully royal, non-Templar treasury before 1303, but he returned some of the business of accounting and disbursing to the Temple that year.[57] It is not clear why, but the point to keep in sight is that among the brothers residing at the Templar fortress when Philip fled there were men who were experts on fiscal matters. It is inconceivable that his coinage reforms, the precipitant of the riots and of his flight, went unmentioned during his stay at the fortress. It will never be known whether this king, punctilious in the way he stood on his dignity, heard and resented hearing criticism of his fiscal practices at the time or perceived some disappointment at his embarrassing, if understandable, flight from the riotous crowds. But it is not implausible that the experience left a sour taste in his mouth.

Philip, at any rate, refused to let go of the matter of the Templars and the rumors surrounding them. At the beginning of May in 1307, he had another audience with Clement V. With regard to the Templars, it was a replay of the king's earlier meeting with the pope at the very beginning of his pontificate (November 1305)—or, at least, the pope seemed to think so. In a letter to Philip of 24 August 1307, the pontiff referred to both conversations and indicated his continued concern.[58] He informed the king that the Knights themselves were scornful of the accusations against them and were eager to defend themselves. Moreover, reports reaching him made plain that the Knights associated the calumnies especially with the French king. Implicit here is the suspicion on their part that the French crown was trying to deflect criticism for the loss of the Holy Land onto the Templars, and away from itself for its failure to mount a Crusade since the death of Louis IX (Saint Louis) in 1270. What was certainly the case was that Philip, despite some encouraging talk, concentrated not on the Holy Land, but on domestic affairs and foreign policy in Europe after the capture of Acre.[59]

The Knights, the pope informed Philip IV, wanted an investigation to clear their names and end the putative vendetta against them. And Clement, at the close of his letter to the king in August, revealed his decision to authorize one. The letter did not, however, provide a legitimate basis for Philip to act on his own authority, although he and his advisers appear to have believed or acted as if they believed that the series of meetings between the king and the pope constituted an endorsement of unilateral action by the crown.[60] On 14 September 1307 Philip secretly put into motion the machinery for the arrest of the Templars.[61] On 13 October the raids on Templar commanderies took place all through the realm. The crown knew who was responsible for the loss of the Holy Land, and this dramatic gesture made it plain.

In form, the seizures of 13 October were, to repeat an earlier observation, a macabre reenactment of Philip's attack on the Jews ten months before, but they were not just that. Philip the Fair virtually owned the Jews; he claimed absolute *dominium* over them and could do with them as he wished.[62] He did not own the Templars. His violation of canon law— the breach of the freedom of the church—looked for a moment as if it would provoke a livid Pope Clement V to some decisive condemnation of the king.[63] For the pontiff did not interpret the meetings and correspondence between him and the king as providing any license whatever to arrest men of the church.[64] At this juncture, the situation might have offered an opportunity for the Cistercians to demonstrate once more their traditional willingness to stand against the French king or, more positively stated, to stand with the pontiff.

A terribly disconcerting series of events complicated matters. The charges against the Templars were revealed to the masters of theology, including Jacques de Thérines, at the University of Paris the day following their arrest, that is, on Saturday, 14 October.[65] They were then made public in "harangues" given in the royal palace gardens on Sunday the 15th.[66] Supporters and detractors of the order were "stunned" at the extent and nature of the charges.[67] They were still more stunned nine days later on 24 October when the recently arrested grand master of the Temple, Jacques de Molay, admitted the truth of some of the crimes alleged against him and his brothers, specifically, abjuring Jesus Christ and spitting on his image, and he repeated his confession on 25 October in front of a special conclave of the masters of theology of the University of Paris, which again included Jacques de Thérines.[68] Was the grand master, this usually very brave man, frightened into lying and implicating himself in heresy, or was he relieved to lift the burden of his apostasy from his conscience? Had he been abused while under arrest despite the crown's assurances to ecclesiastical authorities that torture was not involved?[69] In fact, torture was inflicted, unbeknownst to the masters, hideous tortures: burning the soles of some of the Knights' feet until the bones fell out, hanging weights from their genitals, hauling them on ropes to ceiling heights and dropping them free-fall.[70] But ignorant of these deeds, the masters could only wonder why other arrested Templar leaders concurred so soon after the master's confession that they, too, were heretics. Was it from fear or from shame and remorse?[71] These questions arise because the grand master was soon—indeed on Christmas Eve 1307, two months to the day after making his admission—to recant his confession, and numerous other brothers issued recantations in the wake of his.[72]

There was a certain strangeness in how the ordinary routines of life, university life included, went on. Less than two weeks before the grand master's disavowal of his confession, the University of Paris held the annual Christmas 1307 quodlibets. Palémon Glorieux showed from internal as well as circumstantial evidence and with great probability that Jacques de Thérines's second quodlibetal collection of nineteen questions dates from this period.[73] The professor had prepared his notes carefully; these are some of the most extensive of his discourses. If his audience expected a replay of the previous year, with him addressing the dramatic events of the last few months, in this case, the confessions of the Templars and the violation of the freedom of the church, as he had the expulsion of the Jews and the pope's delay in going to Rome, they were sadly disappointed.

From question one on the differentiation of essence and existence in God to the last question, number nineteen, on the differential power of the passive and active will, he performed as a consummate scholastic theoretician and confined his discourse mostly to the abstract and recondite problems of metaphysics and ontology—with only one significant exception.

The audience, if they were looking for the discursive equivalent of fireworks, would not have thought the declared subject, though less abstruse than Jacques's usual topics that Christmas 1307, was very promising: whether the pope could dissolve a licit marriage, if what God has joined together, no one may sunder (Matt. 19.6).[74] The answer depended on the nature of papal power, and Jacques the ardent papalist might have developed the argument interestingly enough. No doubt he did, although his notes are extremely and uncharacteristically laconic for this question. One thing that he said, however, in affirming the papal plenitude of power over marriage, he did note down. The capacity of the pope to dissolve the most solemn oaths and vows, like marriage, was manifested in his capacity, the regent master asserted, to annihilate the solemn oaths and vows that bound men of religion, monks. It was the pope's duty, that is to say, and most critically (*specialiter*) to discern the "secrets of religious men." It was the confessions of the Templars, he then averred, that made the expeditious use of this authority absolutely necessary.[75] It seems clear that the Templars' confessions profoundly shook the Cistercian master and perhaps temporarily turned him fully against the Knights. Yet two weeks later on Christmas Eve, when the grand master and thereafter his brothers began disavowing their confessions, Jacques was stunned again. A thoughtful person could scarcely know what to believe.

The scholars of the University of Paris dispersed for their much-needed holiday after the Christmas quodlibets. It was typical for those with affiliations elsewhere to return home. It was therefore to the abbey of Chaalis that Jacques de Thérines retreated. The vacation absence of the masters in theology from the university is alluded to in a record dated the Feast of the Annunciation, 25 March 1308.[76] The record makes clear that during the vacation Philip the Fair authorized the sending of a letter of consultation to the university. He wanted the masters' opinion with regard to his own actions against the Templars. Could he act against churchmen without ecclesiastical permission if the danger to the faith were open and substantial? Even if he could not, were not the Templars secular knights against whom everyone recognized a king could justly act? There had been a great many confessions: even if a few refused to confess, was not the existence of so many confessions sufficient to sully the entire order? Should the refusal to confess of only "ten, twenty, or thirty or more" be sufficient to save the order as an institution? With all the secrecy in the order, after all, it was hard to get corroborating evidence for every allegation. If the order were to be abolished, who should receive its wealth, the princes in whose territories the Templar commanderies were situated? Or did the wealth have to go to the donors' purposes, like the Holy Land; and, if so, then who should have the right to determine how it would be used for the Holy Land? Should the French king make the determination for the wealth that came from commanderies in France? These were Philip's queries.

The masters came back to the university long before they responded to these questions.[77] They apologized profusely for their delay in answering the king, whose lineage they praised and flattered. But the delay was necessary not just because the royal letter had arrived while many masters were away. These were grave matters, hard questions. The masters averred that they had discussed them thoroughly and met over and over again before formulating their response. They also tried to be economical in their reply. For they knew, they wrote, that the king wanted clear, sharp statements, which would admit of no ambiguities, no doubtful interpretations. What all this means is that they had great difficulty reaching consensus among themselves, not because the matters were difficult (they were not), but because they were highly charged and the language had to satisfy many parties. Much as the United States Supreme Court in some of its most important and politically fraught decisions tries hard, or used to try hard, to achieve unanimity—one thinks of *Brown v. the Board of Education of Topeka, Kansas*, which outlawed segregation in public education in 1954—the masters in theology wanted to present as united a front as possible. Just as the justices in *Brown* were deeply divided ideologically on the matter of segregation, the masters in theology were divided over the issues raised by the king. Finding the right language (think of the phrase in *Brown* "with all deliberate speed") was the key to reaching consensus, and that took time and effort.

For in substance, there was little to discuss, and this comes out clearly in the response. The masters endorsed almost none of Philip's contentions, explicit or implicit.[78] No prince had a right to move against a churchman or to set up a tribunal to try heresy except, of course, when there was "the threat of an obvious, manifest danger" to the Catholic faith, and when one could presume that the church would ratify the action ex post facto. A useful comparison is Boniface VIII's language in the bull *Etsi de statu* in 1297, when he capitulated to Philip over taxation of the clergy without prior papal consent; the principle was the same.[79] Naturally and as soon as possible, however, the masters cautioned, arrangements should be returned to normal with regard to those arrested, with churchmen judging churchmen and trying heresy. As for whether the Templars were churchmen or secular knights, there had been no doubt for almost 190 years: they took vows; they were churchmen. But the masters were quick to add that the king could act against those who were not professed, mostly employees and servants and of little concern to the crown, but by far the majority of those arrested. As to whether the large number and the content of the professed Knights' confessions sullied the entirety of the order, the masters replied that, in a sense, they did: everyone was disgusted by what he heard, and this justified or, as the scholastic masters preferred to put it, gave sufficiency of cause for the order's deprecation and the enmity of the Christian people. But the masters wrote only about "suspicion," "strong suspicion," and "presumption" of the Templars' guilt arising from the confessions. They did not accept that their guilt was proved. The most they conceded was that there had to be a proper inquiry into the matter.

As for the Knights who refused to confess, the masters acknowledged once more that strong grounds for suspicion existed, since so many of their comrades had confessed. Yet guilt could not be imputed to them on this basis alone. Certainly, they should be sequestered away from the confessed brothers until such time as a final determination was made of the entire affair. But the governing principle emphatically continued to be that this final determination had to take place under the presidency of the church, not that of the crown.

What, then, could the crown do? Would it even get the wealth from the Templar commanderies in France for its own purposes? No, replied the masters. The gifts and bequests to the Knights were less to the Knights than to the Holy Land and the Catholic faith. To the question as to who would manage the resources, if the time came when the Templar Order no longer existed, the masters were indifferent. The appropriate authority, it is implied, would decide, when and if the opportunity arose for it to do so. The language left open the possibility that *ecclesia* might grant the management to the French crown, but it was *ecclesia*'s choice, no one else's.

Jacques de Thérines and thirteen other masters in theology affixed their seals to this reply to Philip as a sign of approval. It is impossible to disentangle his voice from theirs. By its very nature the reply was a compromise. The sycophantic language that opens and closes the reply, far in excess of the ordinary conventional flatteries, was intended to cushion the blow that the reply ran so strongly against the king's position.[80] Yet it is as much Jacques's language as any other's among the masters simply because, whatever he wanted to say, he agreed to say this. It was a price worth paying so that as many as possible of the masters could make a united front for the liberty of the church. Submission to the principle of emergency— conceding the prince's right to move against churchmen and heresy when "there is the threat of an obvious, manifest danger"—may have gone down hard for the Cistercian, but the bull *Etsi de statu*, which most notoriously articulated the principle with regard to taxation of the clergy, was authoritative in 1308.

For the time being the scene shifted away from the university. Clement V now began that arduously lengthy pas de deux with Philip the Fair over the fate of the Templars in France and in other kingdoms.[81] (The pope ordered their arrest throughout Christendom on 22 November 1307 preliminary to a full investigation.)[82] By one estimate, at about the time of the masters' reply to the king's questions, thirty-four Knights had already died in prison.[83] Many others succumbed from torture and hard imprisonment, heroically denying the allegations against them, in the days, weeks, and months to follow.[84] The fate of these helpless men continued to prey upon Jacques de Thérines's conscience, even though his attention was diverted temporarily to other matters. We will encounter him again, a few years later, at the Council of Vienne (1311–1312), making a courageous last-ditch intervention for the Knights.[85]

• • • • •

When, on Annunciation, 1308, the masters in theology of the University of Paris dispatched their reply to Philip the Fair's questions on the Templars to the royal palace, their ranks were divided over whether and, if so, to what extent heresy infected the great military order. The same division affected the secular princes whom Clement V had commanded to arrest and incarcerate the Knights in their lands until such time as a formal ecclesiastical board of inquiry determined the brothers' guilt or exonerated them.[86] But the preponderance of opinion in general among the elites of Europe was that, quite apart from whatever turned out to be the truth about the Templars, heresy was widespread and increasing throughout Christian society. Everyone in authority had to be watchful. In their vigilance, many princes of the church and of the state saw enemies of the orthodox all around them.[87]

Such appears to have been the case with the bishop of Cambrai. His diocese was located in a region that had a reputation for producing laymen and especially laywomen, called Beguines, of extreme devotion.[88] From the early thirteenth century on, there were enthusiastic supporters as well as denigrators of these people and of the authenticity of their spiritual experiences, which included visions, levitation, the stigmata, miracle working, prophecy, and the like. In part, ecclesiastical concerns centered on churchmen's lack of strong institutional control over these laypeople. If more of these devout laypersons formally took vows and came under the spiritual direction and authority of abbots and abbesses, there would have been less cause to worry. Another reason for anxiety was over the conclusion that simple people might draw, indeed might even be urged to draw, from the Beguines' dramatic spiritual experiences, namely, that access to divine grace did not depend on the sacraments or on priests. No theologian, of course, could reject the idea that God might act directly to inspire or give special power to a layperson, priest, or religious, but most people at most times, the argument went, lived in an ordinary world in which the sacraments were the key to the possibility of salvation.

In 1306 or a little before, it came to the attention of Gui *de Collomedio*, the bishop of Cambrai, that there was a laywoman—possibly but not certainly a Beguine—Marguerite Porete, active in his diocese, who had written a short vernacular book known as *The Mirror of Simple Souls* (*Miroir des simples âmes*).[89] The *Mirror*, most scholars now agree, has parts that are "questionable" in medieval orthodox terms, partly because the book is saturated with the unclear, though often quite exquisite, language of ecstatic devotion.[90] Marguerite herself wrote that churchmen could not fully comprehend her meaning unless they were willing to put aside their overarching trust in reason and lose themselves in love and faith.[91] Not everyone who might have been expected to like her book did so, however, for she acknowledged that even some Beguines regarded it as error-ridden.[92] Perhaps she was the target of jealousy within the devotional movements of the time. Bishop Gui was convinced not simply that there were errors in the book, but that the erroneous parts of the *Mirror* were sufficiently dangerous to require its public burning at Valenciennes in 1305 in Marguerite's presence.[93]

The bishop also ordered Marguerite not to write or speak the errors he identified in the book on pain of excommunication and being relaxed to the secular arm for judgment as a contumacious heretic. In the long history of Christian devotion, the *Mirror*, despite Gui's judgment, has fared rather well. Many manuscripts from religious houses survive, testifying to its popularity—and overall compatibility with orthodoxy.[94] On occasion, scribes have revised or glossed passages of questionable orthodoxy in these manuscripts.[95] This practice demonstrates that at least some churchmen took a narrow view of Bishop Gui's (and, later, others') judgment. As far as they were concerned, it was perfectly appropriate to condemn the heterodox passages in the *Mirror*, but Christians could treasure the book as a whole as a tender and moving description, through seven stages of progression, of the quest for mystical union with God.

Marguerite, despite the bishop's decision, continued to speak and to use her little book to spread her message. She sent copies—whole, not censored copies—to other ecclesiastical authorities, like the bishop of Chalons. On the one hand, these authorities did not recognize the same level of danger in the *Mirror* as Gui of Cambrai did, although they were uneasy about how simple Christians might interpret the book's intoxicating language.[96] On the other hand, certain ecclesiastical authorities would later use their testimony to establish that Marguerite had defied Gui's order and ipso facto put herself under the ban of excommunication. By the time

her continuing activities became common knowledge, the pope had translated Gui to the see of Salerno on 22 January 1306. The bishop died at
Avignon while en route.[97] His successor in Cambrai pursued the matter
against Marguerite in concert with the Inquisition.

Jacques de Thérines and the other masters in theology at the University
of Paris could not have been ignorant of the fact that Marguerite had
traveled to Paris by mid-1308, had been arrested, and remained incarcer-
ated in the city for refusing to obey what was now an order issued and
confirmed by a long series of high ecclesiastics.[98] She remained steadfast
despite her imprisonment. The press of the Templar business notwithstanding, the Dominican Guillaume de Paris, who was in charge of carrying out inquisitions into heretical depravity in the kingdom of France,
began to put more time into Marguerite's case. Once again, the scholarly
consensus is that Marguerite's case would not have elicited such a great
dignitary's intense notice, had not the charged atmosphere in Paris, because of the Templar affair and her own obstinacy, influenced Guillaume
to make an example of her.

From the time lag between her incarceration, mid-1308, and her relaxation to the secular arm at the end of May 1310, it seems fairly certain
that the Dominican inquisitor's plan was to use the lengthy imprisonment
as an inducement for her to confess and beg forgiveness before the bishop
of Paris and perhaps the bishop of Cambrai. When she repeatedly refused,
he repeatedly threatened her with the consequences. Ultimately he lost
patience, but he knew that in some circles Marguerite's book was admired.
He decided to consult the masters in theology at the university.[99] On this
occasion, 11 April 1310, Jacques de Thérines and twenty other masters
examined the materials collected against Marguerite, although the employment of the word "examined" considerably overstates what they
did.[100] The deck was stacked against the mystic from the beginning, for
the inquisitor, though he had a manuscript of the entire book with him
and displayed it, provided the masters with only excerpts from the *Mirror*.
Of course, these passages, fifteen in all, consisted of those readily susceptible, especially out of context, to heterodox interpretations. Even if the
book was passed around, several of the masters—Italians like Alexander
of Sant'Elpidio and Gregory of Lucca or the imperial scholar Henry the
German—were almost certainly unable to read the dialect of French in
which it was written and depended on written or oral Latin translations
of the excerpts.[101] There is no evidence that they requested to have the
whole book translated for them preliminary to a decision.

Moreover, although the masters removed themselves from the inquisitor's presence in order to deliberate, they did not deliberate at length.
(This contrasts strikingly with the long and repeated deliberations they
undertook in formulating their reply to the king on the Templar business.

It was far easier to condemn a woman's book and to get more masters to join in doing so than to face up to a king.) One standard of judgment, one might plausibly conjecture, that the professors applied to the excerpts was that of the "simple person," the kind of believer the defenders of orthodoxy were always talking about protecting: would the book mislead a simple person?[102] Consider the fifteenth of the excerpts, rendered in Latin for the masters, Marguerite's statement that the believer's soul, when it was reduced to nothingness in its love of God, "does not care about the consolations or the gifts of God; nor should it care or be able to care, because her entire attention [*tota intenta*] is with God." To care for these things would "impede" (*impeditur*) the annihilated soul's "progress [*intentio*] to God."[103] A simple person might infer an antisacramental theology from this, namely, that the man or woman who has achieved the blessedness of the annihilated soul no longer needed, need not even care for, the gifts of God, the body and blood in the sacrament of the altar.[104]

The decision was a foregone conclusion. A book that contained such an array of dubious statements had to be condemned, for the inquisitor intimated that the excerpts were but the tip of the iceberg.[105] The inquisitor returned to Marguerite with the results of the deliberation, presumably to try one last time to persuade her that if the most learned men in theology in the world found errors in her work, she should acquiesce in their judgment. She continued to refuse, despite seven more weeks of imprisonment to think about it. With the subsequent consent of ecclesiastical legal experts resident in Paris, the inquisitor then relaxed Marguerite to the secular arm on 31 May 1310.[106] Royal officials executed her by burning the next day on the Place de Grève, the same site where, two decades before, the miracle of the consecrated host reputedly occurred, a miracle that Jacques de Thérines only a few years earlier had remembered as a testimony to the power of the sacrament and a support to the weak of faith.[107]

• • • • •

The native of Thérines, monk of Chaalis, and Cistercian master in theology would soon depart Paris. Indeed, the period of his sojourn in the city at the time of the masters' judgment against Marguerite Porete's book was relatively brief, for Jacques had just come back from the chapter meeting at Chaalis for the election of a new abbot. In the event, his brother monks chose him as their leader. All he had to do was return to Paris, complete whatever pressing matters needed his personal attention, and gather up his belongings for the removal to Chaalis. It was in this interval, between his election as abbot and his active assumption of his new role, that Jacques heard the arguments against the *Mirror*, discussed them with the other masters in theology, and affixed his newly minted seal, designating him "abbot of Chaalis," to the censure on 11 April 1310.[108] He then departed the capital, a city where he had been in continuous residence probably from the time of the host miracle on the Place Saint-Jean-en-Grève (1290), uninterrupted except for lengthy academic holidays spent back at Chaalis.

It was a good time to leave Paris. Marguerite's execution—whether or not Jacques concurred with the inquisitor that it, not just the burning of her book, was necessary to protect the weak and simple of faith from heresy—may not have had the immediate effect the inquisitor desired. She died well. She struck the crowds who came to watch her burn as a gentle penitent.[109] It is not clear whether the chroniclers, who report this fact and the great sympathy and tears that went out to Marguerite from the onlookers, meant to imply that she recanted toward the end. One of her devoted followers, Guiard de Cressonessart, however, did do so somewhat earlier.[110] Upon recanting, this Guiard, who had once proclaimed himself, with Doomsday foreboding, the Angel of Philadelphia (Apoc. 1.11 and 3.7ff.), was sentenced the same day as Marguerite, but to perpetual imprisonment. He hailed, as his name implies, from Cressonessart, a little hamlet in Jacques de Thérines's own *pays*.[111] What, if anything, Jacques thought about the Angel is a mystery. There is no evidence that he took any part in his case. Yet he might have had some interesting things to say, for the Cistercian is known to have written an Apocalypse commentary, now unfortunately lost.[112] One would like to know what he would have made of the Angel from his home country, whose heterodox ideas came not only from Marguerite Porete's *Mirror of Simple Souls* but also from Apocalypse commentaries he had read.[113]

3

THE EXEMPTION CONTROVERSY
AT THE COUNCIL OF VIENNE

THE ABBEY OF CHAALIS and the tiny village that abutted it were situated within a short ride of the depths of the forest of Ermenonville. Within the dense sweeps of hardwoods, there were dunes so extensive and bereft of habitation that they gave rise to the name Sea of Sand (*Mer de Sable*).[1] The Sea of Sand is home now to an amusement park, and little remains of the grand Cistercian abbey except the beautiful thirteenth-century Abbot's Chapel, much restored, and a few other fragments.[2] It is difficult, with the comings and goings of tourists to the Musée Jacquemart-André on the grounds of the ruined abbey, to imagine the austere institution with quietly prayerful and learned White Monks, preferring signing to speech and processing in the cloister, in the time of Jacques de Thérines.[3]

Founded in 1136 by King Louis VI the Fat on the site of a former priory of the Benedictine Order, Chaalis took its name from the king's brother, Charles, *Karolus* in Latin. Louis endowed it in Charles's memory.[4] It was "Charles's Place," *Karoli Locus*. In a different dialectical setting, its name might have become the vernacular "Charlieu," as happened with the Benedictine monastery of the same Latin name in the Loire valley, and with the Cistercian Charlieu in the diocese of Besançon not too distant from the Swiss border, but France had such a polyphony of dialects in the Middle Ages that there was little consistency in the language across the north.[5] This fact reinforces the importance of locality to men like Jacques de Thérines. Though professionally a Latin speaker, reader, and writer, he was most at home in the French minidialect of his *pays* when carrying on the business that an abbot had to carry on in the local *patois* with the monastery's gentle and bourgeois neighbors.

The kings of France were generous to Chaalis, without requiring anything material in return.[6] Besides the founder's grants, there were intermittent gifts and confirmations by all subsequent monarchs until Jacques's time as abbot.[7] Many of the gifts were assigned on yearly rents or otherwise brought annual regular income to the abbey.[8] Local lords, inspired by the crown, also became generous patrons.[9] The abbey's great Gothic church was built between the years 1202 and 1219; it was dedicated on 20 October of the latter year by the bishop of Senlis, with the assistance of the bishops of Chartres and Toulouse, whose presence, from such distant parts, is striking testimony to the abbey's prestige in the early thirteenth century.[10] Besides many abbots and some local seigneurs, several bishops of Senlis were interred in the church in subsequent decades, most famously the dedicator of the abbey church, Brother Guérin, a Templar who became bishop at Philip II Augustus's request in the early thirteenth century, and who, as chancellor of France, oversaw the royal administration.[11]

Until Philip the Fair, the French kings loved Chaalis. They so often visited the abbey that the route they took came to be known popularly as the Chemin du Roi, the King's Highway.[12] Likewise, the chapel in which the rulers worshiped with the monks, now called the Abbot's Chapel after the abbot who redecorated it in the sixteenth century, was known in the Middle Ages as the Chapelle du Roi.[13] King Louis IX (1226–1270) sojourned at Chaalis at least eleven times.[14] He admired the forms of devotion and ritual practice that distinguished the monks' lives there.[15] During one visit the brothers showed him the stone slab that served as the table on which they washed recently deceased monks in preparation for their funerals and burial. Moved by the thought of the hallowed dead who had once reposed on the stone, the king kissed the table, explaining that he did so because of its imputed holiness: "O God! How many saintly men have been washed here!"[16]

Louis IX supercharged the abbey's holiness by arranging to have the body of Saint Constance, one of the eleven thousand virgin martyrs of Cologne, and that of a martyred soldier of the Theban Legion given to Chaalis.[17] These were not minor relics. The cult of Saint Ursula and the eleven thousand virgins, whose Christian faith reputedly inspired the lethal frenzy of the pagan Huns, and that of Saint Maurice's Christian legionnaires, who were executed, despite their contribution to a great Roman victory, for their refusal to offer a sacrifice of thanksgiving to the pagan gods, were enormously popular in the thirteenth century. As a result of such benefactions, to the monks of Chaalis Louis IX was like a second founder.[18]

After Louis IX's death the monks treasured one of his cloaks as a relic (it was given to them by a royal chamberlain who was one of the king's close personal friends), and a little later, when Laurent, the prior (subsequently abbot), grew ill with unbearable pain in his back and lower limbs and could no longer walk, he attributed his recovery to the cloak. The story he told in 1282 at the age of fifty-eight to the canonization commissioners investigating the sanctity of Louis IX described how, after enduring two weeks of excruciating pain, he was treated by professional doctors, to no avail. It was the abbey sacristan who brought the cloak and, assisted by another monk, wrapped Laurent in it in all devotion. After sleeping in the cloak through the night, the prior felt delivered from his agony. The doctors testified to the fact that he had dispensed with the poultices they prescribed for his use. It was, they all sincerely believed (or said they believed), the holy king's intervention that cured the prior.[19]

In many ways Jacques de Thérines was an ideal candidate in 1310 for abbot of Chaalis, a monastery with this close relationship with the crown. He had contacts with the highest secular powers in Paris. He was a scholar of renown, as well. Two books that he wrote—one on the body of Christ, the other on the Apocalypse—remain unidentified in extant manuscripts; the information we can derive from allusions to them is inadequate to distinguish them from the mass of anonymous treatises on the same subjects.[20] Some evidence suggests that he was the author of commentaries on parts of the Old and New Testaments, whose quality gave him expert status as an interpreter.[21] And, of course, it was expected that he would gather his Parisian quodlibets into a volume.[22] He also knew a great deal of canon law, although early modern humanists, who implied that he had formal learning in both laws (civil and canon), did so as a consequence of the books he wrote *after* he became abbot of Chaalis.[23]

Nonetheless, there were risks the brothers took in electing Jacques. The quodlibets of 1306–1307 were not exactly ancient history by the date of the monk's election in 1310, although whatever memory there was of their provocative nature could be expected to fade. The fact that King Philip the Fair had not reacted to the quodlibetal question that could be construed as criticizing his expulsion of French Jews—not even when his son enforced a policy in Navarre that mirrored Jacques's preferences— was reassuring in this regard. Jacques's imprudence (or impudence) was forgotten, forgiven, or ignored, as far as anyone knew. If Philip suspected that his son would revoke his policy in a few years, also in line with Jacques's opinions, then the situation might have been different. But there is no evidence that the king thought his expulsion was anything but permanent. The other act that made Jacques's election risky was the stand he took with the other university masters in theology in 1308 against Philip the Fair's continued incarceration of the Templars, even though they were men of the church. But the general loyalty of the university to the crown and the collective nature of the document in which he expressed this view ensured his not being singled out as one of Philip the Fair's particularly troublesome opponents.

While he was settling into what he thought would be his routine as abbot, Jacques found time to supervise the editing of his quodlibets.[24] The manuscript shows evidence of close personal scrutiny.[25] The scribe who wrote it provided a few glosses to Jacques's words where the technical language was difficult or obscure.[26] Beyond the small cluster of scholars at Chaalis, however, the book did not travel. Its limited influence prevented it from inflaming any possible embers of resentment against the Cistercian master in royal circles. There is one very nice passage in which the scribe forgot that he was transcribing in Jacques's voice and referred instead to "the little work 'you' [Jacques] wrote for the chancellor of [the University of] Paris."[27] Glorieux rightly emended the text to "the little work 'I' [still, Jacques] wrote."[28] But the lapse allows us almost to hear the scribe interacting with the abbot in the first few months of the latter's new position. The small book, to judge from the context of the reference, was a defense of the literal truth of Jesus' words of institution in the mass, "This is my body," but why Jacques wrote it and why for the university chancellor are unknown. The chancellor's entreaty attests to the Cistercian's reputation as a scholar, however.

• • • • •

On 12 August 1308 Pope Clement V announced an ecumenical council of the church for 1 October 1310. The preliminaries, however, took far more time and work than he anticipated. In particular, the investigation of the Templars was slowly dragging along. In the event, the pontiff postponed the opening of the council for a year. Two other matters, besides the affair of the Temple, were to be the focus of the council's business: the organization of a new Crusade and the reform of the church. Of course, the concerns overlapped, but the last in particular gave rise to two difficult questions and a spate of polemical outbursts. How would Clement V discipline the exempt clergy who, their critics argued, enjoyed undeserved privileges and caused scandals in the church?[29] Would he halt the strife that was tearing the Franciscan Order apart on the issue of apostolic poverty?[30]

Clement V convened the council, which met at the episcopal city of Vienne on the Rhône River on 1 October 1311. The city's impressive ancient Roman monuments, many fallen into ruin, testified to the initial victory of Christianity over paganism. The council was intended to renew that victory, especially if there was any truth to allegations of the Templars' backsliding into idolatry. The first working session (the first of three) was held in the gigantic and magnificent Cathedral of Saint-Maurice beginning on the 16th of October. What better venue to test the faith of warrior-monks than a church dedicated to the martyred commander of the Theban Legion who refused to sacrifice to idols? The abbot of Chaalis attended the council, undoubtedly leaving the monastery's administration in the prior's hands. His absence was to be prolonged by the fact that Jacques was well known as an advocate of the rights of the exempt orders and was needed in Vienne to confront the attack on exemption led by Giles of Rome, the archbishop of Bourges. As a result, the new abbot's management of Chaalis's affairs was spotty until after the council concluded and he could give his full attention to the task.[31] The three sessions of the council lasted from 16 October 1311 to 6 May 1312, with relatively limited breaks between them, when the clerical attendees returned to their sees, monasteries, and prebends. (Lay participants, like the king of France, were not in regular attendance, of course.) However much Chaalis needed its abbot in residence, it turned out that the Cistercian Order needed his attendance at Vienne even more.

For a century discontent had been growing among bishops who could not exercise jurisdiction over the exempt orders or over specially favored monasteries in nonexempt orders.[32] The bishops' displeasure mirrored that of the vast majority of nonexempt ecclesiastical corporations, which, having no hope of freeing themselves from episcopal jurisdiction, did not see what justified their subordination yet favored privileges for the exempt orders and houses. The authority that the bishops wanted restored to them was not simply judicial. They sought the right of visitation, which meant permission to sojourn at, receive full hospitality from, and investigate all activities in the exempt houses. They also wanted the exempt houses to contribute to the revenue needed to meet the episcopate's crushing financial obligations to the papacy, secular princes, and the care of the faithful.

The most formidable articulation of these views was the *Contra exemptos* of Giles of Rome, an altogether interesting man and a scholar's scholar—the author, known appropriately as *doctor verbosus*, of approximately 140 books and treatises in the course of his career.[33] He was the young Philip the Fair's tutor, but opinions differ on whether he had a great deal of influence on the prince.[34] Though his election to the archiepiscopate of Bourges in 1295 would not have been tolerated without his former pupil's agreement, this does not mean that Giles was "subservient" to the king.[35] In 1301 he defended Pope Boniface VIII's authority, at a time when it was more than just impolitic to do so.[36] As a theologian, he was also an interesting man. Although an Augustinian Hermit, he fully imbibed the philosophical ideas of his Dominican teacher, Thomas Aquinas, and defended them intelligently against the attacks of conservatives, like the bishop of Paris, Etienne Tempier, in the late 1270s.[37] The dominance of conservative elements led to his early retirement from the university, however.[38] From 1281 until 1285 he busied himself in Italy in leadership positions in the Order of the Augustinian Hermits before returning, under papal protection, to Paris, where he taught for a few years. He then assumed the headship of his order in 1292, until he was called to become archbishop of Bourges in 1295. Since he was born in the mid-1240s, he was a man in his late sixties by the time of the Council of Vienne—an éminence grise.

The Templar affair made the whole issue of exemptions all the more urgent. Giles was incensed by the Templars' crimes, which he regarded as proved. Nothing could persuade him otherwise.[39] To the argument that they fought courageously for Christ, he retorted that these were exceptional encounters: the Knights were more often in league with the Saracens, and if they did fight them, they did so for profit (*temporale lucrum*) or for appearance' sake (*ut coram hominibus apparerent*).[40] Even the devil did an occasional good deed, after all, but for the wrong reason.[41]

Giles took a hard line against exemptions, in part (and rhetorically it was his most powerful point) because, in his view, the Templars were an exempt order. If the Knights had submitted regularly to episcopal visitation and had been under the yoke of episcopal jurisdiction, their precipitous fall from grace into sodomy, heresy, and idolatry would be inconceivable.[42] Exemption undermined hierarchy. God ruled the world through his creatures in descending order of authority. It was therefore also unnatural for the pope, God's vicar, to rule lower parts of the church immediately, that is to say, without the bishops' mediation. The good theologian used elaborate figurative tropes to make this point.[43] Exemption, of course, finally meant too much secrecy. The secret receptions and professions of new Knights, the absolute secrecy of Templar chapter meetings, and the secrecy fostered by immunities that prevented communication and common enterprise with other groups—all these created the perfect atmosphere for degeneration from Christian ideals. Secrecy had its place, of course, and some ecclesiastical institutions enjoined similar types of secrecy, but not this whole panoply. Episcopal visitation, he repeated, would have broken the palisade of secrecy around the Templars and stymied their degeneration.[44] All the evils came from exemption.[45]

What was true of the Templars was true potentially wherever exemption was permitted. The exempt clergy grew wealthy, too wealthy, through their immunity to subventions levied by synods. Without serious supervision by bishops, nothing restrained them from violating the rules under which they were supposed to live holy lives. Autonomy led them into arrogance, the deadly sin of pride. They equated justice with whatever they wanted, not with what they deserved. In them there was no true religion.[46] Giles of Rome was not the only author of works against exemption, but his was the most effective and a source of pride to academic types among the Augustinian Hermits, who treasured the professor-turned-archbishop's book.[47]

Jacques de Thérines loathed Archbishop Giles. Nothing short of loathing can explain the vituperative excesses of the polemical tracts he circulated while at Vienne to counter what he considered the Augustinian Hermit's poisonous invective. In 1914 Noël Valois published summaries of the four texts the abbot wrote and circulated at the Council of Vienne in 1311 and 1312.[48] And the few historians who have alluded to the quarrel over exemptions and Jacques's role in it have, with one exception, depended on Valois.[49] It is my intention not to duplicate his summaries but to highlight some of the issues that the Cistercian polemicist raised and to place them in the wider context of ecclesiastical politics in the early fourteenth century.

The tracts, among which the earliest is the *Contra impugnatores exemptionum* (*Against the Impugners of Exemptions*), contain biting but somewhat off-putting ad hominem attacks on the archbishop.[50] To be sure, these were not entirely based on innuendo and gossip, for one allegation was manifestly true, namely, that the archbishop while a master at the University of Paris had openly endorsed propositions and philosophical positions associated with Thomas Aquinas that Bishop Etienne Tempier condemned. The issue that set the Cistercian off was Giles's defense of the proposition, again associated with Aquinas, that God cannot make several angels in the same species.[51] Valois pointed out that Jacques had addressed himself to similar issues in his quodlibets.[52] The view that Aquinas and Giles opposed was that angels consisted of both form and matter—in the case of angels, to use Bonaventure's terminology, "spiritual" matter. The union of the two created individual "personality" in the angels, who otherwise were of the same species, much as the union of form and corporeal matter individuates human beings. Aquinas rejected the idea of immaterial, that is, spiritual matter. For him angels were pure form. Yet they were individuals—Raphael, Gabriel, Michael, Lucifer. Their individuation could be assured and therefore was assured only by the fact that each formed a species unto itself.[53]

The point, which may strike a modern reader as arcane, was not so to Jacques de Thérines. Giles's stand offended him in three ways. First, it contradicted his own philosophical view, which he thought was correct. Second, it defied the magisterial authority of the bishop of Paris to declare what was and what was not consistent with the Catholic faith. Third, and consequently, it exposed Giles's hypocrisy: the Augustinian Hermit's defiance of episcopal censure was not in accord with his insistence that submission of the exempt orders to the authority of bishops would protect the church from error. If there really were potential for errors or errors already flourishing in the exempt orders, how could bishops deal with the problem when they could not stop one deviant, Giles of Rome, from defying them and possibly infecting his students?[54]

This part of Abbot Jacques's counterattack was mild, but he often wrote in a more vehement and less elevated vein. He did not disdain *fama*: public knowledge, we might say, or, less neutrally, rumor.[55] Rumor had it, he reported, that Giles of Rome's retinue comprised a basically dysfunctional gang, an odd lot of thieves and frauds who practiced their chicaneries in Bourges when word of their master's elevation to the archbishopric of the city became known.[56] Using the authority of his new position, members of his retinue preyed upon the wealth of the people of Bourges and so incensed them that the burghers tried to prevent the new archbishop from entering upon his office. Moreover, the citizens of the town were encouraged to do so by Giles's own dismissive and completely unsympathetic response to their complaints. He allegedly denied all responsibility and averred that he could hardly help it that his hangers-on were not angels![57] These accusations undoubtedly owed something to the circumstances surrounding Giles's accession to the see of Bourges. Pope Boniface VIII's predecessor, Celestine V, had approved a different candidate, a Frenchman, but after Celestine's resignation Boniface quashed the selection and appointed Giles, an Italian. Resentments ran high and therefore delayed his installation. In the interval the archbishop-elect and his entourage lived a semi-itinerant existence before entering formally into the see. This was an unhappy period, full of recriminations, on all sides.[58]

As far as Jacques de Thérines was concerned, the rumors were true. Giles was not only a theologian with bad ideas but an insensitive pastor unwilling to do justice to his flock. What else? Everyone knew, Jacques informed his readers and no doubt anyone who cared to listen to him, that the archbishop and his entourage once descended on an exempt abbey and demanded, in place of the modest hospitality freely offered by the generous monks, a full meal *with meat*, a request that particularly repelled the rigorously vegetarian Cistercian. Giles's attendants stole what they wanted (*duos porcos*) when their demand was refused, and they beat the prior of the Cistercian abbey of Loroy, the monastery in question and the oldest Cistercian foundation in the archdiocese of Bourges. As a result of the brutal attack, rumor had it, the prior soon afterward lost an eye.[59] For Jacques, Giles of Rome represented the very type of bishop who, thoughtless and unable to exercise either self-restraint or discipline over his entourage, wanted to extend his "control" to the exempt clergy. Not that such bishops could exercise disciplinary authority any better than abbots did, but, if exemptions were withdrawn, the prelates would have a claim on the resources of the formerly privileged institutions and would use the kind of coercion to enforce those claims that monks were not permitted to employ to defend their properties. The hypocrisy, as the abbot saw it, was patently obvious and deeply sick.[60]

The four treatises evolved slightly over the course of the council in response to objections raised and conversations that transpired during the deliberations. *Contra impugnatores exemptionum*, the first, is impassioned and comprehensive with regard to practical considerations in favor of maintaining the system of exemptions. Its target was particularly the points Giles allegedly argued *minus rationabiliter.*[61] If it swayed anyone, it did so because it pointed out some of the benefits that the system bestowed on the church as a whole.[62] For critics whose objections to exemption were philosophically based, even if they conceded the practical benefits, Jacques wrote a second treatise, which goes by the name *Compendium contra impugnatores exemptionum*, the word "compendium" in the rubric accurately denoting a handbook of scholastically informed arguments.[63] Many critics, of course, based their hostility on what might be termed theological considerations. To counter their objections, Jacques produced a third polemic, the so-called *Quaestio de exemptionibus*, in which he insisted on the compatibility of exemption and hierarchy in the church. After all, he pointed out, many laypeople held special privileges from princes, which were somewhat analogous to the exemptions of privileged clergy granted by popes, but no one suggested that this was unnatural or incompatible with the prevailing status hierarchies of lay Christian society.[64] By the time of the circulation of this third treatise, the abbot's onslaught was paying off, as internal evidence from the fourth and final work shows. There was evidently some attempt at compromise from the critics, who recognized that certain influential presences at the council, including the pope, did not favor a blanket suppression of exemptions. The little handbook Jacques now circulated, known as the *Responsio ad quaedam quae petebant praelati in praejudicium exemptorum* (*An Answer to Certain Recommendations Prelates Have Made to the Disadvantage of the Exempt*), summarized the various arguments of the earlier polemics and warned his supporters not to compromise: to give in on anything to the hostile bishops as a conciliatory gesture was to allow them to pollute the elect (*ponere maculam in electis*) and would embolden them and prepare the way for the future erosion of privileges (*in aliis usurpare*).[65]

Five issues or questions, treated from various standpoints and ordinarily in more than one of the treatises, stand out. The first concerns the relative effectiveness of discipline and obedience in the exempt orders as opposed to the situation among the nonexempt clergy. Second and closely related to it is the question of the practical fruits of exemption: how had the existence of the system of exemptions benefited the church historically? The third issue on which Jacques focused was the particular benefits the Holy See derived from the existence of exempt orders and houses. Fourth, he considered whether the mendicant orders formed a special case in the system of exemption. And, finally, the abbot addressed the Templar scandal and whether that scandal owed anything to the alleged exemption of the order, as Giles of Rome asserted. Many of these themes he had taken up in his days as a Parisian master. Now he addressed them with greater urgency in a city and buildings crowded with the ecclesiastical princes of the Catholic faithful.

With regard to discipline and obedience, the Cistercian argued that the purer the exemption enjoyed by an institution from outside authority, always saving that of the supreme pontiff (in no way to be conflated with an ordinary bishop), and the stronger the disciplinary authority of the head of the institution, the greater the likelihood that the institution would avoid scandals. Criticisms that focused on the bad behavior, for example, of certain collegiate chapters that enjoyed immunity from episcopal authority were off the mark.[66] These collegiate chapters were but loose corporations formed of the priests who served the multiple altars and held prebends in very large churches. A dean headed each chapter. Abbot Jacques pointed to the striking differences between this type of organization and that of the exempt monastic orders. Cistercian monks (just like Premonstratensians, Carthusians, and the like) took vows of absolute and perpetual obedience to their abbots. They did not ordinarily leave the cloister or interact with layfolk, unlike secular priests in collegiate chapters or, as the abbot of Chaalis added pointedly, the friars, whom Giles of Rome admired, who came close to vagabondage in their wanderings and had at best only a tenuous connection to any specific mendicant convent.[67] It was also true that every abbot's power of correction far exceeded that of the dean of a collegiate chapter.[68]

Moreover, in an exempt order—not simply a specially privileged, say, Benedictine, house in an otherwise nonexempt order—there was a hierarchy of disciplinary mechanisms beyond the monastery that reinforced the power of the abbot: *regular* annual visitations from "parent" monasteries; supervision through *regular* meetings, provincial chapters, of the abbots in the filiations, generations, or provinces into which the order was divided; and finally oversight by means of the *regular* annual meetings, General Chapters, of the abbots of the entire order or their lieutenants.[69]

Lesser forms of exemption also led to greed, and greed, as everyone acknowledged, was the seedbed of scandals. Even so, the level of greed among the imperfectly exempt paled in comparison with that of the wholly nonexempt clergy.[70] As long as discipline was inadequate over clergymen in collegiate chapters, over friars in general, and over monks in privileged houses of nonexempt orders, the beneficiaries of the advantages of immunity thought too much in terms of its pecuniary profit. They were motivated to defend their privileges by their desire to maintain this profit, that is, by greed.[71] True poverty existed within the exempt orders—in the cloister.[72] Discipline was so severe that the monks, with almost angelic perfection, abided by their rules, which were emphatic about the avoidance of excess and material comfort.[73] And most especially this pertained to meat, whose avoidance for Jacques de Thérines was among the highest tokens of true brotherhood; if the bishops exercised authority over the vegetarians, they would pollute the latter's monasteries by eating meat (*petunt posse communiter carnes comedere in ordine cysterciensi*).[74] They were more interested in meat than in souls.[75] Friars, on the other hand, were out begging. If they were effective, they garnered a great deal. No superior authority even knew how much. Success at begging was a stimulus to more intensive begging and greater returns. Greed was the fuel that motivated mendicancy.[76] Since the purest and most effective form of exemption required enclosure in the cloister, the mendicants were bound to fall short in the quality of their behavior. In other words, if scandals arose from the behavior of priests in collegiate chapters and even from that of monks in privileged houses in nonexempt orders, it was because these men of the church had too little, not too much, in common with the monks in fully exempt orders.

When he addressed the practical fruits of exemption, the benefits for Holy Church and the common good, the abbot was boundless in his enthusiasm and his claims.[77] The exempt were the example for all Christians. They manifested the greatest piety, the deepest devotion, the fullest abundance of prayers for the living and the dead, the most pleasing acts of mercy, and the strictest self-denial (*in favorem puritatis et asperitatis vitae*).[78] Thus, he declared, the exemptions and privileges of those in the religious orders nurtured the salvation of the Christian people and the exaltation of the Christian religion.[79] Freed and secure from the temptations of the world, they pursued their holy tasks with an energy and single-mindedness of purpose that also had its fruit in intellectual production of the highest order in the service of the church, namely, the best theologians (*notabiles baccallarios ac magistros*) and the most excellent schools to continue to train them, like the Cistercian College of Saint-Bernard in Paris (at which Jacques studied and on whose faculty he served before becoming abbot of Chaalis).[80] But he was unstinting in his praise of all the exempt and imperfectly exempt orders in this regard, Cluniacs, Preachers, Minors, Carmelites, even Giles of Rome's own Augustinian Hermits. It was obvious to anyone who cared to look (*sicut liquide patet*).[81] He likened the exempt to the life force running through the healthy body and, indeed, to the selfless royal bodyguard (*sui proprii corporis . . . milites strenuos et probatos*) in the midst of battle.[82] It is hardly necessary to say that this is a very one-sided and indeed idealized portrait of Cistercian life; a polemicist who indulges in subtlety would be a contradiction in terms.

Yet here and there in these polemical writings Jacques did concede that there were bishops and clergy who were good men and accomplished good deeds.[83] There had even been an archbishop of Bourges once upon a time who was quite decent; the implied contrast with the present archbishop, Giles of Rome, is obvious. This earlier prelate, Guillaume de Donjeon by name, was a saint in heaven, and the so-called French Nation of the University of Paris, comprising scholars from Romance-speaking regions, not including Normandy and Picardy, particularly honored his memory (*de quo etiam natio Franciae in universitate Parisiensi facit festum suum speciale*).[84] It was no accident, however, that he was a good man. He came from an exempt order, the Cistercians, and in fact served as the abbot of none

other than Chaalis in the early thirteenth century before his election to
the archiepiscopal see of Bourges.[85]

Exceptions aside, the secular clergy, particularly the bishops, Jacques
insisted, were a blot upon the church.[86] They practiced nepotism, appointing their know-nothing, stupid, and filthy-minded relatives (*nepotes et cog-
natos nescios et idiotas et dissolutos*) to important ecclesiastical positions.[87]
Greed corrupted them.[88] If they were not feeble of mind, though they
often were, prelates used their intelligence not to any good ends, like the
founding and staffing of colleges, but to fleece their flocks and to oppress
nonexempt monasteries over which they had rights of visitation.[89] They
could be compared to a savage beast (*ad brutum*) seeking prey (*prae-
dam*).[90] They had no desire to repress the excesses of their subordinates
either directly or through the authority of provincial synods, but simply
hoped to seize the exempts' resources through litigation, whether justified
or not (*juste vel injuste*).[91] And their vanity was unbounded. This is why
they waited upon princes and shared in their blood sports—birding, hunting, and war.[92] To be governed by bishops was noxious (*potestas episcopalis
primo sit nociva regimini religiosorum*).[93] Relief from prelates' meddling
and troublemaking (*semotis vexationibus et cunctis gravaminibus*) would
allow the *opus divinum* to achieve the summit of spiritual perfection (*cum
summa perfectione perficiatur*).[94] If the stated goal of the Council of Vienne was to reform the church, then it behooved the pope to begin with
the prelacy, where the rottenness was greatest.[95]

One wonders how such denigrating remarks could influence the bishops, whose numbers dominated the council, to support the system of exemption. The answer is simple. The bishops were inconsequential. Nothing would persuade them anyway. Their virtue had been in a constant state
of erosion since the time of Pope Gregory the Great, as far as the Cistercian
abbot of Chaalis was concerned. Indeed, that great pope foresaw the prelacy's wayward descent and, so Jacques alleged, instituted exemption in an-
ticipation.[96] The bishops had numbers on their side, but the plenitude of
power rested with the pope. Jacques de Thérines was trying his best to
influence Clement V, who wanted both sides in the debate to lower their
voices.[97] Yet the abbot was saying things, even if they were stock arguments and assertions, that must have bothered Clement, in the sense that
he could not dismiss the accusations against the secular clergy out of hand.
Though a bishop himself before his elevation to the papacy, he suffered
the "visitation" of the archbishop of Bourges—Giles of Rome, in fact—in
his diocese of Bordeaux and seems to have felt the demands were excessive.
One of his earliest acts as pope was to exempt Bordeaux from Bourges's
jurisdiction.[98] Nor could Clement wholly ignore the claims to special virtue monks made in defense of their profession. It was, after all, a widely

shared belief, under attack certainly, but still strong, that the monastic life was the highest form of the Christian life and the most beneficial for Christian society.[99] What Abbot Jacques was suggesting was that the highest form of the monastic life itself, that which gave eternal life to the whole Christian people, was the life lived by the monks of the exempt orders.

A special subset of the benefits for Christendom as a whole that resulted from the existence of exempt clergy comprised the benefits for the Holy See. Pontifical power was absolute.[100] All of Giles of Rome's elaborate analogies to show that the pope should rule through his delegates were less similitudes than dissimilitudes (*quae plus habet dissimilitudinis quam similitudinis*).[101] Even if a pope chose to rule through delegates, he could recuperate the delegated authority. The proper analogy was with kings, who did so all the time (*sicut patet de Rege et ballivo*).[102] How did Christians maintain their recognition of the supreme authority of the Apostolic See, which the abbot affirmed over and over again in unequivocal terms?[103] Jacques argued that a clear reminder of that authority (*liquide patet*) was the unmediated nature of the jurisdiction exercised by the Holy See over exempt clergy.[104] Every diocese in Christendom had these institutions. Their regular recourse to the pope to defend their freedom in the face of local onslaughts against them was a powerful reminder to local potentates that supreme authority rested with the successor of Saint Peter. Who, it is implied, could possibly be or historically was more loyal to the Holy See than the exempt clergy, the singular sons of the Roman church (*etiam speciales et peculiares filii Romanae ecclesiae*), whose very existence depended on its authority?[105] If schism carried away a whole region, what institutions, except the exempt orders, could be expected to keep alive the spirit of orthodoxy articulated by the pope in his role as defender of the faith?[106] Even the bishops were kept in check by the existence of and rivalry with the exempt; without the latter they would see no need to seek the pontiff's favor and would declare their independence from his jurisdiction.[107] Finally, to yield (*revocatio seu detruncatio*) on exemptions granted by the pontiffs would certainly be interpreted as a concession, obfuscation, or derogation of authority, as if the Apostolic See were obliged to yield.[108] A pope under the kind of pressure Philip the Fair was applying might find this argument instructive.

Less prominent in Jacques de Thérines's discourse was the question of the friars. The abbot detested mendicancy and said so.[109] Perhaps he shared, unconsciously, the widespread resentment of monks of the older orders toward their mendicant competitors for alms. But he also knew that the mendicant orders were powerful and strong in their support of exemption, since they benefited from the system. He, therefore, also made plain that he favored their retention of exempt status, however flawed it was in practice by inadequate disciplinary structures, the absence of clois-tering, and the friars' excessive contact with layfolk.[110] To the extent that they were truly exempt, the mendicants, like the paragon order, his Cister-cians, also produced saints.[111] But the friars and more particularly the brothers of the Franciscan Order were riven at just this time by the dispute over poverty, encapsulated in the phrase *usus pauper*.[112] To simplify, the issue was whether spurning the ownership of property was sufficient to fulfill the Franciscans' vow of poverty. Dominican critics, all of whom also took vows of personal poverty, but who made no apology for their order's owning property, said no. They regarded the setting up of trusts vesting ownership technically in donors or the pope—the Franciscan way—as a mere legalism. The Franciscans' extravagant claims, based on such ar-rangements, namely, that they and not the Dominicans were living genu-inely devout lives in "real" poverty, were repugnant to the latter.

"Extremists" or "radicals" within the Franciscan Order agreed with the Dominican critique but went much further. For them, the vow of poverty implied an abstinence from the use or enjoyment of property and goods no matter who had formal legal ownership. To Dominican critics this too was absurd. To accomplish the *opus dei* required the use of property pure and simple. People who argued otherwise were naive at best. That they should also project themselves as superior in devotion to other religious merely showed that along with naive ignorance or stupidity went pride. They constituted a blemish on the church. Nonetheless, the so-called ex-tremists and radicals, also known as Spiritual Franciscans, affirmed their views in increasingly strident terms in the late thirteenth and early four-teenth centuries and provoked equal stridency from their opponents out-side the Franciscan Order and within it. As the argument became more and more bitter, ugly words were exchanged. Angry partisans called one another heretics.

Many observers, no one more sharply than Pope Clement V, lamented the scandal of the dispute in an order founded by the most admired man of the Middle Ages, Francis of Assisi.[113] Jacques de Thérines was himself one of those admirers.[114] Many recognized good people and good argu-ments on the various sides of the question. Many were convinced that the two factions had to reconcile their differences. But there were also voices that saw the exemption of the mendicants from episcopal jurisdiction as a contributing factor to the fractiousness and increasingly shrill nature of the dispute. Bishops did not possess the authority to force the friars to keep silent. Thus the mendicants' internal disputes also played out among lay supporters, disturbing the tenor of life in diocese after diocese.[115]

Jacques de Thérines, at this stage in his career and perhaps because he did not wish fully to alienate mendicant supporters of exemption, was circumspect about the dispute. He used an extraordinary analogy to describe it and, thereby, to undermine calls for stripping the friars of their immunity. He compared the friars to Christ's apostles in a different way.[116] That is to say, the apostles, the holiest of men, argued vigorously about who was the greatest among them, just like the friars. The apostles' arguments arose not so much from vanity as from a genuine desire to be the best and do the best for the nascent church. Their arguments were part of a progression to perfection. The Cistercian clearly hoped that the ever more divisive and bitter dispute in the Franciscan Order as to who followed the Rule more conscientiously would resolve itself in charity.[117]

In the meantime, toward the end of the council in 1312, Pope Clement V appointed an ecclesiastical commission to advise him on the *usus pauper* dispute.[118] Abbot Jacques, always obedient to the supreme pontiff, agreed to serve on it although probably with some unhappiness, since the pope put Jacques's archopponent, Giles of Rome, on the commission as well, expecting that they could work together and overcome their own bitter dispute over exemptions.[119] In the end, the commission had quite a diversity of opinions, but its report does not reveal who held which views, noting only that on this or some other issue, one or two masters dissented, were doubtful, or had no opinion. How many tunics could a friar properly possess? How many with a hood? How many without? And so forth.[120] Nonetheless, the commissioners' overall findings gave Clement V the counsel he needed to cobble together a compromise settlement articulated in the bull *Exivi de paradiso* of 6 May 1312.[121] The pope expressed himself in such a way that the Spirituals felt justified in practicing a severer form of asceticism and poverty than that imposed by the rulers of the Franciscan Order on the brothers as a whole.[122] In other words, what the minister general and chapter general of the order commanded with regard to poverty, as the Spirituals understood it, was taken to be the minimum required of the brothers, but it was not absolute in the sense of restricting those who wished to go further in their practice of extreme poverty. This is hardly what the rulers of the order thought *Exivi de paradiso* meant. The so-called settlement was doomed almost from the start.[123]

Doom also hung over the affair of the Templars. For a long time the treatment of the Knights severely tested the abbot of Chaalis's conscience.[124] In his earliest recorded remarks on the Templars (December 1306), before their arrest, he argued against the allegation that it was their status as an exempt order that contributed to their degeneration as a fighting force and indirectly helped lead to the loss of the Holy Land to full Muslim control in 1291. As far as he was concerned, their vocation as shedders of blood and their organization, which precluded cloistering, were not compatible with the strict definition of exemption he favored.

But he does not seem to have been particularly convinced by rumors about their bad behavior, since these had special currency among those opposed to and trying to destroy monastic exemption. Soon afterward, the arrests and the startling charges of heresy, idolatry, and sodomy shook him badly; yet for a while he remained skeptical about their truth, though he supported the use of extraordinary papal (not royal) power to investigate the allegations. His skepticism appears to have dissolved after high-ranking Templars began to confess (late October 1307), only to be reconstituted when they recanted (late December 1307). In 1308, with the other masters of theology at the University of Paris, he joined the advisory opinion on how the Templar affair should be handled, reiterating his view that insofar as the Knights were men of the church, the investigation had to be left to the church. As far as is known, this continued to be his view in the late spring of 1310, when he left Paris for Chaalis to assume his duties as the new abbot, and perhaps until he attended the Council of Vienne the next year.

Since critics like Giles of Rome continued to regard the status of the Templars as a form of exemption and any denial of the fact as mere quibbling, they explicitly extended their attack on the Templars at the Council of Vienne to an attack on exemption *tout court*. The same "quibbling" counterarguments that Jacques had formerly used to oppose them were almost the only ones he had in 1311, so he repeated them.[125] But if the critics rejected the validity of these counterarguments and insisted anyway on assimilating the Templars to the exempt orders and tying their degeneration to their supposed exemption, a different approach was called for. A problem would certainly arise in his opponents' argument if the accusations about the Templars' degeneration were false. I do not know whether Jacques de Thérines was "merely" being instrumental when he discussed the Templars' alleged crimes at the Council of Vienne in 1311. Yet, for whatever reason, this "independent-minded man," as Malcolm Barber styled him, decided to raise serious questions about the whole Templar affair.[126] Again, his real audience was the pope, who, everyone knew, was still torn on the matter.

Many high-ranking Templars had confessed, the abbot acknowledged, and if their confessions were to be believed (*si vera sunt, quae dicuntur*), they were guilty of execrable crimes (*summe detestabilia cuilibet Christiano*).[127] Stunning charges, to be sure—*non modicum stuporis atque admirationis*—but was it truly credible that such men had committed such unspeakable acts?[128] They were already men of standing, some well advanced in their careers, when they entered the order. Yet Christendom was supposed to believe that men of this sort willingly abandoned their virtue and imperiled their reputations at such a stage in their lives.[129] Different categories of people, he continued, could be expected to be differently susceptible to the sins of the flesh, but these men had all confessed to more or less the same crimes. Again, was it credible that commoners and nobles, men of different speech and lands, raised not as bastards but in stable God-fearing households, men who fervently expressed the desire to defend the holy places would all have the appetite to fall to precisely the same temptations?[130]

The incredibility of the whole thing, of course, raised the possibility that the confessions were tissues of lies (*si talia non haberent veritatem*).[131] What would persuade men noted for their bravery to confess to lies in the presence of the masters in theology, including himself, at the University of Paris in October 1307 (*coram tota Universitate Parisiensi*) and even before the supreme pontiff?[132] The implication was clear. Some were tortured unmercifully, some saw them tortured, and many more were threatened with horrifying tortures. In the immediate aftermath, they were gripped by a disabling fear. Time and reflection shamed many at their weakness—their betrayal of their honor—and gave them the forbearance to face the fear and to prepare themselves for their fate. They resolved to tell the truth whatever the consequences, perhaps under the spell of what modern psychologists dealing with torture victims have called "the unconscious magical hope that this time the outcome [would] be different."[133] That would explain their recantations in the face of the rational certainty of execution that followed from changing their stories. Rather than reaffirming the lies and pleading for mercy, which might have got them commutations of their sentences, many chose to accept death. In the archdioceses of Sens and Reims and other ecclesiastical provinces, burnings had already occurred under episcopal license, or rather the recanters "permitted themselves to be burned" (*permiserunt se comburi*); so on this point, according to Jacques de Thérines, doubt was impossible.[134]

Thoughtful men throughout Christendom therefore had misgivings (*materiam dubitationis*) as to the justice of the campaign against the Knights.[135] How widespread these doubts were continues to be a contentious question among historians.[136] Evidence read at the council from lands beyond the borders of France, the abbot pointed out, was not consistent with what was obtained (implicitly, under torture) in France proper.[137] No doubt the king of France was acting with pure motives and ardent zeal, the Cistercian conceded, perhaps grudgingly.[138] But it remained the obligation not of the king but of the supreme pontiff (*summus vicarius Jesu Christi Petrique successor*) to act with all reason in the matter.[139] The plenitude of power on the issue, as Jacques reminded his readers, lay in the supreme pontiff (*in persona Petri*); he was the captain of the metaphorical ship (*regat navem ecclesiae sibi commissam*).[140] It rested in the hands of Pope Clement V and Pope Clement V alone.[141] Of course, whether or not the charges turned out to be true, the whole Templar business remained irrelevant, as far as Jacques de Thérines was concerned, to the discussion of exemption.[142]

•   •   •   •   •

The debate continued.[143] But the pope finally acted—on the matter of exemption and on the Templars. With regard to the first, he laid down guidelines regulating the relations of the exempt orders and houses with the secular clergy. In many ways these regulations amounted to tinkering. They were meant to improve or perfect the system of exemption, as Jacques implored.[144] On the main issue, the pope again sided completely with Abbot Jacques de Thérines, and in a scathing denunciation of secular clerics and their infringement on the immunities of the exempt, he wrote words that Noël Valois thought could have been written by the Cistercian himself.[145] Clement's motives are unfathomable, but it is not implausible that the argument from the traditional support of the exempt orders for the Apostolic See in all its struggles within and outside the church was the key factor that inspired him to endorse the views of the abbot of Chaalis.

As is well known, the Templars fared less well. In council on 22 March 1312 and in the presence of the French ruler, Philip the Fair, and his three sons, the pope, referring to the "infamy, suspicion, [and] noisy insinuation" attending the Order of the Temple, decreed its abolition.[146] Many unconfessed brothers and others who begged mercy were simply pensioned off. Yet although his words evoked the scandal surrounding the order, Clement V did not out-and-out condemn it, the act that the king so zealously hoped for.[147] Perhaps this was a small rhetorical victory for Jacques de Thérines and like-minded clergy with lingering doubts as to the Templars' culpability, but it could not have been very satisfying even to them as they left Vienne to return home from the council.

Papal authorization for the redistribution of the order's property followed the dissolution. Clement V intended the Hospitallers to receive the property so that the resources would continue to contribute to efforts to recover the Holy Land. In Aragon and Portugal, however, the rulers arranged the transfer of the property to newly created military orders whose focus was less on the Holy Land than on Iberia. The new Portuguese order willingly recruited former Templar Knights to its ranks.[148] In France, Templar properties, more extensive and valuable than in any other realm, went entirely to the Order of the Hospital.

In the August following the suppression, it became known that Philip the Fair was openly musing about the problems of the Order of the Hospital and its need for reform, words that sent a frisson through the ecclesiastical hierarchy.[149] But perhaps because he was not quite finished with the Templars, the king never put his thoughts into action. For although Clement V dissolved the Order of the Temple in the spring of 1312, he did not make an absolutely final decision on the highest-ranking individuals, most especially the aged grand master, Jacques de Molay, who had confessed his heresy and then disavowed the confession.[150] His reversal and those of his high-ranking comrades were tantamount to requests for execution. Clement, I believe, was trying to buy time, despite the pressure exerted by the French crown. The pope claimed in late December 1313 that he was overburdened and personally distracted by the business of his office, and everything was going more slowly than outsiders to the deliberate and careful procedures of ecclesiastical justice might wish.[151] Nonetheless, in the grand master's case, the death warrant was finally carried out on the Point Vert in Paris during the night hours of 18 March 1314.[152] It is probably legendary that Jacques de Molay struck the king and the whole royal house with a mortal curse as he succumbed, invoking the Blessed Virgin to see to its execution.[153] But it is true that Philip the Fair died later that year without having the opportunity to show still more zeal for the Catholic faith.

4

AN UNEASY RELATIONSHIP:

CHURCH AND STATE AT THE CISTERCIAN

ABBEY OF SAINTE-MARIE OF CHAALIS

W HEN THE MONKS of Sainte-Marie of Chaalis greeted their abbot on his final return from the Council of Vienne and heard confirmed the reports that had filtered back from time to time from visitors to the house, there was cause for both joy and alarm. On the one hand, their abbot had been instrumental in the successful effort to preserve the exemption of the Cistercian Order and of Chaalis as one of its daughters from all but papal authority. On the other, he had denounced the episcopate, the most powerful estate in the church, insulted one of its most prominent members, the archbishop of Bourges, Giles of Rome, and openly thrown doubt on the Templars' guilt, despite King Philip the Fair's strong stand against them. Being the abbot of one of the greatest monasteries in Christendom was a heavy burden under any circumstances. Some of Jacques de Thérines's actions were bound to complicate his work.

· · · · ·

An abbot's duties in a Cistercian house were similar to but more exhausting than in a typical Benedictine house.[1] Like any abbot, Jacques was responsible for seeing to the maintenance of the fabric of the monastic buildings, including in Chaalis's case the Gothic sanctuary, the so-called Abbot's Chapel (Chapelle Notre-Dame [du Roi]) built in the elegant style of the royal Sainte-Chapelle of Paris, and the farm buildings.[2] He also had to see to the well-being of the inmates of the monastery and others directly associated with it and under his disciplinary jurisdiction, including the *conversi*, or lay brothers, who were to live simple devout lives on the monastic grounds while also helping to carry out the manual labor necessary to sustain the monastery.[3]

Supervision entailed promoting the virtuous behavior of monks and *conversi* and punishing vice.[4] As required, there was a monastic prison for the "hard" cases; perhaps its grim ruins were still visible in the 1840s— or perhaps the grimness of one part of the abbey ruins touched the popular imagination during High Romanticism as appropriate to such a prison, and therefore incontestably the remains of an edifice meant to isolate the few disaffected monks who refused to lose themselves in the collective identity of the corporation.[5] The abbot's responsibilities also extended to supervising the collection of rents, provisioning the house, seeing to the monks' proper attention to the Rule, regulating the *conversi*'s activities, nursing sick monks, and making sure that devotional and liturgical practices were executed properly.[6] At Chaalis this last included the abbot's nightly blessing of each monk individually with holy water. The rite had been observed since at least Saint Louis's time and attracted him greatly. When the brothers first allowed him to watch its performance, he requested that he, too, receive the abbot's blessing in precisely the same way, and the abbot granted his wish.[7] The traditions observed at the abbey also included ones common to the whole order, like summoning the brothers to the bed of a dying monk by the tolling of the bells, laying out the moribund body on ashes and penitential cloth (sackcloth), and continuously performing simple prayers and litanies (responsive prayers) over the dying man.[8] Again, in Saint Louis's presence—perhaps because of his presence—the brothers carried out these devotions with such evident intensity of feeling that he marveled at the scene.[9]

The abbot needed to delegate rather than exercise anything more than occasional direct supervision of the labor force. Most historians agree that the evolution of Cistercian monasticism saw, first, a progressive lessening of emphasis on the performance of manual work (in the fields, for example) by the fully vowed brothers, or choir monks, with such work at first becoming more and more restricted to the *conversi*.[10] But as the size of estates grew, the *conversi* worked alongside hired non-*conversi* laborers.[11] Ultimately, some sort of summary of the problems of keeping, disciplining, and paying the labor force came to the abbot.[12] The information was necessary for accounting purposes.[13]

How many people were included in these various groups? The original foundation (1136) consisted of twelve monks who had migrated from Pontigny, the typical number to establish a new foundation.[14] The number grew spectacularly from this modest beginning.[15] By the thirteenth century Chaalis was a very large monastery. Indeed, only a large monastery could repeatedly entertain the royal entourage, even if the crown did absorb most of the expenses. The abbot had a second in command, a prior, and there were numerous other officeholders as well, including the subprior, treasurer, sacristan, cellarer, *infirmarius*, phlebotomist, and scribes.[16] It would scarcely be surprising if there were 100 monks in Abbot Jacques's time. Rievaulx a century earlier counted 120 to 140 choir monks; Clairvaux about 200; and Dunes, contemporary with Abbot Jacques's time, was home to 180.[17] The number of *conversi* at Chaalis would have exceeded the number of choir monks possibly by a factor of two, three, or even four, judging from the ratio for other large Cistercian communities, even though dependence on and recruitment of *conversi* were slackening in the order.[18] To stay with the examples mentioned, to the very rough estimate of 140 choir monks at Rievaulx must be added the equally rough figure of 500 lay brothers; besides the 200 Clairvaux professed brothers were 300 lay brothers; the 180 choir monks at Dunes were part of a community that included 350 *conversi* as well.[19]

More than merely seeing to the internal life of the monastery, the abbot had to deal with the royal government. In Jacques's time the abbey seems to have avoided the courts as much as possible, probably because of the residual fallout from his actions at the Council of Vienne. Nevertheless, he had to retain someone with legal training in the capital to protect Chaalis's interests in the event that litigation affecting it directly or indirectly came before the high court, the Parlement of Paris. The registration of property transactions entered into by the abbey in districts under the jurisdiction of the royal *prévôt* of Paris required the services of a "lawyer" working or resident in Paris as well.[20] The procurator who represented the abbey in a cause before Parlement on 28 March 1319 (this was about one year after Jacques's abbacy at Chaalis came to an end) was probably on permanent retainer in Jacques's time for these and similar routine duties.[21]

Otherwise there was little enough contact with the government in Paris after the abbot's return from Vienne. The peripatetic royal court almost never settled temporarily at Chaalis in Abbot Jacques's time.[22] So the monastery was spared the need to provide even the modest hospitality that had been offered to the royal entourage at the time of Saint Louis's visits and of Philip III's. In other royal jurisdictions where the abbey engaged in property transactions, like the *prévôtés* of Senlis and Gonesse, procurators registered deeds in the monastery's behalf with the requisite royal authorities.[23] This was, once more, a routine but essential administrative requirement to establish a record that the transactions were consonant with all the applicable provisions of the land law regarding grants to the church.[24]

Relations with his ecclesiastical superiors recurred on a fixed schedule and were much more pressing for Jacques. Regular annual visitations were, of course, a cornerstone of the Cistercian mode of maintaining discipline and virtue in the houses of the order.[25] The abbot was necessarily on call for these visits, which in Chaalis's case occurred under the direction of the abbot of its mother house Pontigny, one of the senior abbots.[26] For his own part, Jacques probably cultivated a special relationship with Chaalis's daughter monasteries, Le Gard in the diocese of Amiens and La Merci-Dieu in that of Poitiers, during visits, although the relationship of mother and daughters had probably been closer in the twelfth century when the foundations were still recent.[27] In 1310, about the time of Jacques's election to the headship of Chaalis, the meeting of the General

Chapter of the entire order formally regularized the practice that during visitations, auditing of the accounts should take place as well.[28] The need to do so was not predicated simply on the desire to prevent embezzlement, although this was naturally a concern in a society whose mental universe saw money as the greatest temptation to wickedness: "the love of money is the root of all evils," 1 Tim. 6.10. But also, since 1235, the General Chapter, its work, and the gracious grants it reluctantly offered for Crusades and "just" wars were supported by prorated contributions from the abbeys in the order.[29] An auditing of accounts provided useful information for assessments.

• • • • •

With local notables, Abbot Jacques's overall concern was to maintain his monastery's possessions intact and to preserve and enhance its financial position. He was also determined to do his best to consolidate its properties and rents. Among the earliest acts in which he was involved as abbot was the acceptance of a feudal property that came from a bequest to the community in 1311.[30] From the middle of the thirteenth century onward, most medieval princes curbed such grants, grants that transferred property into the church's "dead hand," mortmain, so that overlords lost pecuniary rights, like wardship, the right to collect revenues while an heir of the property in question was underage, and relief, the inheritance tax. For the church was never underage, so could never be in wardship, and it never died, so inheritance taxes were never due. There were also recurrent resentments among undertenants who, on account of these grants, began to owe services to the church without, in their view, any hope of receiving the same benefits of protection or maintenance that they would receive from secular lords.[31]

In various grants, especially Saint Louis's, the crown relieved Chaalis from the fines or licensing fees ordinarily levied for the acquisition of such properties.[32] But many abbeys were less careful in this regard, and Chaalis did not always have a Saint Louis on the throne. In 1291 Philip the Fair ordered a general inquiry into amortizations, grants into the dead hand, in an effort to discipline the holders of such properties.[33] Insofar as Chaalis's properties were concerned, the investigation, which was led by a senior courtier and future bishop, Pierre de Latilly, culminated in a confirmation of the grants it had received over the preceding forty-eight years (*a xlviii annis citra*). But the confirmation came at a cost, namely, the payment in 1294 of two hundred pounds thirty-six shillings (200 l. 36 s.) to the crown for the acquisition of lands for which the abbey had not obtained formal relief from licensing fees or could not produce the records to prove it had.[34] This was not an impoverishing sum, but as the equivalent of about a year's salary for a very senior royal administrator, like the master of the forests of Languedoc, it also was not trivial.[35] And it rankled. The documents the monks possessed commanding the inquiry into the amortizations and describing its results, the fine, and the confirmation that followed were kept apart in a neat bundle for ready reference for any future defense of the abbey's claims.[36]

The government's close oversight of amortizations, the punitive fines improper ones entailed, and the fact that undertenants were traditionally rancorous gave an edge to everything touching the bequest that Jacques accepted for the abbey in 1311. The undertenants were especially vexatious in this instance, but the abbot was persistent. He eventually brought all of them into line. It took him six years of cajoling to do so, a time lag no doubt aggravated by his long absences at the Council of Vienne so soon after the bequest; yet in 1317 the undertenants made a formal collective assurance (*assecuratio*) of their willingness to honor the bequest and the dependent relationship between them and the abbot and monastery of Sainte-Marie of Chaalis that flowed from it.[37]

Abbot Jacques's plans for the monastery were in general on hold for much of 1311 and 1312 because of his attendance at the various sessions of the Council of Vienne and the prominent part he played in its deliberations. His second in command, the prior, did not undertake any serious initiatives during his absences, or so the silence of the documentary record suggests. This caution or restriction with regard to the exercise of powers by the prior may have been another factor in the delay in achieving the *assecuratio*. Once the business at Vienne came to an end, however, the abbot fully returned to his duties. We get the merest glimpse of him carrying out his administrative tasks in 1313 from a charter of that year to which he affixed his seal, together with the corporate seal of the abbey, concerning a rent of a measure (*muid*) of grain, involving a local landholder, Pierre de Cugnières, and his wife.[38] But if the year 1313 gives us only a hint that Jacques was focusing his attention on problems touching the abbey's properties, records from the following year indicate that the abbot was already well along in negotiations that were critical to the house's financial well-being. These negotiations began reaching fruition in 1314.

In a series of ten separate agreements in that year, all carefully registered in the presence of the *prévôt* of Senlis, the representative of royal authority in the town and *banlieue* of the same name, the abbot's efforts to transfer properties, including vineyards, from direct exploitation to rentals (perpetual leases) in the nearby terrains of Fontaines (Fontaine) achieved success.[39] The abbey had begun to acquire properties at Fontaines in the mid–twelfth century and continued to do so in the thirteenth.[40] But the early fourteenth century was a period when the holders of large estates all across northwestern continental Europe and in England as well were converting to leasing from direct exploitation owing to changing economic conditions. With population in rural areas at the densest it has ever been, it made fiscal sense to capitalize on land hunger by renting out holdings. The tendency, one that Jacques followed, to make such rentals perpetual, however, would in the very long term undermine the economic benefits of the conversion, as inflation eroded the value of the rents, but the immediate need was too great to permit much quibbling.[41]

To effect the conversion required a patient, diligent, and well-planned strategy of negotiations. The simultaneity of the ten agreements, that is, every one in 1314, establishes the fact. Nor was the campaign—for that is what it was—limited to the abbey's ten properties at Fontaines. Abbot Jacques arranged similar conversions to rentals for a cluster of holdings accessible by the footpath (*semita*) along the small Luat River, a little distance to the south, not far from the present-day airport at Roissy. Once again, the year was 1314. The agreements covered the rentals of four properties along the footpath. In this case, the rental agreements were registered in the office of the *prévôt* of Gonesse, the nearby royal town that was the administrative center of the subdistrict in which the properties were situated.[42] Whole blocks of lands were being converted from the abbey's direct exploitation to rents.

• • • • •

The year 1314, which saw this reassuringly commonplace spate of real estate transactions in the *pays* of Chaalis, was nothing short of traumatic for the *grand pays*, the kingdom of France. The fiery executions in Paris in the spring of the highest-ranking Templars still in custody seemed yet another high point in Philip the Fair's exercise of power, but the other news filtering out of the capital and into the provinces was less flattering to the crown and anything but reassuring or commonplace. The same spring saw the public airing of a scandal in the very bosom of the royal family.[43] The wives of King Philip's three sons were imprisoned for adultery in May. One, who was aware of the others' affairs with household knights, was exonerated from actual participation and eventually won her freedom, but the king obliged his sons to cease relations with their spouses, and a cloud was thrown over the legitimacy of the offspring, a girl, of Philip's heir, the future Louis X. The household knights, two absurdly and tragically irresponsible brothers, Philippe and Gautier Aulnay, who were the young women's lovers for three years, were gutted alive and their penises and scrotums sliced from their mangled bodies. They were then decapitated. The bodies were dragged to a common public gibbet and hung together by their shoulders and arms while the executioners flayed the dismembered torsos and limbs until all the skin fell off in shreds.[44]

Why Philip chose to make public examples of the knights, confirm his youthful sons in the popular imagination as cuckolds, and thus make them the subjects of vulgar tavern-room ridicule and humor is another one of those questions to which no genuinely persuasive answers have been offered.[45] Marriage and the marriage bed were, of course, sacrosanct to the king, and Philip's own marriage was affectionate.[46] It lasted from 1284, when he was an adolescent and still only heir to the throne, until 1305, when his wife Jeanne of Champagne and Navarre passed away in her very early thirties. His wife's death shook him, deepening his morose piety.[47] Later he raised charges against the bishop of Troyes, Guichard by name, who had earlier been accused of poisoning a rival and of embezzlement and connivance with embezzlers of revenues from Jeanne's and her mother's patrimony.[48] The new charges, not unlike those levied against the Templars at the same time, were lurid in content. Guichard was supposed to have poisoned the queen and, before that, her mother. Moreover, being a master of the black arts in league with the devil, he used a waxen figure of the queen to torture Philip's best beloved before dispatching her. The king wanted Bishop Guichard tried and condemned to death. Pope Clement V instead translated him to Bosnia, a fate perhaps not worse than death yet quite horrifying enough for a bishop of orthodox beliefs. The "wild lands of Bosnia," in spiritual rebellion against the Holy See, were the hotbed of the dualist heresy known as Bogomilism.[49] But Guichard went into hiding and probably lived out a very quiet and unobtrusive retirement in Italy, avoiding both fates for a long time.[50]

The point to keep sight of is that Philip's emotional idealization of marriage was manifested in his unwillingness to believe that God would simply call the young and faithful Jeanne away from her affectionate partner. It imparted to him a need to blame someone for his loss (much as I have conjectured that his attack on the Templars deflected criticism from him for his failure to mount a Crusade to the Holy Land); and in a way it made perverse sense that a man like Bishop Guichard, suspected of embezzlement, would kill his victim in a desperate effort and perverted manner to keep her from finding solid evidence against him. (None was ever found.) This moral calculus probably shaped Philip the Fair's reaction to the adulteries of 1314. He wanted and took exquisite revenge on faithless knights, and he immured unfaithful wives. He did not care whether the publicity was bad or not. His virtue and the virtue of his holy lineage required it.

If the adulteries were hidden sins made public, the Flemings' treason in 1314 was open sin multiplied infinitely. The long series of sanguinary wars of intervention in Flemish politics, partly occasioned by Flanders's traditionally close relationship with England (Flemish cloth producers depended on English wool), seemed to have come to an end only a year before and almost completely to the French crown's advantage.[51] The new Flemish rising in July was, as far as the king was concerned, morally unconscionable. Philip summoned the forces he thought necessary to humble the Flemings and their count once and for all.[52] To do so, of course, required the levying of extraordinary taxes. The provinces did not resist granting taxes, although their representatives reminded the king of a promise earlier made that if a truce was worked out, the tax was to be canceled or remitted, its justification having ceased (*cessante causa*).[53]

Everything seems to have gone wrong.[54] Early negotiations for a truce were false starts, and, when subsequent discussions achieved a formal agreement in September, the pact caused bitter resentment among the bloodthirstier of the French nobility, including the king's brother Charles of Valois, who wanted to punish the Flemings' insolence. Rumors persisted about the situation at the front. Was the war really to be prosecuted if a truce was negotiated? Were there traitors subverting the king's will? Should the tax monies raised for an all-out campaign, in the evident absence of such a campaign, be returned? The king dithered, partly because merely preparing for war was expensive and strained resources, but this time northern France, seething for years under his authoritarian rule, began to rise against the Capetian.[55] Dissidents expressed their longing for a restoration of governance as it had been exercised in the now idealized days of Philip's grandfather, Saint Louis. Everywhere provincial leagues of aristocrats drew up lists of grievances against the crown and accusations against the king's ministers; the leagues demanded reform and backed their demands with threats of further resistance.[56]

A healthy king might have met the challenge effectively. Philip, however, was sick, although in my opinion he probably did not realize just how sick.[57] He was exhausted (who would not be from the troubles he was facing?) and decided to break from routine with a brief hunting trip that autumn, using the interval to rest and recuperate his strength for the struggle ahead. While riding one day with the hunting party, he suddenly slumped in the saddle, lost the capacity to speak, and fell to the ground. There was a certain irony in the fact that he was removed to the little town of Poissy, his grandfather's birthplace and the site of a magnificent shrine he was building to Louis's memory and honor, at a time when the country was invoking the saint's example against him.[58] His departure by litter from Poissy to the royal palace at Fontainebleau, where he had been born only forty-seven years before, signaled the end, even though he recovered his speech.[59] As he grew weaker, he cautioned his heir to revere Holy Church, canceled the detested war tax, and pledged resources to the enterprise that until his reign had been the most distinguishing characteristic of the high medieval French monarchy, a Crusade to the East.[60] He died the next day, 29 November 1314.

Soon afterward, the king's body, less its viscera and heart, was interred in a simple ceremony attended only by close family and a few intimates at the royal necropolis of Saint-Denis near his father's and grandfather's tombs. The viscera and heart were reserved for the sanctuary of the nuns of Poissy, as the late king had directed, and immediately carried back there. This was part of what has been deemed Philip's dynastic politics of the royal heart. He endeavored to distribute his predecessors' organs and provide his own for Christian burial around the realm as a form of sacralization, literally melding the holy land with the holy dynasty.[61]

Those who removed the heart were astonished at its size. Philip suffered from microcardia, "abnormal smallness of the heart."[62] The surgeons compared the organ to that of a newborn child or of a bird (presumably a large bird, like a swan, or a bird of prey).[63] The condition of his heart, the result of an unknown and probably unsuspected underlying pathology, certainly caused him to feel exhausted in his last weeks and undoubtedly contributed to the strokelike affliction during the hunting excursion, but even though he was mortally sick he might not have felt anything but extreme fatigue until the stroke. Philip's death, in other words, was unexpected, and it left a political void by throwing responsibility onto people who had not been making any systematic concerted plans to assume it.

The burden of governance fell on Prince Louis, now Louis X, though under the press of circumstances he delayed his coronation for more than eight months until 3 August 1315. His first obligation was to put an end to the unrest sweeping the country and his second to prosecute the war against the Flemings. The success of the latter, if it could be managed, would certainly contribute to the former. He was also concerned with the succession. The legitimacy of his one child was in doubt owing to the involvement of her mother, Marguerite of Burgundy, in the adultery scandal. It remains a mystery as to who was responsible for Marguerite's timely death from hypothermia in April 1315 in an unheated stone garret open to the elements at her prison, the imposing Norman castle of Château-Gaillard.[64] In any case, the death obviated efforts to obtain an annulment of Louis's marriage to her—efforts that, given the long delay preceding the election of a new pope after Clement V's death in April 1314, had been a frustrating matter. The simple fact is that negotiations were ongoing with the Hungarian royal family, from which Louis, freed from the marital tie with Marguerite, secured a bride, Clémence, on 31 July 1315, in time for the coronation at Reims less than a week later.[65]

The rebel leagues that arose under Philip the Fair were pacified by a series of concessions, the so-called charters to the regional nobility (and churches).[66] Norman petitioners received recognition and confirmation of their liberties on 19 March. A number of concessions were made to interests in Languedoc on 1 April, for the opposition was no longer confined to the north. Later in April the new king confirmed the liberties of the

Burgundian nobility. And this pattern continued over the next few weeks, as for example with the elites of Champagne in May, even to the extent of his going back to groups already granted charters and clarifying disputed interpretations of the liberties so recently confirmed.

The king, probably taking the advice of his uncle, Charles of Valois—a path urged on him by his dying father—also yielded to demands for vengeance against his father's ministers.[67] Not all suffered the ultimate fate of the chief minister at the time, Enguerran de Marigny, namely, execution by hanging, after which his corpse remained suspended from the top of a multitiered public gallows for two years.[68] He was hanged along with one Payot, a servant in Marigny's extended family, who swung from a lower tier of the same gallows. Enemies of the former chief minister implicated Payot in a reputed plot with Marigny's kin to make waxen figures with which a sorceress was to torture and kill the royal family. The alleged sorceress was burned. Another man in the reputed conspiracy committed suicide while in custody.[69]

In fact the fury of the vengeance, if not the sense of uncertainty and confusion, ran its course fairly quickly and affected only a relatively small circle of victims.[70] A few men like Bishop Pierre de Latilly, notorious for his exactions of fines under Philip the Fair, including the amortization fines levied against abbeys like Chaalis, were harassed and humiliated by being put on trial. Fortunately for Bishop Pierre he was tried before an ecclesiastical tribunal. The charge, however, was astounding. His enemies accused him of nothing less than poisoning the late king, Philip the Fair, but as the blood lust petered out, fellow clergy exonerated him and the matter was quietly laid aside.[71]

While reprisals were going on, the king promised to make amends for Philip's war tax, but because Louis desperately needed funds to prosecute the invasion of Flanders, on which he pinned his hopes for the real restoration of royal authority, he was not as expeditious in fulfilling his promise as he might otherwise have been. To a certain extent, Louis X tried to shift the cost of the reforms onto the localities in which they were carried out. On 25 May 1315 the king issued an order that acknowledged the concessions that he made to the elites in the territory around Senlis, which included the abbey and many of the properties of Chaalis. The acknowledgment was accompanied by instructions to his lieutenant to collect the funds necessary to carry through on the promised reforms.[72] Less than a week later, on 1 June, the royal entourage visited Senlis.[73] Whether Louis paid his respects to the nearby abbey of Chaalis, as his great-grandfather and grandfather (Saint Louis and Philip III) had been accustomed to do when they visited the royal town, is uncertain. But Louis X was contemplating some fairly radical decisions at this time, one involving Jews. In fact, he had been considering, since at least mid-May 1315, the readmission of Jews to the kingdom.[74] It would not be surprising, since he was in the neighborhood, had he sought out Jacques de Thérines, the man whose views on this matter a few of his councillors must have known, for some last-minute moral assurance in early June that he was planning to do the right thing.

In any case, a month later the first of two royal edicts was published. On 3 July 1315 all royal serfs received their freedom in return for substantial contributions to the royal coffers.[75] A little more than three weeks later, on 28 July, the king announced his decision to allow Jews to resettle in the kingdom of France, reversing his father's expulsion of 1306.[76] He did so in what can be understood as full agreement with Jacques de Thérines's opinion that the expulsion of Jews should never be more than a temporary measure (say, to disrupt a dangerous conspiracy), with the various disconnected groups created by the expulsion being allowed to return somewhat later for the spiritual advantage of the Christian people, whose faith, as the ancient Fathers of the church observed, benefited from the Jews' presence in their midst.[77] An accompanying material advantage for the king was promised, since the representatives of the returning Jews agreed to pay him 22,500 l. immediately and 10,000 l. yearly for the next twelve years, at which time Louis X promised to either renew the agreement or expel them again.[78]

The same month in which he freed the royal serfs and readmitted Jews to the kingdom Louis married Clémence of Hungary. Then in August, immediately after the coronation at Reims, the king set out with an army northward.[79] The various expedients he used to raise money—like the readmission of the Jews, with the addition of revenue from sources unaffected by the concessions made to the rebel leagues, including large grants commanded by Pope Clement V at the Council of Vienne and still being paid by the Cistercians—made the expedition possible.[80] What subsequently rendered it impossible was the weather.[81] The spring and summer of 1315 were terribly wet. Conditions appeared to be getting worse; there were torrential and steady, seemingly never ceasing, downpours in August. War wagons and supply carts bogged down. Horses struggled through mud up to their knees. The king cursed his fate. He wanted to make war in Flanders when war could not be made. He called off the campaign. But the rains refused to stop. Then came incredible snows and cold; then, in 1316, even heavier and steadier rains and a worse winter. The cycle did not want to end. The year 1317 was another ordeal of persistently horrific weather.

• • • • •

In these difficult years for the realm as a whole, the abbot of Chaalis struggled to maintain the properties of his monastery and even to increase their return. We find him involved in one exchange after another—with laymen and ecclesiastics—in the years 1316 and 1317. By and large, the parties to these contracts, on both sides, intended to consolidate their holdings or make collection of revenues more efficient.[82] Typical of Jacques, he tried to forestall later objections to the transactions by having local lords confirm the charters recording the exchanges.[83] He had been loath to use the royal courts in Philip the Fair's reign to defend the abbey's rights, whether because he disliked and distrusted the king or because he thought negotiation and cajoling opponents into agreements was a superior form of protection. In the unsettled interim of Louis X's reign, the abbot did not change his approach.

Once again, close study of the records establishes that Jacques's approach was about as successful as one could reasonably hope in very difficult circumstances. A good illustration is the case of Eustace, a knight, the lord of Francières and a noble who formally raised objections to an exchange of properties, in 1316, in Tremblay between the abbey of Chaalis and the Church of Saint-Symphorien of Beauvais.[84] Lord Eustace was sufficiently angered to bring a formal complaint (*querela*) against the abbey, or to threaten to do so, for entering into the exchange. Abbot Jacques preferred to settle out of court, and he set his mind to reconciling the knight to the new arrangements. To be sure, he had no love for "middling nobles" of Eustace's sort. Outside of their hearing he denounced them as rapacious villains.[85] But as abbot he had to deal with them, rapacious or not, and presumably his smooth words and the promises he made not to upset the relations and the tenor of life that had prevailed in Tremblay before the abbey's exchange of properties with Saint-Symphorien persuaded an aggrieved Lord Eustace de Francières to withdraw his objections to the transaction. In the end, the knight graciously decided to "let the church of Chaalis off from the entire complaint that he raised against it."[86]

It was also in 1316 that Jacques entered into an agreement with the mayor and commune of Compiègne in which the town recognized the abbey's right to market its grain and other goods freely without payment of municipal tolls and without having to use or pay for the privilege of not using the municipal measures ordinarily required of vendors in the market.[87] The monastery had a long history of relations with Compiègne, one of the major royal towns in its vicinity.[88] Now, in the midst of scarcities created by an increasing number of bad harvests, a serious argument erupted between the two institutions over the treatment of the abbey's agents in the municipal market.[89] In particular the agreement spelled out the rights of storage and access that the abbey enjoyed in the municipal warehouse in Compiègne, and it gave the monks redress if they could prove that the town's market officials interfered in any way that caused the Cistercians' goods to suffer damage. The mayor and commune promised restitution in such cases. The monks were to take care, however, not to overstep their privileges.

The agreement went further. Jacques succeeded in persuading the municipality to concede the abbey's right to establish its own separate storage facility and sales outlet (*domus*) in Compiègne or its environs in the future. The brothers would enjoy the same privileges in any new facility that they already possessed in Compiègne's municipal market. Chaalis owned privileged *domus* of this type at Senlis, Beauvais, and Paris. In Senlis, where the abbey had a rather wide array of rights and possessions, the *domus*, known as Petit-Chaalis, was established in 1166.[90] The house in Beauvais, also known as Petit-Chaalis, probably existed from 1171 but was rebuilt around 1240. The Parisian facility came into the abbey's hands in the year 1200. (The monks also collected an annual rent in Paris, thanks to Philip III's generosity, on property near the market.)[91] Excavations suggest that all these buildings had extensive cellars (*caves*) for grain and wine.[92]

Since the opening of any such facility in Compiègne implied a considerable transfer of sales out of the municipal marketplace, the mayor and commune's concession was potentially a financial detriment for the town. The abbot, therefore, agreed that his monks, their lay brothers, and their servants would levy municipal sales taxes on purchases made at the facility and would hand these over to the municipal market officials. Inability to collect these taxes, should the situation arise from the refusal of the purchasers to pay a municipal market tax outside the physical space of the municipal market, was supposed to be reported to the town's market officials. They would then take action despite the Cistercians' ownership of the facility. Finally, if the abbey allowed *extranei*, merchants who were not formally agents of Chaalis, to use the facility temporarily or at long-term lease to vend grain and other goods, these merchants were not to enjoy any of the privileges that the town granted to the abbey in the agreement. The abbot saw to the confirmation of this agreement by the appropriate secular authority, in this instance the "Châtelet," that is to say, the royal *prévôt* of Paris.[93]

• • • • •

While the relentless rains fell in 1316, a frustrated Louis X grew ill. As he lay dying on 5 June 1316, he was only twenty-six years old. Clémence of Hungary, his wife of less than a year, was pregnant, a fact that gave him some hope that despite the misfortune of an unfinished war he might fulfill at least one of the duties a king owed his people, the fathering of a legitimate heir. In the event, a posthumous son, John (I), was born on 15 November, only to die a few days later on the 19th or the 20th.[94] From the time of King Louis's death in June until the child's birth six months later, the late king's brother, Philip the Tall, with the consent of the baronage expressed in assembly, 16–17 July, acted as regent.[95] When his infant nephew also died, the regent announced his own accession to the throne as Philip V, but the declaration evinced some murmuring against his claim, murmuring that arose from Louis X's belated "recognition" of his daughter by his disgraced first wife, an act that, the daughter's partisans argued, vested rights of succession in her.[96] No one thought yet to invoke the so-called Salic Law against inheritance by women.[97]

None of this would have come about if the king's posthumous son, John, had survived, but his demise left it an open question as to who should rule in France. Rumor would later have it that Louis X himself was poisoned by his brother.[98] But as if this were not enough to taint Philip the Tall, it was also bruited about that he had tried to do away with little John by poison and even thought his plot had been carried out successfully. However, Philip's enemies, so the story went, spirited the baby away and put a different newborn to serve as a corpse in his place. A pretender claiming to be John did later appear during the Hundred Years' War but, despite some fleeting celebrity, garnered no sustained political following.[99] In the long run, these deaths, many others to come, and the innuendos and suspicions surrounding them undermined the monarchy's claims to integrity and contributed to a sense of paranoia at the very heart of the court.[100] Far more important in 1316 was the fact that the rumors gave partisans of Louis X's daughter, chiefly her mother's Burgundian relatives, the courage to mount a modest opposition to the regent's accession, but Philip the Tall never lost a step.[101]

Even before his rather speedy coronation at Reims on 9 January 1317, Philip began to behave in the manner of the traditional *débonnaire* king, in the medieval sense of the term, generous to a fault, distributing gifts to a wide variety of groups, including ecclesiastics.[102] Much of this was surely intended to encourage support of his claim to the throne. A cascade of additional gifts and gestures followed the coronation and encouraged more support. With respect to the church, the newly crowned ruler began an extensive program of confirming his royal predecessors' grants, with Philip V himself then issuing charters in his own name to enhance the grants.[103] This was never a fully comprehensive policy though, for the king played favorites among the orders. The Cistercians were most favored.[104]

Jacques de Thérines was not slow in obtaining benefits for his monastery from the new king. The close connection between the crown and Chaalis had eroded since the days of Louis IX and Philip III, who had confirmed prior grants of property and rights, made new grants, and extended special privileges to the abbey on twelve and eleven occasions, respectively.[105] In 1290, five years after he became king, Philip the Fair in his first charter to Chaalis gave the abbey a blanket confirmation of its rights.[106] Momentarily, it seemed as though he would treat the abbey as his predecessors had treated it. Soon after, he confirmed an exchange of property made between the abbey and Lord Simon de Soisy, a knight, and his wife.[107] But then came the inquiry into amortizations, as a result of which the abbey had to render up more than 200 l. to the crown in 1294.[108] During the great struggles with Boniface VIII, which occupied the next ten years, and in which many in the Cistercian Order were prominent supporters of the papal position, Philip appears to have given little or nothing to Chaalis, although he continued, like his predecessors, to stop at the abbey during his travels.[109] Possibly as a modest gesture of reconciliation after Boniface's death in 1303, the king confirmed several concessions (*de pluribus concessionibus*) that he had made to the abbey. This occurred in 1304.[110] And payments, presumably attending the concessions, were made by Ascension Day the following spring, 1305, to the tune of 108 l.[111] But thereafter— the last decade of his reign—he was in no way the abbey's benefactor and appears to have visited just once (mid-April 1311), before Abbot Jacques set out for the Council of Vienne.[112] Whether at this time Philip or members of his entourage used the opportunity to lobby the abbot for the royal position on the Templars is unrecorded. If so, the effort was spectacularly unsuccessful, to judge from the Cistercian's impassioned declarations at the council.[113] Every indication, indeed, is that the historically close relationship between Sainte-Marie of Chaalis and the French crown, already weakened in Pope Boniface VIII's time, was in total suspension during Jacques de Thérines's abbacy. Philip's successor, Louis X, did not live long enough to fully reconstitute the old ties between the monarchy and the monastery.

Thus Jacques's success in claiming Philip the Tall's beneficent attention was all the more welcome to the community of monks at Chaalis and valuable to the abbot, particularly if there was sentiment among the monks that Jacques's opposition to the crown had been the cause of Philip the Fair's lengthy indifference. In January 1317, the new king issued a preliminary confirmation of the charter of protection originally granted to Chaalis by Louis VI at the founding of the abbey and a blanket confirmation of the monastery's rights and privileges.[114] Formal confirmation followed in February.[115] In a separate instrument, later that year in July, the king promised royal safeguard to the abbey in his own name.[116] With these three acts, the curtain fell on a generation of indifference.

• • • • •

The granting of Philip V's charters to Chaalis was the stimulus for the last great project that Jacques de Thérines carried through at Chaalis, the creation of a new and comprehensive reference book in Latin with details on all the abbey's possessions extracted from the original charters (*carte*) then in its archives.[117] Although François Blary consistently refers to this book as the "Cartulary of 1399," and it has an early modern note in French toward the front, asserting that it was assembled in 1394, it would be more accurate to name it the "Cartulary of 1318."[118] No record enrolled in the manuscript in the original hand can be dated later than 1318, although there are many, many additions in later, very different, and frequently careless hands down into the 1390s.[119] As is typical of such codices, the original scribe left a number of empty folios distributed after each section of the cartulary for future enrollments, and in this instance, subsequent scribes often made heavy use of them. This explains why the present manuscript on superficial observation seems somewhat careless, an impression that no one looking at it in its original state would have had.[120] I am not arguing that the manuscript, properly appreciated, is uniquely splendid among Cistercian or any other sort of cartularies, but that it excellently serves its purpose, while its organization and the timing of its creation reveal its patron's intentions.[121]

The dominant organizing principle of the cartulary, at least up until the closing two sections, is topographical.[122] A reader who needed to know the details of grants made to the abbey over the course of its history in its immediate vicinity (*De possessionibus circa abbatiam*) would turn to folios 7v–29v, for example. To find out what the abbey held in and around Beauvais, he had only to consult the grants and confirmations (*Hec sunt carte de Belvaco*) recorded in chronological order beginning on folio 371.[123] To repeat: of the twenty-eight sections in this enormous document (399 folios, nearly 800 pages) organized in this way, not one *in the original hand* ends with a record more recent than the year 1318.[124]

What gives Jacques's cartulary an especially nice character, however, are the closing two sections. All his mature life the Cistercian as a master in theology at the University of Paris and as an abbot was concerned about the privileges of the exempt orders. His quodlibetal questions of 1306–1307 and the four treatises on the subject composed for the Council of Vienne in 1311 are always angry and often eloquent monuments to this concern.[125] He was particularly anxious to forestall the ignorance of future abbots with regard to the immunities that the French kings and the supreme pontiffs had granted Chaalis. To this end he had the scribe conclude the new cartulary with the two sections alluded to, one devoted to notices of royal privileges (*Tituli privilegiorum regalium*), the other and last to notices of papal privileges (*privilegia pontificum romanorum*).[126]

As one might expect, the latest royal privilege was the omnibus of King Philip V dating from 1317.[127] Royal privileges granted thereafter were kept in a separate bundle.[128] The papal privileges granted Chaalis constituted the concluding section of the manuscript; the omnibus privilege that was secured in Jacques's own time from Pope Clement V closed this section and, indeed, the entire manuscript in the original hand. To be sure, Clement V's confirmation is completely formulaic and repeats verbatim an earlier confirmation of Pope Boniface VIII, but since Boniface had subsequently granted further privileges to Chaalis—appointing a religious, the abbot of Saint-Aubert of Cambrai, to be guardian of the immunities of the house, in one instance, and conceding its exemption from tithes and other exactions in another—Clement V's blanket confirmation was all the more inclusive.[129] The simple concluding formula reads, "Clement V, who confirms all the privileges conceded to us both by the Apostolic See and by kings and princes and every other sort of person."[130]

• • • • •

As the scribe of the "Cartulary of 1318" was finishing his work, Abbot Jacques de Thérines prepared to leave Chaalis to become head of one of the four daughters of Cîteaux, the great monastery of Pontigny, and thus, after the abbot of Cîteaux, one of the four traditional abbot fathers of the entire order.[131] The "Cartulary of 1318" was a monument of his achievement as an administrator and protector of the rights of his brother monks at Chaalis. It was also the instantiation of his career-long determination to put theory into practice in the defense of the historic privileges of the whole Cistercian Order and of all exempt orders. The headship of Pontigny was the reward as well as a new and heavy burden, but for reasons that will now be laid out, his election was not wholly unexpected.

5

OLD FIGHTS AND NEW:

FROM EXEMPTION TO *USUS PAUPER*

THE YEAR 1314 WAS an *annus horribilis* for the French crown, beset as it was by adultery scandals, misfortunes in waging war, the specter of armed rebellion, and Philip the Fair's death. The demise of Pope Clement V on 20 April was but another occurrence contributing to a general sense of crisis. No one knew what relationship a new pope would work out with the kingdom of France, the "eldest daughter" of the church. The cardinals meanwhile were directionless, bitterly though not quite hopelessly divided, with a substantial and particularly intransigent anti-French faction among them. Since a two-thirds majority was necessary for a pope's election, a stalemate developed, despite repeated meetings and deals proposed. When the Holy Spirit, as prophetic claims had it, finally worked its will upon the cardinals, aided by the increasingly ominous threats of princes, the papal interregnum had already lasted for two years and three months.[1] The choice announced on 7 August 1316 fell on yet another southern Frenchman, Cardinal Jacques Duèse, born in Cahors in 1244 and thus in his early seventies.[2] His advanced age may indicate that the electors looked on him as a brief placeholder while the jockeying process of settling on a vigorous younger man as his successor continued.[3] But the wait was long. Duèse, who took the name John XXII, would preside over the Apostolic See for almost twenty very tumultuous years, 1316–1334, until he died at the age of eighty-nine or ninety.[4]

The new pope was an *érudit*, a former professor, too little educated in theology for his pretensions as an interpreter of the divine word, but a gifted student of canon and Roman law.[5] He tried to stay abreast, too, of the latest intellectual fashions.[6] He was severely ascetic in his personal habits and remained so, even as the papal court at Avignon, where he took up residence, began more and more to assume those characteristics of bureaucratic sophistication or of excess, as its critics bemoaned, that have come to define it in many popular if exaggerated modern appraisals.[7] Aside from his eccentric views on the impossibility of full bliss (the beatific vision) and of full perdition before the Last Judgment, he was a theological conservative, suspicious of contemporary devotional movements that were both invigorating religious life and at the same time challenging the narrow definition of orthodoxy he favored.

As a fiscal bureaucrat, Pope John XXII was first-rate.[8] One consequence of the papal treasury's bureaucratic sophistication during his pontificate was the more efficient extraction of revenues from ecclesiastical provinces throughout Latin Christendom, excepting the Holy Roman Empire, where the pontiff engaged in a bitter struggle with Ludwig of Bavaria (1314–1347), a claimant to the imperial throne, over papal authority in German royal elections. The struggle was altogether as savage and debilitating for the church in the empire as that between Boniface VIII and Philip IV the Fair had earlier been for France, perhaps more so, since it led Ludwig to support men whom John XXII considered heretics, and even to acknowledge the authority of an "antipope."

•   •   •   •   •

Having been a bishop before becoming pope, John XXII carried with him some of the concerns that most bishops felt in the early fourteenth century. They were jealous of their authority, zealous to restore it where they thought it slipping, and determined to root out the infection of heresy by the use of this authority. For example, although they ceded significant powers to "inquisitors of heretical depravity," mainly Dominican and Franciscan friars, during the thirteenth century they often, if not always, worked hand in glove with the inquisitors rather than protesting their commissions or their practices.[9] A major area in which the bishops perceived an illegitimate weakening of their authority is one with which we are already familiar, namely, the existence in their dioceses of exempt and privileged ecclesiastical corporations, including the Templars before their suppression. Their critique of the system of exemption, including their argument that the Templars' privileges, tantamount to exemption, helped explain the Knights' allegedly vice-ridden behavior, failed to bring the system to an end at the Council of Vienne in 1311–1312. Most of the bishops undoubtedly felt disappointed but resolved that there was nothing left to do after Pope Clement V, having pondered their criticisms, spoke so emphatically in favor of exemption.

The new pope, however, revived the bishops' hopes. Despite the resolution of the issue of exemption at the Council of Vienne, John XXII was reluctant to admit the continuing need for exempt orders. While acting on Pope Clement V's behalf on business in France in 1310, he had benefited from a mandate the pontiff issued compelling exempt and nonexempt orders alike to support his mission financially, a method of sustenance the late pontiff resorted to and justified on more than one occasion.[10] This fact could be used to argue that exemption should not extend to fiscal matters. As bishop of Avignon he attended the council, where he cast his lot with the Templars' opponents. He was therefore perfectly familiar with

Abbot Jacques de Thérines's arguments in favor of exemption, the latter's insistence on the irrelevance of the Templars' moral state to the question of exemption, and also his plea for greater skepticism about the charges against the Knights. Aware from the early months of his pontificate that funds needed for projects dear to his heart, like a new Crusade, were not coming to Avignon in the amounts he expected, the new pope, while undoubtedly sensitive to the backlogs in collection attending the lengthy papal interregnum, put part of the blame on the system of exemptions.

In an effort to confirm his suspicions he challenged the Cistercians to defend their immunities once again, and to do so successfully or submit to reform.[11] It was no accident that he put a pair of "insidious questions"— to use Jean-Berthold Mahn's phrase—to Jacques de Thérines and another even more senior monk, Simon, the head of Pontigny and therefore one of the five abbot-fathers of the order.[12] The strongest point or argument against exemption had always been the slippage from virtue opponents of the system believed was inevitable when outside authorities, in particular bishops, were barred from investigating allegations of improper conduct in the exempt establishments in their dioceses and punishing it, if they found the allegations to be true. The questions Pope John XXII explicitly raised were two. First, did the Cistercian Order, the model of an exempt order, need reformation? Second, could it not contribute significantly greater subsidies to future Crusades?[13]

In fact the pope's two questions raised several subsidiary ones. The suggestion that the order might need reformation implied that there were widespread abuses within it, and that these were direct consequences of exemption. The question of subsidies for future Crusades implied that the pontiff regarded the order's gracious grants and other coerced contributions to Crusades and just wars in the past as legitimate. For him, it was a given that the order's immunity no longer extended to exemption from war taxes. The issue was simply whether the order was capable of giving more, and, if the answer was no, whether this incapacity owed itself to inefficiencies and financial improprieties critics could legitimately associate with exemption.

Owing to his dignity Abbot Simon of Pontigny should have been the senior partner in drafting the response, but he was a very old man and on the verge of a precipitous physical decline when the pope's request reached him toward the end of 1317. He had been abbot of Pontigny since about 1290, twenty-seven years, and the post would not have come to him had he not at the time already been an exceptionally senior member of the order.[14] So the task fell to the abbot of Chaalis, who drafted a response that, he reported, carried the aged senior abbot's endorsement.[15] By now, Jacques's skills at defending the order and its exemption were honed to a remarkable sharpness, but he was also aware that his earlier arguments, which John XXII knew, were not persuasive to the pontiff, and that he needed to come up with additional ones.

The report, edited by Noël Valois and summarized at length by him in two different places in almost the same words, is "a little masterpiece."[16] Jacques took pains to be polite, perhaps almost too polite, but John XXII had "an excessive confidence in himself" that flattery only confirmed.[17] The abbot stressed the pontiff's plenitude of power, first of all, and the splendor of his office.[18] An exempt order fell under the Apostolic See's direct authority.[19] How was it possible to accept critics' arguments that exemption implied absolute independence? It would be as much as admitting that the pope's supervision was nothing, when in fact it was *SUPER-vision* (like the proverbial eyes of the lynx) and had the strength imaged in the eagle's visage.[20] That papal authority came into play on top of the extraordinary levels of internal supervision that characterized and differentiated exempt orders from nonexempt orders should convince anyone, Jacques insisted, that the possibility of a massive falling away into vice or heresy was utterly impossible.[21] The system of supervision, including confinement to the cloister (*restringuntur occasiones evagationum*), made strict adherence to the Rule commonplace. Exempt monks gave themselves actively to manual labor (*interdum manibus laborantes*) when they were not reading the daily lessons and praying potent prayers for themselves and for the Christian faithful.[22] They were strict vegetarians who made no concessions to eating meat unless a sick brother might benefit from it (*extra infirmatoria Ordinis*). Austere and ascetic in their own habits, a style of living that might appeal to an ascetic pope, they were nonetheless generous to all who needed alms (*sibi sunt parci, aliis liberales*). It was their splendid success in religion and the works of charity, in brief, in the monastic life that was at least one justification for earlier popes' conferral of exempt status on them.[23] Or so the abbot of Chaalis maintained.

Another argument from one former professor that might appeal to another who still kept up with the intellectual debates at the universities was the strong support the Cistercians gave to education.[24] The order produced scholars who served the great universities, not least the University of Paris. The professors taught Cistercians and non-Cistercians alike, particularly in theology, the science of those matters that most touch upon salvation (*in his potissime que pertinent ad salutem*). The Cistercians' commitment to continue in this path, Jacques noted, was firm and without reservation. The General Chapters endorsed the expansion of schools and studies (*ut studia multiplicentur et numerosius dilatentur*).

Was every Cistercian or, by implication, every member of every exempt order or exempt house without sin? The abbot quoted scripture (1 John 1.8): "If we say that we have no sin, we deceive ourselves, and the truth is not in us."[25] Everyone sins. But the Cistercians were monks who, by having a keen sense of their sinfulness and their propensity to sin, took steps to fight sin, Jacques asserted, and to ask for forgiveness and renewed strength when they fell into sin.[26] All this was, of course, in line with the continuation of the biblical words (1 John 1.9), "If we confess our sins, he is faithful and just to forgive us our sins, and to cleanse us from all unrighteousness."

The frequency of the sinning, not God's inclination to forgive and purify, was the very point the critics were always making. So what if Cistercian abbots and monks confessed once a week at least, as Jacques claimed? What did it matter that those over whom the abbots had authority, like the *conversi*, were obliged to live up to their obligation to confess regularly not less than once a year? The Cistercian Order's opponents seized on the notion that the very need to confess, and to enforce the obligation of confession on sinners reluctant to admit their wrongs, was an argument against the purity or superiority of the men in exempt orders.

The counterargument further developed by the abbot was intended to flatter a pope with a keen, even urgent, sense of his status in the long aftermath of Clement V's pontificate, and with the ever growing perception that the power of the church was facing a serious challenge from the purveyors of heresy. For over the exempt orders, Jacques reminded John XXII, as if he needed to be reminded so soon after the abbot first made the point, there hovered the imposing edifice of Cistercian supervision culminating in that most absolute and sublime of authorities, the supreme pontiff of the Roman Catholic Church—presuming, that is, that the supreme pontiff would conscientiously exercise his divinelike powers.

Perhaps, the abbot of Chaalis intimated, the issue was not individual monks' or abbots' or lay brothers' fall from grace, but defects in the order itself, some genuinely systemic problem or set of problems that actually encouraged sin. Jacques was unwilling to argue that such defects were impossible.[27] For nothing on earth achieved perfection. The question for him and, therefore, his answer for John XXII, concerned the best way to remedy such defects. He returned once more to the fact that the Apostolic See had sufficient wisdom to identify and address imperfections in the system of exemption, and the ministers of the order were willing to accept correction from such a wise source (*a vestre Sanctitatis prudencia directivam omnem reformacionem recipere*). Ideal reform, in other words, was reform that would improve and increase, not abolish, exemption.[28] Here the abbot was recycling with a slight twist an argument he had used at the Council of Vienne, namely, that the problems identified in the partially exempt orders were better solved by increasing their level of exemption (and, therefore, quality of internal supervision and strictness of claustration) than by suppressing their privileges.[29]

So much for the pope's first question: if reform was needed, then he should carry it through, and it should eventuate in a more exalted, a closer to perfect, form of exemption. The abbot of Chaalis treated the second question, on the Cistercian Order's capacity to increase its financial contribution to Crusades, in a less schematic fashion. He, of course, acknowledged the glory of the Crusade to a pope who desperately wanted to be the instrument of the recovery of the Holy Land.[30] But he refused to engage at an abstract level the implicit issue of whether the order's gracious and coerced payments of war taxes in the past compromised its exemption or by long use or prescription had achieved quasi-legal status. He preferred merely to describe the effects of paying the taxes and to have the pope draw his own conclusion as to whether they were as negative as he depicted them.

No one could deny that the first priority for men of religion on the matter of the Holy Land was prayer.[31] Pope Clement V particularly begged Cistercians' prayers for a new Crusade, Jacques might have pointed out to Clement's successor.[32] Without prayer and God's help, which came from prayer, there would be no victory against the sworn enemies of Christ. Moreover, without the works of mercy that monks performed, God would not aid the Crusade. Yet how could monks do these works? The abbot presented figures derived from his careful examination of the General Chapters' records. According to his reckoning, Cistercians in France had contributed 60,000 l. *tournois* to the French crown for the war against the English in Gascony (1294–1297).[33] Independently the king's own officials in a memorandum around the time of the war recorded the Cistercian grant also as 60,000 l.[34] The initial tax, levied without papal permission, led to the first great crisis between King Philip the Fair and Pope Boniface VIII, and to the capitulation of Boniface on the issue.[35]

The grant of 60,000 l. was just the beginning of the misery, because Cistercian houses simply did not have the disposable surplus at the time. They were forced to borrow, and borrowing meant paying interest (*ad usuras*). By Jacques's reckoning, once again, the total sum the Cistercian abbeys rendered to crown and creditors together was approximately 100,000 l. *tournois* for the war.[36] And this was the outlay merely for one war. Wars had been and were being waged everywhere. That the French never seemed to stop fighting the Flemings is the other illustration Jacques stressed, as a Frenchman himself.[37] But he acknowledged that the problems ensuing from these hostilities were replicated in any number of theaters of conflict (*et alibi*), with deleterious consequences—additional war taxes, heavy interest payments, royal and princely seizures of goods, even the extensive destruction of monastic properties in the vicious strife.[38] On top of all this Avignon craved more. It commanded payment of annual taxes of a tenth of income, from which the Cistercians ought to have been exempted. These taxes went to princes, in fact, with the result that the Holy See continued to be in need, but the now impecunious order, whatever its desires, had little to offer to offset the need.[39] And then there were the onerous stipends (*pensionibus annuis*) the order paid to the cardinals charged to protect the order.[40] In sum, the abbot of Chaalis asserted, the Cistercian Order, the whole order, had obligations all told to the tune of 500,000 l. *tournois*, and each of five of the greatest abbeys, four of which were in France, had obligations as high as 100,000 l. each.[41] These figures—total obligations of half a million when five houses alone had individual obligations of 100,000 l. each—need explication.

Peter King acknowledged that Jacques's statements in some particulars found confirmation in the records he looked at on the finances of the Cistercian Order in the fourteenth century. He found evidence of costly stipends for the cardinals, the payment of yearly subsidies earmarked for Avignon (or the princes who were promising to go on Crusade), requisitioning of goods from Cistercian abbeys in the war zone of the Franco-Flemish borderlands.[42] He also recognized problems in the numbers, but he went too far in regarding all of them as absurdly high. Indeed, his reasons for rejecting the entire array of Jacques's figures were strange. First, King argued that the abbot hardly knew what wars were going on elsewhere and so concentrated on French wars.[43] Why this should have led Jacques to overestimate the cost of the wars for the Cistercian Order as a whole in taxes and damage from requisitions and violence is unclear. Logically it should have led the abbot to underestimate the burden. That Jacques limited himself to two specific illustrations of war's effects, namely, those associated with the Anglo-French conflict in Gascony and the Franco-Flemish conflict in the north, may be proof that these mattered most to him. After all, they had the most direct impact on French ecclesiastical politics and the long unhappy tensions in Cistercian-crown relations, tensions he had to endure. But he acknowledged the waging of other wars, and it is hard to believe that he "did not really know what wars had occurred outside of France" (Peter King's words).

The fact is that the Anglo-Scottish wars of Edward I and Edward II, especially intense and brutal in the teens of the fourteenth century, the Welsh Rebellion (1314–1316) in Edward II's time, the savagery following the Scottish invasion of Ireland in 1315, and the civil war in Germany (from 1314 on) were extremely well reported.[44] It would not have taken much effort either, given the annual meetings of the General Chapters attended by abbots or monk-delegates from monasteries throughout the order, to learn of the effect of this violence on Cistercian houses in the war zones.[45] War and requisitions of resources severely weakened and sometimes nearly destroyed several Cistercian monasteries in Britain at this time: Holme Cultram, Neath, Llantaram, Maenan, and Cymer.[46] The records of Neath monotonously itemize its losses to war and the ways in which the monks had "been plundered of their goods." Borrowing and falling into crippling debt were characteristic of a number of these British foundations, as well as of Clairvaux and Vaucelles and some imperial foundations, such as Dunes, Cambrai, Ter-Doest, Daimbach, Argenton, and Val-Dieu.[47] Daimbach and Argenton, indeed, were Cistercian nunneries whose representatives, around the time Jacques wrote, spoke of the "burdens of [their] debts," in the first case, and about being "oppressed most heavily . . . by debts," in the second. To try to preserve body and soul, some hard-pressed houses sought to transform their estates from direct exploitation to leasing, as Chaalis under Jacques was doing.[48] Vaulerent is an example, and there are others.[49]

Then there was the frighteningly persistent bad weather ruining crops and causing animal pestilences. Jacques remarked on it gloomily.[50] Such weather, particularly in the previous three years, was virtually unheard-of, a claim that was not an exaggeration.[51] To Peter King, however, this comment merely showed Jacques's limitations as an observer. Jacques, according to him, was solely interested in the weather and its effects in France. He had no idea that this weather and its consequences, the Great Famine, beginning in 1315, affected all of northern Europe from the British Isles to Slavia.[52] Yet once more, it is hard to see how this limited vision, if that is what it was, led Jacques to overestimate the impact of the weather and the famine on the Cistercian Order as a whole. Logically, again, it should have led him to underestimate the effect.

In any case, the abbot certainly was on the right track. The extreme plight of houses like Villiers, Val-Saint-Lambert, and Orval makes the point.[53] As the year 1315 drew to a close, the brothers serving the Cistercian abbey of Villers (Brabant) abandoned their house and dispersed to more fortunate establishments on account of the prolonged bad weather, the failure of crops, disease, and mortality. Val Saint-Lambert in the Liègois under precisely the same pressures dispersed in 1316; conditions did not permit a return until the 1320s. The Orval abbey scriptorium prepared letters of introduction for the monks of the house when it looked as though there would be no other choice but for them to leave the diocese of Trier and disperse "with bitterness of heart" to other Cistercian monasteries.

Cistercian houses, insofar as they were able, Jacques asserted, were spending every penny possible on alms for the burgeoning number of poor in these famine times. Admittedly, he could not really know whether reports of this were true, but he would have been repeating what he had heard at the General Chapter or read from its records. Something like the scenario he described was being played out by Abbot Eylard of the Cistercian monastery of Aduard near Groningen, who was getting a reputation as a saint in 1315 for his generosity to the lay poor (his giant pot from which he daily served them soup became a relic), and for his brotherly alms to hard-hit religious houses, not all of them Cistercian.[54] And, thanks to the General Chapter meetings, Jacques de Thérines had access to information on the Cistercian monks of Riddagshausen in the diocese of Magdeburg, whose heroic efforts to feed their hundreds of needy dependents in 1316 were becoming the stuff of legend.[55] I presume the former professor had also heard that "the university initiated an appeal in 1316 for increased benefice support from the church," as a result of the decline of income owing to the bad harvests on the estates providing their income.[56]

But what ought one to make of Jacques's overall figures? Even if we accept that the Cistercians and just about everybody else in northern Europe were suffering, could outstanding obligations really have reached the levels the abbot suggested? Peter King was adamant. He did not think this was remotely possible: "the figures are fantastic." Further, he wrote, "It must be remembered that in modern times the use of arabic numerals has made it easy to understand high numbers, so that billions, millions and thousands present no difficulties even to children." (Ah, modernity!) "In the Middle Ages," however, he continued, "when such quantities were usually expressed through cumbrous roman numerals, many people, even among the learned, had difficulty in conceiving them. This was undoubtedly the case," he concluded, "with Jacques de Thérines, or his copyist."[57]

At the time the abbot wrote his response there were approximately 700 male monasteries in the Cistercian Order.[58] No final reckoning on the number of female houses, although it was well above 130, is yet possible, but the nuns, judging from gracious grants to the Crusades, probably contributed only 2 or 3 percent to the order's overall income.[59] Jacques did not write of the debts (*debita*) of the order but of its obligations, and he or the copyist did so in prose, not dreaded roman numerals (*in quingentis milibus libris turonensium obligatus*, and *in centum milibus libris turonensium obligate*), which would have included outstanding debts as well as regular budgeted annual expenditures. If obligations ran to 500,000 l. French, then the average level of obligation was a little over 700 l. *tournois* per abbey, perhaps £150 English, quite a credible figure. If the estimate covers the nunneries as well, the average would plummet to about 600 l. French or £125 English. In the order, there were houses like Clairvaux, enormously wealthy or rather under enormous obligations, and tiny Welsh houses, which at the time were scarcely scraping by. As Jacques pointed out, it was the burden of poverty that was the root cause of the dispersal of monks to other monasteries (*multi conventus, ratione paupertatis, his diebus per ordinem sunt dispersi*).[60] Moreover, Jacques claimed that he was backing up with hard data statements about the order's deleterious financial state that had recently been reported orally to the pope (*nuper in vestra presentia*).[61] John XXII, whatever else he was, was extremely knowledgeable on fiscal matters. He would have spotted wild exaggerations with ease.

One must doubt, however, that any single house had obligations reaching 100,000 l. *tournois*. The error in Jacques's figures is here. I am inclined to think that he intended 10,000 l. instead of 100,000. The order's total overall obligations amounted to approximately 500,000 l. Five houses in the order, four of which were in France, had especially onerous obligations amounting altogether to 50,000 l. This is a reasonable surmise, and it is the information, I am arguing, that Jacques meant to convey. If income and expenditures were supposed to be roughly in balance in the largest Cistercian abbey in the county of Burgundy (the Franche-Comté), for example, its budget was about 2,000 l. per year.[62] A 10,000 l. obligation for a much greater Cistercian house is entirely plausible and not out of line with that of other major institutions. Canterbury Cathedral Priory, for which there are excellent contemporary fiscal accounts, had an annual budget of £2,000 English, equivalent to approximately 10,000 l. French in the standard money of account, *tournois*. It had deficits when translated into *tournois* of 2,455 l. in 1316, of 1,425 l. in 1317, and of 2,670 l. in 1318. Its average annual obligations in these years therefore amounted to 12,190 l. *tournois*.[63] This is somewhat higher than the level of obligations (budget plus debts) that Jacques de Thérines was attributing, again quite credibly, to each of the five greatest abbeys in the Cistercian Order for the truly horrifying financial years his estimates cover.

The error in the text sent to the pope, 500,000 for 50,000, is very simple to explain. It arose, if I am right, from a mistake in the draft of the report where *in quingentis*, 500,000, was written or abbreviated instead of *in quinquagentis*, 50,000, for the total obligations of the five most distressed abbeys. The scribe or copyist of the formal report then broke this figure down into five units of 100,000 rather than five units of 10,000. A regrettable slip, no doubt, but also one easily corrected by a fiscally adept pope earlier given an oral synopsis of the report, as opposed to a condescending modern historian. Certainly the error offers no very persuasive evidence of a brain-addling incapacity to deal with numbers in the billions, millions, and thousands as any child can do today.

The pope's shrewdness in fiscal matters would immediately have made him curious about something else, though. How much of the difficult financial situation described was the result of poor management? Jacques's answer has already been anticipated. No one was right to impute bad administration to the ministers of the order.[64] War and royal war taxes, bad weather and poor harvests, alms for famine victims, debts and usury upon usury—the best management could not withstand such an onslaught of demands (a *multiplex ratio*, as the old scholastic put it). Yet there was more. The abbot could not help but recall the humiliation of his own monastery and of so many other French monasteries, which had been forced to pay amortization (*de amortizacione*) fines to Philip the Fair for acquiring feudal property, even when they held their lands peacefully, in some cases for a century or more (*licet eas pacifice tenuerimus per centum annos et amplius*).[65] And, echoing a theme from his own experience as an abbot and the continuing concern of the General Chapter, he vented his contempt for *nobiles mediocres*, rapacious minor nobles who wanted to take exempt Cistercian monasteries to secular courts on whatever unjust pretext in order to extort their goods.[66]

Nonetheless, the abbot concluded, perhaps there was a way for the order to contribute money to the recovery of the Holy Land. The good pastor, the pope, could authorize each individual house, for they, not the order, had sovereign rights over their property, to alienate their lands to willing buyers.[67] This practice was becoming common among fiscally stressed ecclesiastical corporations.[68] Did the abbot need to mention that the Blessed Virgin Mary, as the patroness of Cistercian monasteries, owned all these lands whose sale the pope would be allowing?[69] Jacques did not make the point explicitly, but John XXII—an enthusiastic devotee of the Virgin's cult, author of prayers to her eternal honor and glory, and the pope who was instrumental in popularizing the recitation of the *Ave Maria*—hardly needed reminding.[70] The abbot of Chaalis did mention, however, the indignation that would arise among donors and the resulting and horrifying decline of alms, hospitality, prayers, and the divine cult, so necessary for eliciting God's support for the recovery of the Holy Land.[71] On the one hand, the abbot added, if the pontiff went ahead and authorized these sales, the monasteries could not get the just price for the lands. With the background of his own recent real estate transactions for Chaalis in the famine time, he estimated that sales would generate scarcely half what the properties were worth in normal times (*de quibus medietas justi pretii his diebus*).[72] On the other hand, to reject the radical solution of the alienation of Cistercian properties was to hope for better times, a merciful respite from wars, an end to annual taxes of a tenth, and a cessation of all the other harms of the present day, and perhaps, just perhaps, allow the order to breathe again and serve the Holy Father (*posset Ordo noster aliqualiter respirare, et placeret vestre Sanctitati*).[73]

"L'éloquence de Jacques de Thérines détourna le pape de ses desseins," wrote Guillaume Mollat, the premier historian of the Avignonese papacy.[74] The ugly little old man, a characterization that Noël Valois employed for the rail-thin pope who was scarcely five feet tall, was no doubt moved by the flattery of his office.[75] He was possibly persuaded by the arguments, too, especially Jacques's tactful silence on whether the war and Crusade taxes levied on the Cistercians were just too heavy or were illegitimate in themselves. But perhaps the most important factor in persuading the pontiff to leave the Cistercians alone was the chorus of lamentations coming out of the north contemporary with Jacques's report about conditions there that reinforced the abbot's picture: the University of Paris masters' petition, to which the pope agreed, for supplements to their benefices because of income shortfalls; monastery after monastery in the north seeking relief from papal levies or begging papal support for creative ways to raise money, such as by selling annuities or even getting a special dispensation to receive the profits of former Templar granges; and independent reports about the cascading threat of rapacious local elites like Jacques's *nobiles mediocres*.[76] Whatever the reason, the abbot of Chaalis was once again instrumental in preserving the privileges of the Cistercian Order.

• • • • •

Not too long afterward word reached Chaalis that Jacques de Thérines's companion-in-arms in this most recent struggle to defend the order, the aged Abbot Simon of Pontigny, was dead. The monks of Pontigny saw to his burial in a site in the abbey that also held the earthly remains of Simon's mother and father. The monks, as the epitaph carved for their late abbot testified, prayed Christ that he and they would be admitted to the company of the blessed in God's eternal kingdom.[77] Then they set about the task of choosing a new abbot. Electing an abbot at the senior abbeys required the consultation of the abbots of monasteries in the filiation, and the choice often, though not always, fell on an elder monk who was not already resident in the senior house.[78] The name of Jacques de Thérines—for all the reasons he was elected abbot of Chaalis almost a decade before, and now with the addition of his several spirited defenses of the Cistercian Order—would have arisen immediately as a possibility, and a Pontigny abbot chosen from among the monks at Chaalis was not without precedent.[79] His success in repairing his own monastery's relations with the French ruling house after the death of Philip the Fair was not to be ignored. And his reputation as a successful administrator, which was known through the workings of the General Chapter, contributed, too, to making him seem a good candidate. Finally, the recent close collaboration between Jacques and Simon in responding to Pope John XXII's questions easily suggested the abbot of Chaalis as Simon's successor at Pontigny.

"If we say that we have no sin, we deceive ourselves, and the truth is not in us." A model abbot needed more than a sharp tongue, a fine mind, administrative acumen, or even courage in the strife-torn and fear-ridden world of early fourteenth-century French high politics. In theory he was to have that well of piety and devotion that enabled the monk to save the sinful Catholic faithful. Three statements found in the epitaph later inscribed for Jacques at Pontigny suggest that he struck his contemporar-

ies as possessing these virtues. Although epitaphs typically employ laudatory and sometimes exaggerated language to describe the merits and
achievements of the people they memorialize, the individual statements,
unless completely conventional, ordinarily have some relationship to the
real life story of the person recalled.

One of these statements compared Jacques's holiness to that of Saint
Edmund of Abingdon, also known as Edmund Rich, Edmund of Canterbury, and Edmund of Pontigny. The abbey of Pontigny was the cult center
of Saint Edmund, the archbishop of Canterbury who was interred there
in the year 1240, when he died unexpectedly while away from his see.[80]
The French had long bragged unfairly that Edmund, an extremely devout
and ascetic man, chose to die in exile from England in the kingdom of
France, where there was a hallowed tradition of sheltering his persecuted
predecessors, most famously Saint Anselm, Saint Thomas Becket, and Ste-
phen Langton, King John's adversary.[81] To be sure, Edmund had serious
problems in his political relations with King Henry III of England, but
the archbishop's trip, though occasioned by some of these problems, was
to have taken him to Rome for consultations. En route he had second
thoughts, probably because word reached him of the deterioration of political conditions in Italy, and also because of the onset of a grave illness,
from which he did not recover. With the great abbey church of Pontigny
nearby, which had once been home in exile for Becket, it seemed altogether reasonable that another primate of the English church be welcomed there, this time for burial.[82] Archbishop Edmund's adversary,
Henry III, visited the tomb in 1254, a little more than seven years after
Edmund's canonization, in order to do public veneration to his memory
and to try to put an end to the French canard that he had exiled Edmund.

Jacques was said to be "Holy like Saint Edmund, pure and without
lust" (*Sanctus ut Edmundus fuit absque libidine mundus*). These are hardly
words that refer to Edmund's or Jacques's resistance to monarchs. The
defining event in Edmund's devotional life, the centerpiece of the hagio-
graphical texts written in his honor, was a vision he had while a student
at Oxford. It was a vision of a small boy, in fact the Christ Child. But
Edmund, not yet perfected in his holiness, failed to recognize the boy's
true identity. Upbraided by the Lord for his failure, the future archbishop
instituted a practice whereby every night for the remainder of his life he
traced the letters of the name Jesus of Nazareth on his forehead, and he
became an enthusiastic devotee of his virgin mother's cult.[83] Enthusiastic
is too mild. He immediately took a vow of chastity, binding himself in a
spiritual marriage with the Virgin Mary. He wore a wedding ring sym-
bolizing the marriage and allegedly placed another on the finger of one
of the Virgin's statues in the Church of Saint Mary in Oxford. It is no great
leap of the imagination to argue that the epitaph reference to Jacques's

Edmund-like holiness and his chastity, his "purity . . . without lust," evokes the abbot's remarkably intense devotion to the Virgin's cult as well.

Later in the epitaph, indeed, this devotion is made explicit: Jacques de Thérines was "fervent in the love of Mary" (*fervens in amore Mariae*). The phrase is immediately followed by a description of Abbot Jacques (Latin, *Jacobus*) as a "second Jacob, thus carried to the stars in his spiritual yearnings" (*Cum duplex Jacobus sic fertur ad astra talentis*). This third and last pertinent reference, of course, is to the dream of the patriarch Jacob in Genesis: "And he dreamed, and behold a ladder set up on the earth, and the top of it reached to heaven: and behold the angels of God ascending and descending on it" (Gen. 28.12). It seems fairly clear from all three statements taken together that the monk's devotion to the Virgin and his devotional practices in general were exemplary as far as his Cistercian brothers were concerned, and gave him an additional characteristic that recommended his candidacy for the abbacy of Pontigny.

• • • • •

Jacques de Thérines's duties as the new abbot of Pontigny, which he was fulfilling by mid-1318, were very similar to those he had left behind at Chaalis.[84] He managed the same oversight of the fabric of the buildings, monastic discipline, and the workforce, the same keeping of accounts and negotiating disagreements with local seigneurs, the same efforts to productively exploit the estates of the abbey, the same responsibilities as annual visitor to houses in the filiation (he now had to visit Chaalis) as well as to the visitors who inspected Pontigny and to the General Chapter, which met every September.[85] Even the physical environment was similar. A very strong argument suggests that the Gothic church at Chaalis owes its features to the Burgundian Gothic of Pontigny rather than to the Ile-de-France Gothic of the churches in its immediate vicinity.[86]

Despite the similarities of these duties to those at Chaalis, it must be remarked that all of Jacques's efforts were now being undertaken for a monastery immensely more involved with local elites. Its own purchases of property, like an expenditure of 1,500 l. *tournois* in 1295, oiled the regional economy.[87] Evidence also indicates that the abbey was a major contributor, as a lender, to nobles who needed large caches of capital for projects in which they were involved or for payments they had to make to higher authorities. Countess Jeanne of Alençon and Blois made formal acknowledgment of having borrowed 2,000 l. *tournois* from the abbey in 1287.[88] Countess Marguerite of Tonnerre made a formal recognition of receiving a gift (!) from Pontigny in 1292 of 3,000 l. *tournois*.[89] Jacques's predecessor as abbot of Pontigny, Simon, was exceedingly adept at and busy with securing aristocratic support and the overall financial integrity of the institution.[90] This included obtaining proper amortizations for the lands that lords granted to the abbey.[91] It was Jacques de Thérines's responsibility to maintain both.

The abbey of Pontigny was also a major pilgrimage shrine as the site of Saint Edmund's tomb.[92] It was at least Jacques de Thérines's formal responsibility to supervise access to the relics, and to see to the registering and collection of evidence of the miracles. Contact with laypeople was largely confined to *conversi*, secular priests, or perhaps lay employees rather than choir monks.[93] A great many pilgrims were women. They were not permitted to enter the abbey precincts, but Edmund's relics were exposed for them at the abbey gates on Saturdays (*in porta . . . presentibus reliquiarum custodibus*).[94] Evidently there was a crush of people in winter on the Saturdays around the time when the saint's feast was celebrated, 16 November. Many of the women were afflicted with blindness and were seeking to have their sight restored. The *custodes* of the relics regulated access very carefully to preserve decorum. This meant that many women were out in the cold for lengthy periods. If the choir monks decided that there were too many of these pilgrims to fit in all their devotions in the allotted time, the *custodes* urged them to return to their homes and make a new trip on another Saturday, presumably if they had not come from distances that made this impractical.[95] All of these comings and goings needed to be carefully monitored, and ultimately the responsibility of supervision lay with the abbot, who was motivated to avoid even the hint of scandal where women were concerned.

There were also distinct additional responsibilities that Jacques, as abbot of Pontigny, now had as one of the five senior abbots. This small group, which included the abbot of Cîteaux, the titular head of the order, and the abbots of Clairvaux, La Ferté, Morimond, and Pontigny, constituted an executive committee within the body of the *diffinitores*, the specialists who saw to most of the business that touched the order as an institutional unit.[96] But there were some specific tasks reserved for the senior abbots. It was upon them that the duty of visiting Cîteaux itself rested.[97] In 1314 the oversight and control of financial matters for the General Chapter was also formally enjoined on them, presumably because someone had to watch the other *diffinitores*, and for the same reason that committees on audit and budget exist on modern boards of directors to oversee even the most trustworthy treasurers and committees on investment and finance of those boards.[98] One aspect of their control was actualized by a ruling in 1317 that each of the four senior abbots, along with the abbot of Cîteaux, was to have a key to the strongbox at Cîteaux where the order's agents—who received money and letters of credit from the various abbeys and provincial chapters—deposited their collection.[99] The letters of credit were capitalized and local coins were exchanged for more standard currencies at the great series of emporiums known as the Fairs of Champagne.[100] At the General Chapters of 1318 and 1320 Jacques was a recipient of a directive issued to all five senior abbots "to send in reports about the economic state of their daughter houses, and how much they had paid at the last Collection," and, in general, to maintain good records for the ongoing work of the *diffinitores*.[101] This was no easy task. There were forty-four male monasteries and an unknown but significant number of female houses in Pontigny's filiation.[102]

•   •   •   •   •

The foregoing discussion evokes an abbot totally immersed in the duties of his monastery and the work of the Cistercian Order. In fact, almost as soon as Jacques became abbot of Pontigny, Pope John XXII intruded once more on his peace of mind. The issue was a life-and-death one. And the pope's turn to Jacques de Thérines for an "authoritative" opinion smacks of an attempt to stack the deck against the very men, a group of Franciscan friars, whose lives were at stake. From Jacques's statements at the Council of Vienne the pontiff knew his views of the mendicant orders, such as the Franciscans. Their imperfect form of exemption, as Jacques regarded it, which tolerated wandering about and frequent contact with layfolk, was dissatisfying to the Cistercian. Their mendicancy in fact bred not humility but pride, as far as he was concerned. And yet he recognized that those who chose the mendicant life were, like their founder Francis, good—if in their case somewhat misguided—men, whose arguments about how best to achieve poverty he likened to the arguments the apostles had in the early church. Insofar as they were productive, the arguments had a kind of holiness about them, to the extent that they were part of a process that aided the visible church on its road to perfection, just as the apostles' discords had.[103] The truth, however, was apparent to everybody. The disputes among the friars were not productive, but angry and self-defeating. They were tearing the mendicant movement apart. In 1312 Pope Clement V enjoined the factions not to stoop to the level of calling any of their opponents heretics.[104] By 1318, however, "heretic" was the most common slur hurled among the parties in the bitter dispute.[105]

Sixty-four of the so-called Spiritual Franciscans were in rebellion against the superiors of the order and the minister general Michael de Cesena, elected in 1316.[106] The issues went back decades but came to focus on the habit that the dissidents preferred to wear, variously described as wretched, short, patched, vile, and so forth. They believed that this was the form of the habit prescribed in the Franciscan Rule and worn by Francis.[107] Of course, there were other issues as well, particularly touching the *usus pauper*, but in fact they all revolved around the central claim of fidelity to the founder's intentions.[108] Clement V in the bull *Exivi de paradiso* of May 1312 imposed a judgment compelling brothers to obey the prescriptions of their superiors, but the Spirituals, insofar as they respected this judgment, did so by regarding the prescriptions as a minimum requirement that fulfilled the letter, not the spirit, of Francis's Rule. There were those who fulfilled only this minimum and no more, the so-called Conventuals; there were others, namely, themselves, who exceeded it and were more austere.[109] Since the Conventuals regarded their superiors' orders as binding and not to be exceeded, and since they perceived, probably rightly, that the Spirituals therefore looked upon them as unworthy recipients of Francis's legacy, they pressured the Spirituals to conform. The Spirituals, openly defying their superiors, began to leave their convents and live apart. The long papal interregnum after Clement V's death worsened the situation. By the time of Jacques Duèse's election as pope two years later in August 1316, his view and possibly the consensus in the hierarchy were that decisive action had been delayed too long.[110]

The disobedience was intolerable, as far as Pope John XXII was concerned. He came to feel that negotiations, which were proving to be futile, would never resolve the disputes.[111] On 7 October 1317, therefore, he issued the bull *Quorundam* (or *Quorumdam*) *exigit*. Its fundamental provision was to confirm authority over the habit to the superiors of the Franciscan Order, thus putting into stronger language what he and many canonists regarded as the true intent of *Exivi de paradiso*.[112] "Poverty is great," the bull concluded, "but unity is greater; obedience is the greatest good if it [unity] is preserved intact."[113] The hierarchy of virtues here is clear enough. Disobedience came at a cost. The minister general railed at the sixty-four dissidents now under arrest to submit.[114] From fear or from lingering doubts about their right to refuse to obey, since the Franciscan Rule also laid enormous stress on obedience to the supreme pontiff and the successors of Francis, thirty-nine submitted, while twenty-five held firm.[115] As far as John XXII was concerned, the twenty-five who refused were holding on to ideas that were contrary to the teaching of the Catholic faith.

In the late winter or early spring of 1318—more precisely, sometime before 3 May but after 14 February—the pope decided to put together a blue-ribbon commission of theologians to decide whether the Spirituals' views formally constituted heresy.[116] To repeat an earlier observation: owing to the pope's hostility the deck was stacked against the men whose views the commission was to assess.[117] The pontiff chose, among others, the minister general Michael of Cesena for the commission. Years later Michael would defy the same pope over the latter's interpretation of apostolic poverty and flee his wrath.[118] At this point, however, he agreed with John XXII on the need for all Franciscans' obedience to the superiors of the order and to the pontiff. Besides Michael of Cesena the commission included three other friars (a Franciscan, a Dominican, and a Carmelite), one Benedictine, six bishops, and one cardinal. Several of these commissioners, like Berengarius de Landorra and Vitalis de Furno, had earlier participated in recommending the judgment embodied in Clement V's bull *Exivi de paradiso* in 1312 and cautioning about the more extreme views of the Spirituals.[119] The final member of the group was Jacques de Thérines. He was the only commissioner from a fully exempt order, and he had a history of being openly contemptuous of bishops, friars, and nonexempt clergy.[120] He must have found the personnel of the commission distasteful, to say the least—almost as bad as eating meat.

That the pope selected the new abbot of Pontigny, therefore, appears anomalous at first glance. It is probably best explained by three considerations. First, Jacques was a veteran on the matters at issue; he had served Pope Clement V on the ecclesiastical commission at the Council of Vienne in early 1312 that advised the pontiff on the *usus pauper* dispute.[121] A second reason John XXII called on Jacques de Thérines was that in all of his polemical work Jacques argued vehemently, even obsessively, in favor of the plenitude of papal power and the need for absolute obedience. The Spirituals' denigration of papal authority, which their enemies made so much of, surely encouraged the pope to turn to a stalwart champion of papal supremacy for the commission. Third and finally, although there is no explicit evidence for this contention one way or the other, John XXII had Jacques de Thérines in his debt insofar as the pope had yielded to the abbot's defense of the Cistercian Order and retreated from his plan to reform it and to end its exemption. I think he was calling in that debt.

The specific statements the commission was to evaluate were presented in three groups.[122] First, the Spirituals obstinately (*pertinaciter*) counseled disobedience (*non est obediendum*) to any command to cease wearing their type of habit. Was such counsel heretical? They were also said to assert that no mortal man (*nullus mortalium*) who impugned their type of habit had the right to force them to take their habits off. For anyone to do so was to act contrary to the true meaning (*intelligentiam*) of the Rule of Saint Francis, the gospel, and the faith, and to behave no differently from the Jews who expelled Christ from the synagogue. Was this assertion heretical? The Spirituals went further and insisted that men who brought legal action (*procedunt*) against those who wore their habits contravened the gospel and the faith. Was this heretical?

The second and third groups of statements that the pope asked the commission to consider, which were said to build upon those of the first group, returned to the question of obedience, but in particular obedience to the supreme pontiff (*in virtute obedientie*). The Spirituals, in the second group of statements attributed to them, rejected the pope's right to issue the constitution *Quorundam*, which commanded obedience (*obedirent*)

to the rulers of the Franciscan Order with regard to any and all specifica-
tions about the size and quality of the habit and the kinds and quality of
food and drink of which brothers were to partake. The third set of attributed statements to be evaluated for their heretical content included the
assertion that neither for the pope nor for prelates was *Quorundam* to be
obeyed, because the constitution was contrary to the counsel of Christ
and the Franciscan Rule, against which the pope has no power (*contra que
papa non potest*).

Not surprisingly the commission concluded that the three articles were
manifestly heretical.[123] They contravened evangelical truth. They denied
the supreme pontiff's power and authority. They were an effort to pull
into the Catholic faith *opinio*, false novelties, that contradicted the creed.
The Catholic faithful were bound together, the creed reminded all Christians, in the communion of saints, past, present, and future. The church
was one. To entertain novelties was tantamount to an attempt to sever the
oneness, the body of Christ, and to destroy the communion of saints by
introducing differences between the beliefs of the dead in Christ and those
of the living.

The commissioners' subscriptions have a certain monotony about
them.[124] The verbs avowing the condemnation of the articles vary only
slightly, when they vary at all, from one theologian to another: *dico, judico,
credo, assero, affirmo*, or some combination of these. No theologian de-
fends any article; the commissioners condemn them all (*omnes, supra-
dictos, suprascriptos, predictos, dictos*) and every one of them (*quemlibet
eorum*). Two commissioners described themselves with the conventional
formula asserting their unworthiness (*licet indignus*) to hold the offices
they occupied. Two supplemented their condemnations of the articles as
heretical with the otiose addition that the articles also "contained damned
[or condemned] heresies" (*et damnatas hereses continere*). Two members
of the commission extended their wrath to the people propounding the
articles. They recommended that the obstinate chatterboxes be condemned as heretics along with their opinions (*pertinaces assertores eorum
fore sicut hereticos condemnandos*).

Jacques de Thérines took a uniquely different path to reach the same
condemnation, a path entirely consistent with his lifelong views. Unlike
any other member of the commission, he offered the argument that the
Spirituals' attack on papal authority was most insidious not in and of itself,
though this was terrifying, but because it undermined a principle at the
core of his understanding of the perfected life. For on the pope's power
depended the integrity of monastic rules (*a quo statuta quecunque regu-
laria trahunt roboris firmitatem*).[125] If the pope's authority were successfully set aside on this point, it followed that there was no way one could
legitimately argue that the kind of monastic life brothers lived in the Cis-

tercian Order could survive. For it depended—it depended absolutely, as Jacques de Thérines never ever tired of repeating—on the supremacy of papal authority. Without that anchor, one might say, the monasteries that he particularly loved so much, those of the exempt orders immediately under papal supervision, might as well be subject to ordinary bishops. This would ruin them and destroy the highest form of the religious life—a fate far worse than death, for in Abbot Jacques's moral universe it would put at risk the very hope of sinful mankind's salvation, which depended on the prayers and acts of mercy in the religious life of exempt brothers.

Informed of the judgment and aware that its consequences would in time be made painfully clear, the ranks of the twenty-five broke. Twenty yielded; only five still stood their ground.[126] Before the Inquisition, following a formal trial, turned them over to secular authorities to be burned at the stake the following May, however, one more submitted, accepting perpetual imprisonment rather than enduring "martyrdom."[127] The other four were burned publicly in Marseille on the 7th.[128]

• • • • •

After this extraordinary interlude Jacques de Thérines concentrated his energies on the administration of the abbey of Pontigny. But his tenure as abbot was not to be without controversy. His "submission" to the bishop of Auxerre was delayed for nearly a year, owing to the press of other business, but it was expected that he would take the formal oath of "subjection, reverence, and obedience" that had been required of his predecessors. It was a tricky business. The oath had a saving clause limiting the subjection, reverence, and obedience to that which was consonant with the exemption of the Cistercian Order, the issue that overshadowed the abbot's whole career. However limited the oath, the bishop and chapter of Auxerre, in whose diocese Pontigny lay, insisted on it. On 7 November 1319 around the canonical hour of tierce, at the solemn ringing of the cathedral bell (*ad sonum campanae*), Jacques and Henri, the Cistercian abbot of Roches, also in the diocese of Auxerre, approached the altar and agreed to take the oath. They did so after agitated discussion (*post nonnullas altercationes*).

Each abbot had a copy of the oath he intended to swear. But the two oaths differed. Jacques intended to swear, "I, Brother Jacques, abbot of Pontigny, of the Cistercian Order, promise to you bishop father, and to your successors canonically constituted and to the Holy See, that, saving [the privileges of] my order, I will perpetually show subjection, reverence, obedience, enjoined by the holy fathers, according to the Rule of Saint Benedict." Henri's version was very similar, but he also specified that his abbey was "of the diocese of Auxerre" after noting its inclusion in the

Cistercian Order. Jacques appears to have regarded this specification not as otiose but as perhaps implying episcopal jurisdictional over the Cistercians, which he did not believe the diocesan authorities possessed. He did not have these words in his version of the oath.[129]

The bishop and chapter were astonished at both men's insolence. Even Abbot Henri's specification "of the diocese of Auxerre" was insufficient because the oaths deviated from earlier forms. The cathedral clergy insisted that the abbots directly acknowledge that the oaths should include the phrase "to you, the bishop, and the chapter of Auxerre or to the church of Auxerre," as early forms, they also insisted, had always stipulated. They promptly produced earlier records of the oaths to prove their case, and they read them aloud to the two Cistercians (*ostendebant et legebant, seu legi faciebant, coram ipsis abbatibus*).[130]

Jacques and Henri asked for time to examine relevant records in good faith (*bona fide*) and promised to report their conclusions to the bishop and chapter by the next Easter. The seculars agreed and then permitted the abbots to mount to the high altar (*magnum altare*) and swear the oaths as the latter wished, with the understanding that they would be resworn in the appropriate form by Easter 1320, if the evidence supported the bishop and chapter's position. It is clear that the Auxerrois contingent received the newly sworn oaths *nomine ecclesie Autissiodorensis* and confidently talked about them in these terms.[131] It is also clear that Jacques and Henri had to yield.[132] Surviving evidence indicates that the Auxerrois seculars were in the right, although their preferred wording did nothing to establish episcopal jurisdiction over the Cistercians in the diocese.[133] Nonetheless, this was a rare defeat for the indefatigable abbot of Pontigny.

Meanwhile other matters pressed in upon the abbot, including the daily and burdensome routines of running Pontigny. Much of this mundane but heavy work—heavy for a man as conscientious in his duties as Jacques de Thérines—is buried in anonymous charters recording arrangements between Our Lady of Saint Edmund of Pontigny, as the abbey was often called, and local seigneurs.[134] A glimpse into what is meant is provided by an impressive dossier accumulated by the abbey on fishing rights in the Armançon River, the abbey's watercourse. In 1290 a concession was made whereby locals were allowed to fish in a stretch of the river for personal, noncommercial, purposes. The charter describing the arrangement limited the gear to small hoop-nets and nontrolling lines (*aux troubles et à ligne dormante*).[135] Basically this was fishing from the bank. But the concession opened the door to abuse. The agreement of 1290 may have been the formal recognition of a long custom, one that many locals did not believe the abbey could regulate or interfere with. Even though the very existence of the charter suggested otherwise, the situation was out of hand thirty years later.

Abbot Jacques, obsessed as always with defending the privileges and immunities accorded to Cistercian houses, appealed to the *bailli* of Troyes to intervene so as to prevent the local *prévôt* of Saint-Florentin from fishing or permitting any other fishing in the abbey river. On 14 August 1320 the *bailli*, Symon de Montigny, ruled in Pontigny's favor at the meeting of his assize court held at Saint-Florentin; the abbot and monastery would have been represented by a procurator, still another agent whose work Abbot Jacques had to monitor carefully. The *bailli*'s judgment also commanded the *prévôt* to swear publicly that he would thereafter preserve the abbey's rights from harm (*Item nous avons fait jurer quil gardera les privileges des dits religieux*).[136] The number of copies and confirmations of this judgment in the archives indicates, however, that preserving these rights inviolate was anything but easy in the years, indeed centuries, to come.[137]

Routine though carking matters of this type cut into the time the abbot could allot to his principal task, prayer to save the Catholic faithful. Undoubtedly he saw his duties as abbot as a necessary toil. Everything he did and every moment he spent protecting his monks from the intrusions of the outside world gave them greater opportunities to do the *opus dei*. Every time he successfully defended a claim to resources that generated the income requisite to the pursuit of charitable works, he was contributing indirectly to the salvation of the world. Any shirking of his tasks for the personal and individual pleasures of prayer and contemplation necessarily put the collective work of the choir monks at risk of being compromised. Or so he undoubtedly tried to persuade himself during moments of introspection.

The occasional breaks from administrative routine compromised the abbot's search for solitude even more, in part because he had a reputation for being so good at what he did, and because he had such prestige as a successful polemicist and theologian. Men continued to seek his advice and judgment on pressing matters. Four days after winning the case against the fishermen of the Armançon, Jacques joined a group of local churchmen whom the bishop of Auxerre asked to make up a commission to decide on where the relics of Saint Amatre were resting.[138] Amatre had been the fourth bishop of Auxerre and ruled the nascent see in the mid–fourth century. His claim to fame, besides his own holy life and renunciation of wealth, was his designation of Germain, the great evangelist saint, as his successor. Germain, an illustrious and proud lay aristocrat, so the legend goes, loved to hunt and to hang his trophies, the bloody severed heads of the great beasts he slaughtered, from a magnificent tree to bedazzle the local rustics. Amatre detested the practice, because it encouraged the still incompletely Christianized rustics to adore the tree itself: an act of arbor worship characteristic of the Gallo-Roman pagans from whose ranks they had so recently been brought to the Catholic faith. He had the tree felled. Having become aware of the act and consumed by anger, Germain paid a visit to the audacious bishop, but Amatre, with superhuman courage and saintly foresight, faced his adversary down and demanded that the aristocrat accept the tonsure and take up the rule of the see on his death. The strange encounter transformed the swaggering and violent young nobleman into an ascetic and missionary, one of whose acolytes would be a pious little girl, Geneviève, subsequently the patron saint of Paris.

It was a good story. It was well worth having Saint Amatre's body. But who did have it? The canons regular of the Priory of Saint Symphorien, who preferred to call their church Saint-Amatre (*que nunc B. Amatoris vulgariter nuncupatur*), situated on the periphery of Auxerre, claimed that they did, despite the counterclaim of the cathedral chapter of Auxerre.[139] Bishop Pierre de Grez, the same bishop who defeated Jacques de Thérines on the matter of the oath the abbot swore to the church of Auxerre, was as insistent on the rights of his church as any other conscientious prelate. He launched his own investigation and, not surprisingly, decided that Auxerre's claim was more trustworthy than Saint-Symphorien/Saint-Amatre's. But the priory, not surprisingly either, impugned the bishop's decision, since he was not disinterested, and continued to insist that Saint Amatre was at rest in the priory precincts.[140] It was at this stage that the bishop decided to constitute a blue-ribbon commission to assess the evidence. Among its members was the abbot of Pontigny, Jacques de Thérines, but also an array of other churchmen who could be considered above the fray, including the abbot of the prestigious Benedictine monastery of Vézelay, which claimed to possess Mary Magdalene's relics, and the abbot of Saint-Germain of Auxerre (the site of Amatre's successor's entombment), as well as the abbot of the exempt Premonstratensian monastery of Saint-Marien of Auxerre.[141]

The commission, meeting on 18 August, heard that Saint Amatre was originally interred at the site where the priory stood; from this neither side in the dispute dissented.[142] But there were no written records at the priory as to whether his relics remained there. The commissioners were presented with old cathedral martyrologies, however, that recorded a feast for 12 July celebrating the reception of the saint's relics at Auxerre. There was also the evidence of the verb tense that the cathedral canons used when they paid their annual ceremonial visit to the Priory of Saint-Symphorien/Saint-Amatre. They referred prayerfully to the saint "who rest*ed*," not "rest*s*," in the priory church (*qui in praesenti requievit* [not *requiescit*] *ecclesia*), and they had the documents to prove it. Finally, there was the evidence of a very old reliquary at Auxerre that was opened for the commissioners. Inside were found pictures and reliefs of Saint-Amatre's life (*in cujus superficie vita et gesta dicti beatissimi confessoris impressa in imaginibus* *et insculpta*) plus written proof that when the reliquary had been opened in 1238, eighty-two years earlier, it already had this ornamentation.

Of course, the evidence was capable of being faulted and challenged, and the commission weighed it carefully over the ensuing several weeks. The claim was that the commissioners were deciding where more appropriately (*principalius*) the Catholic faithful could seek the intercession of the saint, the Priory of Saint-Symphorien/Saint-Amatre or the cathedral.[143] The more appropriate place, of course, was also the place where offerings would accumulate. Indeed, the showy nature of the commission and the investigation undoubtedly stimulated greater devotion to Saint Amatre's cult. In any case, on 20 September 1320 the commissioners issued their findings and advisory opinion favoring the cathedral's claim in a notarized record that was also sealed individually with their seals.[144] The bishop then formally and with great ceremony declared the matter settled.[145]

• • • • •

While Bishop Pierre de Grez was solemnly declaring his church to be the home of the ancient saint of the Auxerrois, Jacques de Thérines was attending his order's General Chapter meeting, which began around Saint-Lambert's Day, 17 September. All of the abbots of the order or their representatives were supposed to be in attendance every year, unless they were granted moderated schedules (every four, five, or seven years) because of their abbeys' distance from Cîteaux. Despite the vaunted system of supervision in which the General Chapters loomed so large, as Jacques de Thérines depicted it, the attendance requirement was often honored only in the breach.[146] And the frequency of attendance by abbots, as opposed to their representatives, was declining precipitously. By midcentury, owing partly to the terrible ravages of the plague and partly to the Hundred Years' War and its truces, when brigands and unpaid soldiers ruled the countryside, sometimes as few as twenty-five abbots managed to attend, a decline from which the medieval order never fully recovered.[147] Nonetheless, in the period of Jacques's abbacies the meetings were still immensely large. Although they took place at Cîteaux, most of the abbots put themselves up in nearby Dijon. Where else could lodging be found for between one thousand and two thousand attendees and servants?[148] Several abbots shared rooms in the city that their abbeys had purchased in a building owned by Cîteaux, and offered lodgings to those abbots and representatives whose monasteries' finances could not bear the expense of buying their own.[149] Although particularly acute in the bad years of the famine, the problem of the high cost of attendance at the General Chapter was a long-standing one.[150]

The meeting in 1320 was altogether troubling. The great house of Clairvaux in particular was in desperate fiscal straits, and the General Chapter recognized that the only possible solution or stopgap to the hemorrhaging of its financial outlays was the alienation of some of its extremely valuable urban properties in Paris, properties whose rents helped underwrite the work of the schools of Saint-Bernard in the capital. The hemorrhage was described vividly in the records as stemming from burdensome debts owed to a wide array of lenders (*plurimos creditores*) and from unwise fiscal decisions, namely, perpetual rents that the monastery had to pay annually to its investors and pensioners (*redituum perpetuorum . . . apud nonullas personas*). The alienations were intended for obvious benefit (*evidenti utilitate*). Only through the alienation of properties could there be relief for Clairvaux and renewal of its fiscal integrity (*ad reformationem status ipsius et oneris predicti relevationem*).[151]

The king, Philip V, needed to be informed, in part because the General Chapter was approving the alienation of properties granted in the thirteenth century by none other than Alphonse of Poitiers, Saint Louis's brother. The king's confirmation permitted the alienation, which included a furnished house, vineyards, and some land and underbrush, as well as rents, which were capitalized. He permitted the "rerouting" of one of Alphonse's endowments to the support of the schools that Clairvaux founded. He insisted, too, that the monks continue to pray and celebrate annual masses for his ancestor's soul, despite the alienations.[152] Jacques de Thérines secured authentic copies or arranged for them to be sent to Pontigny for the archives there.

It was a depressing meeting, indeed, but as suggested by his memoir to Pope John XXII a few years before, it was not entirely surprising to the abbot that a great Cistercian house, Saint Bernard's own house, might succumb to the humiliation of alienating its properties. The times were very hard. Abbot Jacques returned to Pontigny to begin another, what was to be his final, year in service to the order he loved.

EPILOGUE

UNCEASING STRIFE, UNENDING FEAR

AS JACQUES DE THÉRINES'S ADMINISTRATION of the Abbey of Our Lady of Saint Edmund of Pontigny was coming to an end, a steady stream of information on the nearly apocalyptic horrors of the wider world intruded into the peaceful precincts of the cloister. Since the return of Jewish exiles to France in 1315 in line with the abbot's opinions, the situation for the settlers had proved lamentable.[1] Violence against Jews from the very moments of their reentry into the kingdom, fueled by the long experience of popular hatred, was also fed by the sense of intrusion many French felt at the resettlement.[2] There was also the question of old debts. As effective as the crown's seizure of Jewish account books was in 1306, it was not perfect. A number of debtors went undetected and paid nothing to their new creditor, the king, in the years that followed. The government granted Jews who resettled in 1315 permission to produce evidence identifying these debtors and then mounted a campaign to find them and force them to repay their loans, with two-thirds going to the badly strapped royal treasury and one-third to the original Jewish creditors.[3]

The amazing thing is that as this campaign went forward, the government of Louis X and then of Philip V legislated temporary relief for debt-ridden farmers suffering from the disastrous crop failures of the time, carried through on its own promises to free serfs while urging seigneurs to free theirs (all should be free, *francs*, in a kingdom called *France*), and otherwise inclined its ear to the complaints of the rural population through special investigations into crime and bureaucratic oppression.[4] Yet by resettling the Jews and enforcing collection of old and now new debts to them, the administration tainted itself in the eyes of many subjects, and administrative attempts to respond to the Great Famine were ineffective in any case and do not appear to have done much to recuperate the government's tarnished prestige.[5] The sources report repeated incidents of vigilante "justice" against alleged Jewish crimes.[6]

One way the crown tried to recover its prestige and please God, thereby endeavoring to bring an end to the famine, was to fulfill a long-standing pledge to wage holy war against the enemies of Christ in the Holy Land.[7] In hindsight, given the weak state of the economy in 1320 when the call went out for a Crusade, it seems an almost absurd response to the multiple crises facing the government.[8] The sincerity of Philip V's intentions has been questioned, probably in a misguided attempt to see the project as merely a way to raise money and divert it to other pressing needs.[9] To be sure, no formal Crusade was launched, but the call did evoke a popular response that spring, the so-called Shepherds' Crusade, whose trappings were to some extent "messianic" in that participants seem to have construed the intended struggle as a means of offering the hope of redemption for a beleaguered kingdom.[10] In one interpretation the long series of accusations of sorcery against political enemies, within and outside the Capetian court, contributed to a kind of social-mental disequilibrium for which crusading, understood as an act of openness and courage with goal-oriented simplicity and clarity, was the remedy.[11] The hypermasculinity of the call to violence may also have been particularly attractive to adolescent boys, shepherd-types, even if they never quite dominated the ranks of the movement.[12]

Chroniclers note that the Shepherds' transition from marching off on Crusade to marauding was swift.[13] The would-be holy warriors' violence in fact came to be directed at upper-class Christians and at Jews in northern France. The territorial sweep included areas surrounding Pontigny. Indeed, a series of tense jurisdictional confrontations pitting ecclesiastical authorities in the dioceses of Sens and Auxerre against local secular interests in the late teens of the fourteenth century grew ever more violent under the impact of the Shepherds' uprising.[14] The *Jours de Troyes*, the supreme court of the county of Champagne, would ultimately adjudicate some of the most serious and unsettling acts of violence.[15] In the north and subsequently in southern France and Aragon the number and savagery of the atrocities—murders upon murders into the hundreds in some localities—and the instances of forced baptisms mounted.[16] Pope John XXII, hardly partial to Jews, indeed rather more contemptuous than most popes, even supporting acts of expulsion, nonetheless denounced the escalating frenzy of violence in letters to secular rulers and prelates on 19 June 1320.[17]

The Shepherds' Crusade waned after several months under the vigorous repression finally mounted against it in France and Aragon.[18] Yet economic, psychological, and physical conditions—bad weather, widespread scarcities, high prices, lingering famine, animal and human pestilence, high mortality, cynicism, and despondency—did not vanish; life for ordinary people remained prone to the most appalling misery. Christendom was weak and divided as a result or was imagined to be. It was in these circumstances that rumors arose that lepers, in league with the already vilified and persecuted Jews and encouraged by Christendom's foreign Muslim enemies, were plotting to poison the wells and other sources of drinking water in order to destroy the Christian people.[19] Like sorcery, poisoning, it has been suggested, is the preferred method for murder imputed to the threatening "Other," because of its secrecy or more precisely because of the cowardice of the perpetrators, who will not reveal themselves and kill honorably "like real men."[20] Conversely, and somewhat strangely, it was real men, heroes, as history unfortunately demonstrated to medieval readers, against whom poison was particularly effective. Indeed, death by poison was seen to some extent as valorizing public claims for heroism made on a fallen man's behalf.[21] (The existing scholarship does not endorse the use of the gender-neutral phrase, "person's behalf," here.)

Letters purportedly translated from Arabic gave the formula of the substance that was to be the means of the mass murder: "human blood, human urine, magical herbs, snakeheads, toads' feet, stolen consecrated hosts, hairs from the heads of young maidens."[22] These imaginings about the nature of the poison, with the obvious sexual and anti-Jewish elements implicit in the ingredients (virgins' tresses, stolen/desecrated hosts), and the rumors of the plot can be plausibly understood as a critique of the crown for its failure to mobilize for war, for its toleration of Jewish resettlement, and for its incapacity to succor its people in the famine. The critique drew additional intensity by coupling Christendom's confessional adversaries, internal and external, with lepers and all the repugnance and fear that leprosy evoked.[23] Belief in the plot led to a new wave of vigilantism in which hundreds of innocent Jews and hundreds, perhaps thousands, of innocent and largely defenseless lepers were burned to death.[24] Pyres sent the smell of burning flesh heavenward.

In the region where the abbey of Pontigny was located and its properties concentrated, the number of leper houses was exceedingly large; between the abbey and Troyes, the nearby capital of the county of Champagne, there were no fewer than twenty leprosaria.[25] As with many other sorts of ecclesiastical institutions the leper houses' accumulation of wealth provoked envy. Disputes with local elites over the financial obligations and the limits of the leprosaria's immunities and privileges were frequent, prolonged, and sometimes sharp-edged, as evidenced by a series of confrontations over contributions to protecting market rights in Sens in 1319.[26] In this case the sergeants assigned by the *prévôt* of Sens to patrol the market belonging to the Popelin, the leprosarium of the town, were angry over their pay. They insisted that they should be paid from the receipts of one of the best market booths, and they wanted twenty-two shillings rather than a lower customary payment to divide among themselves.

It is hard to assess the merits of their case. Had the market grown in importance, along with the onus of the sergeants' duties, but their wages not mounted in tandem with these developments? Were the skyrocketing prices of the famine years a contributing factor to the sergeants' discontent? The administrators of the Popelin leprosarium insisted that the guards would receive only the customary rate, which was five shillings.

The monetary gap, with the sergeants wanting more than four times as much as they were offered, is extraordinary and may speak genuinely to their need rather than to their greed. But the *bailli* of Sens, when called upon to adjudicate the dispute, decided firmly in favor of custom. Five shillings it was, and five shillings it would remain. Accusations of chicanery, unfair practices, and avarice against the administrators of leper houses and, by implication, against lepers, did not necessarily or seamlessly lead to belief in the wilder accusations of the plot to kill the Catholic faithful. But the unsettled circumstances during the vigilantism, like the earlier destabilizing violence of the Shepherds, provided an opportunity for theft and otherwise settling scores.

Government officials at various levels of administration, including the municipal, vigorously joined in the frenzied effort to exact vengeance, arresting suspects and torturing them. Reports of the lepers' torture in the pope's own town of Avignon, probably on orders of the municipal council, and of Jewish complicity in the lepers' plot reached the royal courts of Majorca and Aragon.[27] King Philip V never publicly called the truth of the plot into question, and although he acted judicially against the "stinking lepers," as he was wont to call them, he indulged in the full range of violence, including torture and execution by burning of those convicted of plotting.[28] He also ordered widespread confiscations of the properties of leper houses and on occasion permitted the refashioning of their administrations to the benefit of the heirs of the seigneurs who had founded them. The latter seems to have been true, for instance, with respect to the leprosarium of the village of Saint-Florentin, where Pontigny had extensive holdings.[29] Philip's confiscatory measures effectively destroyed another neighboring institution, the leprosarium of Appoigny, though the king allowed its patrons to reconstitute it on a reduced scale after the panic subsided.[30]

All through the region royal agents pursued lepers and Jews who were accused by other terrified and victimized lepers and Jews of participating in the plot (*super venenosis pocionibus aquarum*).[31] Paul Lehugeur, Philip V's modern biographer, considered the king's treatment of the alleged conspirators the moral and psychological equivalent of the atrocities his father had inflicted on the Templars.[32] The crown also ordered Jewish communities to pay a punitive fine of 150,000 l. for their supposed part in the plot. They were too poor, in fact, to pay more than half of this.[33] The much beleaguered Pope Clement V had once felt obliged to praise those French agents whose zeal for the Catholic faith, misapplied though it was, led to the kidnapping of Boniface VIII in 1303; similarly, the crown acknowledged that popular extrajudicial risings against and murders of the alleged conspirators in the plot to destroy the Christian people were, although jurisdictional affronts to royal authority, still praiseworthy in that they were motivated by the sincerest devotion.[34]

It was in August 1321 that the most murderous phase of actions against the Jews and especially the lepers came to an end.[35] Jacques de Thérines died about two months after this. Thus even in the island of peace and prayer that was Pontigny, he had immediate evidence of the outrages against the reputed conspirators and of the innumerable rejections of his long held opinion that Jews ought not to be killed. On the other hand, he probably did not live to see the further and official repudiation of his views on expulsion.[36] That is to say, in 1322, or rather, to be more cautious, sometime between late 1321 and 1323, the crown chose to send all the Jews of the kingdom of France into exile once again.[37] It is vaguely possible that the old abbot would have regarded the move as just, if he believed that Jews were really involved in a plot and therefore constituted a dangerous *confederatio* to exterminate the worshipers of Christ.[38] But the man who would not yield on his doubts about the Templars' guilt is not likely to have uncritically credited the equally fantastic charges against lepers and Jews or to have been morally at ease with the victims' extrajudicial mass murder.

•　•　•　•　•

Perhaps he was too ill to make his views known—whatever they were. Sometime during the day on the feast of the Apostle Luke, 18 October, in the year 1321, according to the epitaph created for his tomb at the abbey of Pontigny, Jacques de Thérines, his failing body lying on sackcloth and ashes if the monks suspected the end was near, breathed his last while the brothers, summoned by the death knell to his presence, intoned the penitential psalms. They carried his corpse for washing to the stone slab provided for that purpose in all Cistercian monasteries before the final obsequies and simple shroud burial in the church.

The epitaph inscribed on the abbot's tomb was a fine piece of Latin verse in eight long lines, each of fourteen or fifteen syllables and each with a caesura usually after the first six of these. The syllable preceding the caesura in the first line, -*us*, rhymed with the last syllable in the line. The second line duplicated the pattern. Lines three and four had the same form as the first couplet, but a different rhyme, -*ae* (medieval Latin -*e*). The couplet that followed, lines five and six, then reverted to the original rhyme, -*us*, although the poet cheated a little at the end of line five by using -*is*. The final couplet altered the scheme and made a formal chiasmus: the syllable before the caesura of line seven is -*es*, but instead of repeating the same syllable at the end of the line as he consistently did earlier, the poet chose -*ae* (or really, in medieval Latin, -*e*). It is this syllable, -*e*, that then precedes the caesura of the final line, while -*es* is the closing syllable of the verse. It is a pretty pattern.

```
------a / -------a
------a / -------a
------b / -------b
------b / -------b
------a / -------a
------a / -------a
------c / -------b
------b / -------c
```

There are other contrivances, too, that, together with the extremely laudatory sentiments, probably help explain why scholars before now have not tried to squeeze much information out of the epitaph. Noël Valois hated it and was quite unwilling to take any of it seriously, not even the date of Jacques's death, which he presumably suspected was fudged to make rhyming easier. In his words, Jacques died on 18 October 1321, "si l'on s'en fie à l'épitaphe prétentieuse qui se lisait autrefois dans l'église de Pontigni."[39]

> This plot of ground holds him. He was a deeply learned teacher,
> Holy like Saint Edmund, pure and without lust;
> Father of this church, and fountain of theology,
> Model of a pious life, fervent in the love of Mary,
> A second Jacob, carried to the stars in his spiritual yearnings,
> Distinguished interpreter of the two testaments.
> In 1321 during the daylight hours of Saint Luke
> He leaves this light. Let him be at rest, O Christ![40]

In the spring (late May and early June) following Jacques de Thérines's death and burial, the new king, Charles IV the Fair (1322–1328), the last of the three sons of Philip the Fair, paid his respects at the abbey of Chaalis.[41] He became king on 3 January 1322 after his brother Philip the Tall died, some said by poison, a suspicion that was becoming de rigueur in the paranoid atmosphere of court politics on the occasion of a royal demise.[42] The late king left no male heirs. Philip's exclusion of Louis X's daughter from succession provided a precedent for the exclusion of his own daughters and the transmission of the throne to Charles the Fair, who was crowned at Reims on 21 February. On Charles now rested the hope of dynastic continuity: so social commentators, like the poet Watriquet, reminded readers.[43]

Jacques de Thérines's successor as abbot of Chaalis, Jean Picard, to whom the new king presented himself, was known as a decent fellow. The Latin epithet given him was *Probus*; one might say "Man of Honor."[44] Perhaps words he spoke on the occasion of King Charles's visit persuaded the monarch to make a rather unusual pilgrimage for a French king that summer, namely, to the Cistercian abbey of Pontigny.[45] There in August Charles came into the presence of the tomb of Saint Edmund of Canterbury and of that of his spiritual likeness, Jacques de Thérines.

Charles IV remained in the region for a long time dealing with a multitude of serious political matters, but if Abbot Jean Picard hoped the king's visit to Pontigny might be the commencement of a process in which the crown played an active role in honoring his predecessor, that hope was disappointed.[46] Jacques de Thérines's considerable accomplishments quickly receded into oblivion. After a relatively rapid diffusion of and a short period of interest in his written works in France, Italy, and German-speaking territories (to judge from the distribution of the manuscripts), they lay almost unread and largely unpublished for several hundred years.[47] That mistranscription of his name by a humanist scholar, mentioned at the outset of this book and uncritically adopted by his savant successors over the centuries, turned the monk from the *pays* of Thérines into an otherwise undocumented Sicilian wanderer, a horrid fate for a man who loved and defended the confinement of the cloister, even though, as with his hero Saint Bernard, necessity compelled him to spend more time than he liked outside it.

It is worth repeating that the process of Jacques's effacement was so effective that the men and women of his hometown could not discover until a hundred years ago and then only with great effort that an extraordinary human being once walked their village streets and counted himself a native son. It has seemed worthwhile to tell Jacques de Thérines's story, for in many ways it is the story of France in a politically terrifying period of its existence, one of unceasing strife and unending fear. And it is the story, too, of the church, and especially that part of the church on whose integrity and freedom the Cistercian believed and insisted that so much of the salvation of humankind depended. It was in service to this understanding and this representation of the world that he lived and struggled and died.

NOTES

CHAPTER 1
ENCROACHMENTS ON ECCLESIASTICAL AUTHORITY:
TAXATION, CLERICAL IMMUNITY, AND THE JEWS

1. Valois, "Jacques de Thérines," pp. 179–80.

2. Antonio Mongitore, who repeated this opinion in 1708 (*Bibliotheca Sicula*, vol. 1, fol. 304), was one of the few authors uncomfortable with it: "an ex praeclara Panormitana Familia de Thermes an vero ex Urbe Thermarum, divinare non audeo."

3. Cf. Lawrence, *Medieval Monasticism*, pp. 110, 158.

4. Another Thérines native of Jacques's time (if Valois's identification is correct, "Jacques de Thérines," p. 179 n. 4) exemplifies this pattern, the master of arts and beneficed clerk in the diocese of Beauvais, Gérard de Thérines. For the text on which Valois draws, see *Lettres communes de Jean XXII*, vol. 2, no. 7646.

5. I am extrapolating from Valois's tentative identification, "Jacques de Thérines," p. 179 n. 4. For the document to which he refers that gives more information on Jean's career than Valois provides, see *Lettres communes de Jean XXII*, vol. 2, no. 7514; *CUP*, 2:220, no. 763.

6. A good parallel is the family of the Franciscan archbishop of Rouen in the thirteenth century, Eudes Rigaud. Eudes grew up near the castle town of Brie-Comte-Robert. His intelligence took him to Paris and a university career before he became a Franciscan. His brother Adam and a nephew of the same name also entered the church, the first as a Franciscan (he attached himself to his brother's ecclesiastical *familia*), the second as a secular canon and, subsequently, dean of the cathedral chapter of Rouen. See Jordan, "Archbishop Eudes Rigaud," forthcoming. The pattern existed as well for women; cf. the careers of the women of the Norman noble family known as the "de Harcourt"; Field, *Writings of Agnes of Harcourt*, p. 4.

7. On the cathedral school and library of Beauvais, see Lesne, *Ecoles*, pp. 314–16, and Omont, "Recherches sur la bibliothèque de l'église cathédrale de Beauvais," pp. 2–4. The chief legal officer or *officialis* of the cathedral of Beauvais was ordinarily a master trained at the University of Paris (Baldwin, "Masters at Paris," p. 155); from such a man, a student like Jacques de Thérines would have learned about university life in the capital.

8. Glorieux, *Répertoire des maîtres*, 2:250 and 262, no. 367, and Glorieux, in Jacques de Thérines, *Quodlibets I et II*, p. 13. For the establishment and early history (including architectural) of the College of Saint-Bernard, see Dautrey, "Eglise de l'ancien collège des Bernardins," pp. 497–514; Dimier, *Saint Louis et Cîteaux*, pp. 124–26; LaCorte, "Pope Innocent IV's Role," pp. 289–304; and Obert-Piketty, "Promotion des études," p. 65, who dates the formal establishment of the college somewhat earlier than the 1245 date favored by LaCorte.

9. Bianchi, *Censure et liberté intellectuelle*, p. 216.

10. On Jean de Weerde, see Glorieux, *Répertoire des maîtres*, 2:254–57, no. 362; on the miracle stories, above, p. 14.

11. Glorieux's dating (*Répertoires des maîtres*, 2:262, no. 367) supersedes that (1304–1306) of the editors of *CUP*, 2:121, no. 658, and of Valois, "Jacques de Thérines," p. 180.

12. *CUP*, 2:121, no. 658: they were requesting from the king the benefice "Sancti Lupi juxta Taverniacum duntaxat assecuto, cujus beneficii fructus amisit cadente super hiis tempestate, de meliori providere dignemini secundum etatis sue statum et merita probitatis. Valeat in Domino vestra majestas altissima, qui statu prospero multiplicet et augeat dies vestros."

13. Vémars and Taverny were in the historic *département* of the Seine-et-Oise (Paris and its *banlieue*), which has since been broken up. At present they are in the *département* of Val d'Oise.

14. For an exhaustive treatment of the events narrated in the next several paragraphs, see Digard, *Philippe le Bel et le Saint-Siège*, 1:207–369. See also Jordan, "Capetians from the Death of Philip II to Philip IV," pp. 302–13.

15. King, *Finances of the Cistercian Order*, pp. 60, 90–94; Buczek, "Medieval Taxation," pp. 42–72.

16. On the matters addressed in this paragraph, see King, *Finances of the Cistercian Order*, pp. 30–32, 48–52; and Jordan, "Cistercian Nunnery," pp. 311–20.

17. The phrase "war fever" is Denton's, *Philip the Fair and the Ecclesiastical Assemblies*, pp. 20, 26–27, and 71. See also Buczek, "Medieval Taxation," pp. 72–74.

18. Denton, *Philip the Fair and the Ecclesiastical Assemblies*, p. 21.

19. Ibid., p. 20; Buczek, "Medieval Taxation," pp. 75–76.

20. All translations from the various bulls issued by Boniface VIII during his struggles with Philip the Fair are taken from Tierney, *Crisis of Church and State*, pp. 175–79, or are my own. On the propaganda war between Boniface and Philip, the old book by Scholz, *Publizistik*, is still helpful.

21. Denton, *Philip the Fair and the Ecclesiastical Assemblies*, p. 20, draws on, but also amends, the work of Baron Kervyn de Lettenhove, "Etudes sur l'histoire du XIIIe siècle." Relations between Philip IV and the Cistercians (and the count of Flanders) in the mid-1290s are treated at length in Kervyn's study (cols. 1833–52); the dossier on Cistercian resistance occupies in particular cols. 1837–38. See also Buczek, "Medieval Taxation," pp. 76–78.

22. Favier, *Philippe le Bel*, p. 277.

23. On Boniface VIII's "retreat," Buczek, "Medieval Taxation," pp. 79–80.

24. Favier, *Philippe le Bel*, pp. 284–85.

25. Michaud-Quantin, "Politique monétaire," p. 149; Jordan, *Louis IX*, p. 209.

26. For continued Cistercian uneasiness, see Buczek, "Medieval Taxation," pp. 81–87.

27. Dickson, "Crowd at the Feet of Pope Boniface VIII," pp. 279–307.

28. On Roman mercantile and social-political elites' exploitation of the jubilee, see Anheim et al., "Rome et les jubilés," pp. 53–82. The local clergy benefited less, perhaps, but enjoyed the excitement; cf. Barone, "Clergé romain et le jubilé,"

pp. 23–28. A recent estimate revising the Roman population upward from 30,000 in the year 1300 to 40,000–80,000 would still leave the antique city of 1,000,000 inhabitants terribly underinhabited; cf. Hubert, "Rome au XIVe siècle," pp. 43–52.

29. For the more general political context in France and the narrative from which the observations in the next several paragraphs are drawn, see Jordan, "Capetians from the Death of Philip II to Philip IV," pp. 306–9. Translations of the various texts are my own or, when available, those of Tierney, *Crisis of Church and State*, pp. 184–92.

30. Cf. Beaune, "Rois maudits," p. 14.

31. D'Avray, *Death and the Prince*, p. 80.

32. Pegg, *Corruption of Angels*, brings research on this issue to a new level of sophistication and insight.

33. Given, *Inquisition and Medieval Society*, pp. 91–165.

34. Ibid., pp. 206–8.

35. Digard, *Philippe le Bel et le Saint-Siège*, 2:49–104, is comprehensive. See also Favier, *Philippe le Bel*, p. 344.

36. For a discussion, see Favier, *Philippe le Bel*, p. 347.

37. Digard, *Philippe le Bel et le Saint-Siège*, 2:105–45.

38. As to the anachronism, since the "term 'estates' does not appear" in the context of assemblies before 1316, see Lalou, "Assemblées générales sous Philippe le Bel," p. 7.

39. Dupuy, *Histoire du differend*, "Preuves," pp. 117–18: "contra dominum Bonifacium Papam octavum . . . diversa enorma et horribilia ac detestabilia crimina, quorum quaedam haeresim sapient manifeste."

40. Digard, *Philippe le Bel et le Saint-Siège*, 2:146–85; Favier, *Philippe le Bel*, pp. 385–90.

41. Favier, *Philippe le Bel*, pp. 391–92.

42. Digard, *Philippe le Bel et le Saint-Siège*, 2:186–209; Favier, *Philippe le Bel*, p. 392.

43. On his pontificate, see Favier, *Philippe le Bel*, pp. 394–97.

44. This enormously complex story, including its relationship to other high matters of state (like the imperial election), is narrated in full in Lizerand, *Clément V et Philippe le Bel*, pp. 151–314. For the papal absolution, years later, of Guillaume de Nogaret, the royal minister who led the kidnappers, see the *Regestum Clementis Papae V*, 6:420–21, no. 7503.

45. Cf. Strayer, *Reign of Philip the Fair*, p. 272.

46. Dupuy, *Histoire du differend*, p. 19 (French version; the Latin translation accompanies).

47. This accusation contributed to a witticism with which the French denigrated Boniface VIII's memory in 1310: Boniface gained the papacy like a wily fox, ruled it like a predatory lion, and died like a miserable cur; Lizerand, *Clément V et Philippe le Bel*, p. 191. Applied to Boniface, the witticism was probably already a commonplace ("Intrasti ut vulpes, regnas [*or* regnabis] ut leo, morieris [*or* exibis] ut canis"); see, for example, *Weltchronik des mönchs Albert*, p. 68, and Ebendorfer, *Chronica pontificum romanorum*, p. 441.

48. Tierney, *Crisis of Church and State*, p. 190.

49. Digard, *Philippe le Bel et le Saint-Siège*, 2:132–33.

50. Kervyn de Lettenhove, "Etudes sur l'histoire du XIIIe siècle," col. 1909; Courtenay, "Between Pope and King," p. 580.

51. Cf. Favier, *Philippe le Bel*, p. 359; Strayer, *Reign of Philip the Fair*, p. 273 n. 115.

52. Cf. Denton, "Taxation," p. 253; Buczek, "Medieval Taxation," pp. 89–95.

53. Strayer, *Reign of Philip the Fair*, p. 240; Courtenay, "Between Pope and King," p. 580.

54. Cf. Lewry, "Papal Ideals and the University of Paris," pp. 386–87; Courtenay, "Between Pope and King," pp. 588–89.

55. I am dissenting here from Strayer's conclusions in *Reign of Philip the Fair*, pp. 276–77.

56. Dupuy, *Histoire du differend*, p. 20 (French version; the Latin translation accompanies).

57. Schmidt, *Bonifaz-Prozess*, p. 85. See also Favier, *Philippe le Bel*, p. 376. (Cf. Kervyn de Lettenhove, "Etudes sur l'histoire du XIIIe siècle," col. 1910.) The detention of a number of other prelates, whom Schmidt enumerates, also contributed to the fear.

58. Kervyn de Lettenhove, "Etudes sur l'histoire du XIIIe siècle," cols. 1909–10. On the succession, a clear gesture to make peace with the crown, see Strayer, *Reign of Philip the Fair*, p. 240.

59. Dupuy, *Histoire du differend*, p. 28 (French version; the Latin translation accompanies). Cf. Courtenay, "Between Pope and King," p. 582.

60. Kervyn de Lettenhove, "Etudes sur l'histoire du XIII siècle," col. 1916 n. 6, where he cites the chronicler of Saint-Denis: "L'abbé de Cistaux seul, à eux non assentant, avec indignation et disdaing tant du roy comme des prélas." Kervyn provides additional examples of Cistercian resistance, cols. 1909–10, 1916.

61. Cf. Valois, "Jacques de Thérines," p. 180.

62. Lists of Jacques's works (manuscripts and incipits) may be consulted in Glorieux, *Répertoire des maîtres*, 2:262–63; Oudin, *Commentarius*, fols. 728–30; Sanderus, *Bibliotheca belgica*, pt. 2, p. 106; and Fabricius, *Bibliotheca latina*, 4:310. His quodlibetal questions are published in Jacques de Thérines, *Quodlibets I et II*, with the discussion of Jews at pp. 157–59.

63. Scordia, "Images de la servitude fiscale," pp. 611, 620.

64. Aquinas, *Quodlibetal Questions 1 and 2*, p. 34.

65. Biller, "Views of Jews from Paris," p. 200 n. 40.

66. Ibid., pp. 200–201.

67. Ibid.

68. Ibid., pp. 187–207.

69. Cf. Scordia, "Images de la servitude fiscale," pp. 616–17.

70. Jacques de Thérines, *Quodlibets I et II*, p. 7: "Sa pensée ne peut pretendre ni à la vigueur ni à l'originalité de tel ou tel de ses contemporains. . . . Il est à ranger dans la catégorie des maîtres consciencieux, honnêtes, mais non transcendants, qui forment le fond de tableau du XIIIe siècle finissant ou du XIVe commençant."

71. I refer to the edition authorized by Pope Leo XIII: Aquinas, *Opera Omnia*.

72. Blary, in passing, considers Jacques a member of "a particularly fecund intellectual center," that is, the abbey of Chaalis; *Domaine de Chaalis*, p. 8.

73. Jacques de Thérines, *Quodlibets I et II*, 1.8, pp. 125–31.

74. Ibid., 1.16, pp. 165–66, discussed in Valois, "Jacques de Thérines," pp. 187–88.

75. Jacques de Thérines, *Quodlibets I et II*, 1.11, pp. 148–50, discussed in Valois, "Jacques de Thérines," p. 188. Canonists were slow to permit marriage between a rape victim and her ravisher, but in the early thirteenth century Pope Innocent III recognized its validity; Brundage, *Law Sex, and Christian Society*, pp. 209–10, 250, 312, 338. In many jurisdictions marriage after the fact quashed the charge: Brundage, p. 531; Hanawalt, "Whose Story Was This?" pp. 132–33.

76. Glorieux, in Jacques de Thérines, *Quodlibets I et II*, pp. 14–20. See also Valois, "Jacques de Thérines," pp. 184–92.

77. Two examples: Jacques de Thérines, *Quodlibet I et II*, 1.9, pp. 131–44, "Vtrum prudentia prestituat finem uirtutibus moralibus," and 1.21, pp. 183–92, "Vtrum iustitia sit nobilior uirtus omni alia uirtute morali."

78. Ibid., 1.22, p. 192 (defective), "Vtrum felicitas consistat in actu intellectus uel uoluntatis," and 2.15, pp. 294–302, "Utrum uirtutes morales sint ponende in uoluntate uel in appetitu sensitiuo."

79. Ibid., 2.8, pp. 251–53.

80. Glorieux, in ibid., p. 19.

81. Jordan, *French Monarchy and the Jews*, p. 203.

82. On the demography, see ibid., p. 202.

83. For the information in this paragraph, see ibid., pp. 203–5.

84. A detailed treatment of the matters discussed in this paragraph is available in ibid., pp. 203–6, 214–38. See also Assis, "Juifs de Montpellier," p. 11.

85. Quodlibet 1, in which the Jewish question is found, is dated Christmastime 1306, in the week of December 10–15, while the questions in quodlibet 2 were debated in the academic year 1307–1308, probably 1307; see Glorieux, *Répertoire des maîtres*, 2:262, no. 367, and Glorieux in Jacques de Thérines, *Quodlibets I et II*, p. 11.

86. Several scholars have noted and commented on this quodlibet, but although I have learned much from them, my interpretation does not depend on theirs. See Martin, *Mentalités médiévales*, p. 451; Klepper, "Jewish Expulsion"; Dahan, *Intellectuels chrétiens*, pp. 547–48; and Biller, *Measure of Multitude*, pp. 381–82 (in general, Biller's use of quodlibetal material is one of the most creative I know).

87. Valois, "Jacques de Thérines," pp. 188–89.

88. The most thorough study is now Mundill's, *England's Jewish Solution*.

89. Jacques de Thérines, *Quodlibets I et II*, p. 157: "Et arguitur quod sic; quia sicut in una regione nolunt dare pecuniam sine usura."

90. Ibid.: "ergo si usura est causa quare debeant expelli, sequitur etc."

91. Ibid.: "Contra: quia facta antiquorum patrum sunt imitanda. Sed antiqui patres eos permiserunt uiuere inter christianos." For a discussion of the continued authority of the traditional Augustinian argument in the High Middle Ages, see Hood, *Aquinas and the Jews*, pp. 1–18.

92. Jacques de Thérines, *Quodlibets I et II*, pp. 157–58.

93. Ibid., p. 158.

94. Valois, "Jacques de Thérines," p. 188, asserts, perhaps too strongly, that Jacques was "plein d'indulgence pour les Juifs." Mahn, *Le Pape Benoît XII*, p. 79,

following Valois, calls his views of the Jews (and of the Templars, above, chapter 2, pp. 51–54), "généreux et sensés."

95. Among the fullest treatments of the events and legends about the alleged desecration are Rubin, *Gentile Tales*, Einbinder, *Beautiful Death*, pp. 155–79; and Jordan, *French Monarchy and the Jews*, pp. 192–94. The miracle was at the center of an earlier quodlibetal question, soon after 1290, attributed to Master Henry of Ghent, but to which Jacques made no allusion. Master Henry imagined the alleged Jewish perpetrator of the outrage as willingly submitting to baptism after having witnessed the bleeding host, and then he addressed the issue as to whether punishment could licitly be inflicted on the new convert for his attempt to desecrate the host; Marmursztejn, "Du Récit exemplaire au *casus* universitaire," pp. 37–64.

96. Jordan, *French Monarchy and the Jews*, p. 194.

97. Ibid.

98. Jacques de Thérines, *Quodlibets I et II*, p. 158.

99. Ibid.: "continua desolatio et dispersio eorum facit ad Christi gloriam et honorem et ad eorum multiplicem confusionem."

100. Ibid.

101. Ibid., pp. 158–59.

102. Glorieux points out that we have, in the preserved manuscript of the quodlibets, not the questions in Jacques's own hand but a scribe's redaction relatively soon after; ibid., p. 21.

103. Jordan, *French Monarchy and the Jews*, pp. 9–10.

104. Jacques de Thérines, *Quodlibets I et II*, p. 159: "Intelligendum est tamen quod tantum possent multiplicari et confederari in aliquo regno et tam grauiter offendere christianos et eos infestare quod ad tempus possent expelli de aliquo regno."

105. Ibid., p. 159: "Quod tamen pro semper expellerentur non uideretur expediens propter causas predictas."

106. Jordan, *French Monarchy and the Jews*, pp. 214–15.

107. Ibid., pp. 232–33.

108. For the context and some speculation on what Louis's defiance (in Navarre) and later repudiation (in France) of his father's policies meant in his personal development, see Jordan, "Princely Identity and the Jews," esp. pp. 268–72.

109. Jordan, "Home Again," pp. 27–32.

CHAPTER 2
THE POPE IN AVIGNON AND THE CRISIS OF THE TEMPLARS

1. Lizerand, *Clément V et Philippe le Bel*, pp. 37–38.

2. Menache, *Clement V*, p. 23.

3. Glorieux in Jacques de Thérines, *Quodlibets I et II*, p. 11.

4. Menache, *Clement V*, p. 6.

5. Lizerand, *Clément V et Philippe le Bel*, pp. 45, 114, 130, 350.

6. For a brief discussion of his views, see Valois, "Jacques de Thérines," pp. 189–91. Menache, *Clement V*, p. 89, depends on Valois.

7. Jacques de Thérines, *Quodlibets I et II*, 1.13, p. 153.

8. On Dolcino (or Dulcino), see Töpfer, *Das kommende Reich*, pp. 292–324, or, more briefly, Lambert, *Medieval Heresy*, pp. 194–95.

9. Jacques de Thérines, *Quodlibets I et II*, 1.13, p. 154: "Stante ergo tali heresi in Italia utrum papa debeat remanere Burdigalis uel ire in Italiam."

10. Menache, *Clement V*, p. 301. See also Töpfer, *Das kommende Reich*, p. 323.

11. On Dolcino's ideas and movement, see Töpfer, *Das kommende Reich*, pp. 292–324, and, again more briefly, Lambert, *Medieval Heresy*, pp. 193–95, and Burr, *Spiritual Franciscans*, pp. 109–10 and 389 n. 4.

12. The "errors" summarized in this paragraph may be found in Jacques de Thérines, *Quodlibets I et II*, 1.13, p. 154.

13. Töpfer, *Das kommende Reich*, pp. 295–97; Lambert, *Medieval Heresy*, p. 194.

14. For orthodox (and alternative) teaching on the keys, see Froehlich, "Saint Peter, Papal Primacy, and the Exegetical Tradition," pp. 1–44 (Innocent III was instrumental in the early thirteenth century in the classic formulation of orthodox teaching). See also Principe, "School Theologians' Views of the Papacy," pp. 45–116, and idem, "Monastic, Episcopal and Apologetic Theology of the Papacy," pp. 117–70. For a briefer conspectus, cf. Pelikan, *Christian Tradition*, pp. 46–48.

15. Lambert, *Medieval Heresy*, pp. 193–94.

16. With respect to Dolcino's understanding of Francis, see ibid., p. 194.

17. On Joachitism and orthodox reactions to it, see ibid., pp. 186–97.

18. Cf., for a representative medieval interpretation of the kind mentioned, Richard of Saint-Victor's in "De Statu interioris hominis," in *PL*, 196:158.

19. Jacques de Thérines, *Quodlibets I et II*, 1.13, pp. 154–57.

20. Ibid., p. 157: "dicendum quod licet urbs romana sit sedes principalis summi pontificis, tamen. . . ."

21. Ibid., pp. 154, 157.

22. Töpfer, *Das kommende Reich*, p. 322; Lambert, *Medieval Heresy*, p. 195.

23. Lizerand, *Clément V et Philippe le Bel*, pp. 58, 130–31, 210, 226, 363. (For the dates of Fra Dolcino's arrest and execution, see Glorieux in Jacques de Thérines, *Quodlibets I et II*, p. 11.)

24. The argument, which was probably being bandied about as a joke or slur, was that by being in France the pope might humble French churchmen through the impositions of the ravening peripatetic papal court, which demanded lavish hospitality, consuming their wealth and thereby harnessing their pride and other vices ("quia in Francia facit [papa] maius bonum decrassitando prelatos siue extrahendo nimiam pinguedinem prelatorum Francie quantum ad diuitias temporales que prestant eis occasiones superbiendi et aliorum malorum"); Jacques de Thérines, *Quodlibets I et II*, 1.13, p. 154. See the discussion in Valois, "Jacques de Thérines," pp. 190–91.

25. Jacques de Thérines, *Quodlibets I et II*, 1.13, p. 157.

26. Above, p. 48.

27. Menache, *Clement V*, pp. 205–6. A few managed to evade capture; Barber, *New Knighthood*, p. 301. Some lords, like the prince-bishop of Liège, resisted carrying out Philip's orders in their lands; Marchandisse, "Entre défiance et amitié," pp. 33–34.

28. On the Templars' origin and rise, the scholarship is enormous in quantity; in general, I follow Barber, *New Knighthood*, pp. 1–63. Forey, "Military Orders," pp. 184–216, is a splendid brief overview. Demurger, *Vie et mort de l'ordre du Temple*, is the classic treatment in French; see esp. pp. 15–52.

29. Barber, *New Knighthood*, pp. 252–53.

30. Ibid., pp. 190–93.

31. Ibid., pp. 250–57.

32. Ibid., pp. 266–78.

33. On Philip II's employment of the Templars, see Baldwin, *Government of Philip Augustus*, pp. 165–66; for Philip the Fair's, above, pp. 26–27.

34. On the later history of the order, sketched in this paragraph, and the problems of the Holy Land, see Barber, *New Knighthood*, 148–78.

35. Thier, *Kreuzzugsbemühungen unter Papst Clemens V*, pp. 33–57.

36. For a full discussion, see above, chapter 3, p. 46.

37. Jacques de Thérines, *Quodlibets I et II*, 1.21, pp. 183–92 (for the entire question; the section on exemptions occupies pp. 191–92).

38. Ibid., p. 191: "sicut patet in Templariis."

39. See above, chapters 3 and 5, pp. 41–54 and 74–78.

40. Jacques de Thérines, *Quodlibets I et II*, 1.21, p. 191.

41. Ibid., 1.8, p. 130. (N.B.: It is Glorieux who exercises editorial prerogative and adds Bernard's name after *beatus*; it is not in the MS.) Cf. Jacques's preference to cite Bernard when any number of other "saints" could be mentioned by name (1.4, p. 74: "multi sancti et specialiter beatus Bernardus dicunt . . .").

42. Above, pp. 28–29.

43. Above, chapter 3, pp. 51–52.

44. Jacques de Thérines, *Quodlibets I et II*, 1.21, p. 192: "patet quod non es simile de laïcis et clericis." Cf. Valois, "Jacques de Thérines," pp. 191–92.

45. Jacques de Thérines, *Quodlibets I et II*, 1.21, p. 192: "exempti hiis diebus plus faciunt ad confirmationem fidei et eius exaltationem quam non exempti, et sunt plures doctores et excellentiores clerici. Item episcopi sunt insufficientes et non querunt salutem animarum sed solum suas procurationes pecuniarias et extorsiones; nec promouent sufficientes, nec habundant in clericis sed in excessibus et pompis."

46. Above, p. 22.

47. Jacques de Thérines, *Quodlibets I et II*, 1.21, p. 192: "loquebatur [Bernardus] et pro tempore suo quo episcopi erant sancti et deuoti et habebant zelum religionis."

48. On secrecy, see Barber, *New Knighthood*, pp. 183–87. The texts are accessible in Upton-Ward, *Rule of the Templars*, pp. 72–73, 107, 112, 143, nos. 223, 225, 391, 418, 550–51.

49. For the texts prescribing obedience, see Upton-Ward, *Rule of the Templars*, pp. 29, 74, 80–81, 88–89, 169–71, nos. 39, 41, 274–75, 313, 664, 667, 675.

50. Barber and Bate, *Templars*, pp. 243–44, no. 66.

51. On coinage reform, Strayer, *Reign of Philip the Fair*, pp. 395–96. On the Jews, above, chapter 1, pp. 12–17.

52. Spufford, "Monetary Practice," pp. 63–67; Strayer, *Reign of Philip the Fair*, p. 396.

53. Shatzmiller, *Shylock Reconsidered*, p. 98.

54. Strayer, *Reign of Philip the Fair*, p. 396.

55. Jordan, "Jews, Regalian Rights, and the Constitution," p. 14. The incident is there misdated 1305 instead of 1306.

56. Strayer, *Reign of Philip the Fair*, p. 396.

57. Ibid., p. 174; Demurger, *Vie et mort de l'ordre du Temple*, p. 295.

58. Barber and Bate, *Templars*, pp. 243–44, no. 66.

59. Cf. Stickel, *Fall von Akkon*, p. 91.

60. Menache, *Clement V*, pp. 209, 217; Barber, *Trial of the Templars*, pp. 47–48.

61. Barber and Bate, *Templars*, pp. 244–48, no. 67.

62. Jordan, "Jews, Regalian Rights, and the Constitution," pp. 1–16.

63. Cf. Barber, *Trial of the Templars*, pp. 70–71.

64. Menache, *Clement V*, p. 207.

65. Lizerand, *Clément V et Philippe le Bel*, p. 93.

66. Ibid.

67. Menache, *Clement V*, p. 206.

68. For the text of his confession, see Barber and Bate, *Templars*, pp. 252–53, no. 69, and for the general context, Favier, *Philippe le Bel*, pp. 440–42. On his appearance before the masters, Lizerand, *Clément V et Philippe le Bel*, p. 98. Later in his life Jacques de Thérines publicly recalled this dramatic confrontation; see above, chapter 3, p. 53.

69. Cf. Menache, *Clement V*, pp. 215–16.

70. Barber, *Trial of the Templars*, p. 56.

71. Menache, *Clement V*, p. 216. Another high-ranking brother had on 21 October preceded de Molay in confessing; Barber and Bate, *Templars*, pp. 251–52.

72. Menache, *Clement V*, pp. 217–18.

73. In Jacques de Thérines, *Quodlibets I et II*, p. 11.

74. Ibid., 2.7, pp. 250–51.

75. Ibid.: "et tamen hoc potest; et specialiter quia per hoc possunt sciri secrete religiosorum, quod expedit sicut patet de Templariis."

76. Lizerand, *Dossier*, pp. 63–66; Barber and Bate, *Templars*, pp. 258–60, no. 71.

77. For their response, Lizerand, *Dossier*, pp. 66–70; Barber and Bate, *Templars*, pp. 260–63, no. 71.

78. Menache, *Clement V*, pp. 219–20.

79. Above, chapter 1, pp. 4–5.

80. The following are examples of the language of subservience and flattery taken from the beginning and the end of the response (the translations are Barber and Bates's in *Templars*, pp. 260, 262): "in complete submission always ready and willing to manifest grateful and devoted service to his royal majesty"; "May your surpassing goodness deign to keep us, your humble, devoted chaplains, in your care." Clerics under the special protection of the crown, like those who served the University of Paris, which had a royal charter, were accorded the title chaplains of the king; Lehugeur, *Philippe le Long*, p. 344 n. 4.

81. The most levelheaded and comprehensive synthesis on these developments is Barber's *Trial of the Templars*. Cf. Favier, *Philippe le Bel*, pp. 467–80.

82. Barber, *New Knighthood*, p. 303; Menache, *Clement V*, p. 216.

83. Menache, *Clement V*, p. 221.

84. Ibid., p. 228.

85. Above, chapter 3, pp. 51–54.

86. Barber, *New Knighthood*, p. 303.

87. Tierney and Painter, *Western Europe*, p. 452, sum it up nicely: in the fourteenth century "Europe was pullulating with new forms of religious vitality and with new religious movements that were often hostile, in varying degrees, to the established regime."

88. In general on the Beguines, see McDonnell, *Beguines and Beghards*. See also Babinsky, "Introduction," in Porete, *Mirror of Simple Souls*, pp. 6–20.

89. The standard edition is Verdeyen's *Margaretae Porete Speculum*. Several readily available translations exist (Babinsky's, Crawford's, and that of Colledge et al.). In general on the events surrounding Marguerite, see Babinsky, "Introduction," in Porete, *Mirror of Simple Souls*, pp. 20–26. On whether she was formally a Beguine, see below, n. 92.

90. Colledge et al., in their "Introductory Interpretative Essay" to their translation (pp. xxxv–lxxxvii), carefully lay out the ideas of the *Mirror* and their relation to "orthodox" Christian spirituality.

91. *Margaretae Porete Speculum*, ante-Prologue, p. 8.

92. Ibid., p. 344, cap. 122. Whether Marguerite was a Beguine herself is called into question in Colledge et al., "Introductory Interpretative Essay," in Porette, *Mirror of Simple Souls*, p. xlviii.

93. The general narrative presented here and in the following several paragraphs is the standard one reconstructed by scholars from the small dossier of surviving legal documents published in Verdeyen, "Procès d'Inquisition," pp. 47–94. See also Lea, *History of the Inquisition*, 2:575–78; Langlois, "Marguerite Porete," pp. 296–97; and Lerner, "Angel of Philadelphia," pp. 343–64.

94. Cf. Babinsky, "Introduction," in Porete, *Mirror of Simple Souls*, p. 26.

95. Emery, "Foreword," in Porette, *Mirror of Simple Souls*, pp. xxii–xxiii.

96. Verdeyen, "Procès d'Inquisition," pp. 86–87. Also, Colledge et al., "Introductory Interpretative Essay," in Porette, *Mirror of Simple Souls*, pp. xl–xli.

97. Scholars differ on the dates of Gui's episcopate (cf. Lea, *History of the Inquisition*, 2:576n; Langlois, "Marguerite Porete," p. 296). I follow Gams, *Series episcoporum*, pp. 527 and 919.

98. Lea, *History of the Inquisition*, 2:123.

99. Verdeyen, "Procès d'Inquisition," p. 52.

100. For the record of the examination, ibid., pp. 50–51. Also, Langlois, "Marguerite Porete," pp. 296–97. On the question of thoroughness Verdeyen (p. 54) is equivocal.

101. On these masters, see Glorieux, *Répertoire des maîtres*, 2:317–20, nos. 406–8. The text, while offering two of the excerpts in Latin, as was proper in an official ecclesiastical document, does not reveal whether the excerpts actually passed around to the masters were in Latin or in French dialect.

102. A subsequent condemnation of the *Mirror* on 9 May 1310 accuses its author of having made her book, as if it were a good thing, available "pluribus aliis personis simplicibus"; Verdeyen, "Procès d'Inquisition," p. 78.

103. Verdeyen, "Procès d'Inquisition," p. 51: "Quod talis anima non curat de consolationibus Dei nec de donis eius, nec debet curare nec potest, quia tota intenta est circa Deum, et sic impediretur eius intentio circa Deum." This is not an exact translation of any passage in the French version of the book as it has come down to us in later codices, but is similar to many passages and was undoubtedly in the original, according to Verdeyen (p. 52).

104. Cf. Babinsky, "Introduction," in Porete, *Mirror of Simple Souls*, pp. 43–44; Lea, *History of the Inquisition*, 2:123.

105. This is, to be sure, my interpretation of the displaying of her book and then the passing around of excerpts, as if, that is, it was so full of these and similar statements that the case was stronger than even the excerpts alone suggested.

106. For the acts leading up to her relaxation to the secular arm, the relaxation itself, and the canonistic endorsement of it, see Verdeyen, "Procès d'Inquisition," pp. 55–65, 78–86. Also, Lea, *History of the Inquisition*, 2:575–78.

107. Above, chapter 1, p.14.

108. "Jacobo abbate Caroliloci"; Verdeyen, "Procès d'Inquisition," p. 50.

109. Ibid., pp. 87–93, brings together all the relevant chronicle texts. One of these chronicles reports how "she manifested, as she died, many noble and devout signs of penitence" ("Multa tamen in suo exitu poenitentiae signa ostendit nobilia pariter et devota").

110. Lerner, "Angel of Philadelphia," pp. 343–64. Also, Verdeyen, "Procès d'Inquisition," pp. 65–77.

111. Cressonessart (modern, Cressonessacq, département Oise, canton Clermont, arrondissement Saint-Just).

112. Glorieux, *Répertoire des maîtres*, 2:263; Valois, "Jacques de Thérines," pp. 192–93.

113. The conclusion of Verdeyen, "Procès d'Inquisition," p. 77.

CHAPTER 3
THE EXEMPTION CONTROVERSY AT THE COUNCIL OF VIENNE

1. The most convenient histories of medieval Chaalis and Fontaine-Chaalis (alternatively Fontaine-Cornus or Fontaine-Corps-nuds, after a historic local noble family) are Dimier, "Oise cistercienne," p. 608, and idem, "Abbaye de Châalis," p. 639.

2. For reference to the extensive restorations, see Dimier, "Abbaye de Châalis," p. 639.

3. On sign language in the Cistercian Order, see Kinder, *Cistercian Europe*, p. 58, and the bibliography cited there. For an evocative description of the ruins of Chaalis, including the cloister, before development took over, see Chatel, "Notice sur l'abbaye de Chaalis," pp. 137–44.

4. Gordière, "Chaalis," p. 110; Blary, *Domaine de Chaalis*, p. 8. One occasionally encounters the date 1137; cf. Dimier, "Oise cistercienne," p. 608; idem, "Abbaye de Châalis," p. 639.

5. The number of times even excellent scholars identify Jacques as abbot of Charlieu rather than Chaalis is striking. See, for example, Lizerand, *Dossier*, p. 70 n. 2; Schulte, *Geschichte der Quellen*, p. 378; and the instance noticed in Carolus-

Barré, "Saint Louis et les translations des corps saints," p. 1101 n. 69. For an alternative etymology, see Dimier, *Saint Louis et Cîteaux*, p. 108.

6. I doubt that the record edited in *HF*, vol. 23, "Submonitiones anno M.CC.LIII factae," can be used as evidence against this assertion. This is a list of, among others, ecclesiastical corporations that contributed (or were summoned to contribute) cartage to the feudal host in 1253 when King Henry III of England seemed on the verge of invading France, whose king was abroad on Crusade. Unfortunately, the document is defective in many places, and it was the editors who arbitrarily substituted Chaalis—as one provider of carts (*carri*)—for a copyist's gibberish. An admittedly incomplete and also defectively transcribed list of the "Noms des abbayes qui doivent charroi au roi" (reedited in *HF*, 23:731–32) does not include Chaalis.

7. Dimier, *Saint Louis et Cîteaux*, pp. 108–9; Gordière, "Chaalis," p. 110, and above, chapter 4, pp. 69–70.

8. Despite the fragmentary nature of royal treasury records, this is quite clear; see the fiscal accounts for All Saints 1285 in *HF*, 22:624, 632, and those for All Saints 1299 in *Comptes royaux*, vol. 1, nos. 521, 901, which establish the continuity of these yearly payments, in one case for 40 s., in the other for 6 l. 7 s. 8 d.

9. Müller, *Analyse du cartulaire*, p. 20 n. 5; Dimier, *Saint Louis et Cîteaux*, p. 109; Gordière, "Chaalis," pp. 109–20.

10. Dimier, "Oise cistercienne," p. 608; Gordière, "Chaalis," p. 109.

11. For these interments, see Dimier, "Abbaye de Châalis," p. 639; Müller, *Senlis*, p. 139; Longpérier, "Crosses de bronze doré," pp. 259–60. On Brother Guérin, see Baldwin, *Government of Philip Augustus*, pp. 114–18.

12. Caudel, "Voie romaine," p. 21.

13. Flammermont, "Recherches sur les sources," p. 37.

14. My count is based on the number of times the king is known to have visited Senlis in the immediate environs of the abbey; cf. Le Goff, *Saint Louis*, p. 535. See also Blary, *Domaine de Chaalis*, p. 8.

15. Le Goff, *Saint Louis*, p. 618; Dimier, "Oise cistercienne," p. 608; idem, "Abbaye de Châalis," p. 639; idem, *Saint Louis et Cîteaux*, pp. 110–11.

16. Le Goff, *Saint Louis*, p. 341; Dimier, *Saint Louis et Cîteaux*, pp. 111–12. See also Klaniczay, *Holy Rulers and Blessed Princesses*, p. 254, for how this behavior compares with other forms of royal and princely devotion.

17. *GC*, vol. 10, col. 1511; Carolus-Barré, "Saint Louis et les translations des corps saints," p. 1101 n. 69; Müller, *Senlis*, p. 140; Dimier, *Saint Louis et Cîteaux*, p. 109.

18. Dimier, "Abbaye de Châalis," p. 639; idem, *Saint Louis et Cîteaux*, p. 109.

19. Carolus-Barré, *Procès de canonisation*, pp. 176, 235–36. Farmer, *Surviving Poverty*, p. 53, analyzes this miracle in the context of the other healing miracles of Saint Louis; Dimier does so in the context of miracles worked on Cistercians and attributed to Louis, *Saint Louis et Cîteaux*, pp. 127–34.

20. Above, p. 40.

21. Cf. his epitaph, *GC*, vol. 12, col. 448: "In testamentis praeclarus scriba duobus."

22. For a fuller discussion, see below, nn. 24–28.

23. Cf. Visch, *Bibliotheca*, p. 166; Oudin, *Commentarius*, fol. 728.

24. That Jacques had these redacted as abbot is explicit in the scribe's closing sentence of the quodlibets (Jacques de Thérines, *Quodlibets I et II*, p. 321): "Expliciunt duo quolibet uenerabilis magistri jacobi abbatis karoliloci ordinis cyster[ciensis]." On Cistercian scriptoria, see Kinder, *Cistercian Europe*, pp. 336–38.

25. Cf. Glorieux in Jacques de Thérines, *Quodlibets I et II*, pp. 20–23.

26. Glorieux in ibid., p. 21.

27. Ibid., 2.6, p. 250: "et ibi vide in opusculo quod feci [*for* fecisti] pro cancellario parisiensi."

28. Ibid., p. 250 n. 1.

29. Above, pp. 41–49.

30. Above, pp. 49–51, and above, chapter 5, pp. 88–92.

31. Above, chapter 4, p. 60.

32. On the struggle over exemptions in the century leading up to Jacques de Thérines's career, see Mahn, *Ordre Cistercien*, pp. 119–55; Buczek, "Pro defendis ordinis," pp. 88–109; and Müller, *Konzil von Vienne*, p. 492.

33. Lajard, "Gilles de Rome," pp. 439, 545–47. The list and summaries of Giles's works are at pp. 442–565. His *Opera Omnia* are now being published (see bibliography). For the epithet *doctor verbosus*, see Dyson, in Giles of Rome, *On Ecclesiastical Power*, p. iv.

34. Strayer, *Reign of Philip the Fair*, p. 8, doubts it. Biller, *Measure of Multitude*, p. 344, is less doubtful. See also Lajard, "Gilles de Rome," p. 422.

35. Cf. Strayer, *Reign of Philip the Fair*, p. 7 n. 20.

36. Ibid., pp. 93–94.

37. Lajard, "Gilles de Rome," pp. 423–24; Keck, *Angels and Angelology*, p. 19.

38. Monahan, in Giles of Rome, *On Ecclesiastical Power*, p. xi. For a thorough review of the context for academic controversies at the University of Paris, see Thijssen, *Censure and Heresy*.

39. The text of Giles's attack on the Templars is edited in Müller, *Konzil von Vienne*, pp. 689–90. See also Lajard, "Gilles de Rome," p. 546.

40. Müller, *Konzil von Vienne*, p. 690.

41. Ibid.: "Et si dicatur, quod quandoque strenue bellabant contra Saracenos, dicendum, quod et diabolus facit aliqua bona, sed illa facit intentione fallendi, sicut August. ait."

42. Ibid., p. 689: "de facto videmus in Templariis, qui occasione suae exemptionis lapsi sunt in apostasiam perfidiae." Lajard, "Gilles de Rome," p. 546.

43. Lajard, "Gilles de Rome," pp. 545–46.

44. Müller, *Konzil von Vienne*, p. 689: "Si autem Templarii non fuissent exempti, sed fuissent a suis ordinariis visitati, scita fuisset perversa professio eorumdem."

45. Ibid., p. 690: "Nunc autem ista mala propter exemptiones Templariis evenerunt; quia Praelati eos non poterant visitare."

46. Müller, *Konzil von Vienne*, pp. 495–96; Lajard, "Gilles de Rome," p. 546.

47. For reference to other authors in the controversy (pro and con), see Lajard, "Gilles de Rome," p. 547; Müller, *Konzil von Vienne*, pp. 496–502; and Rivière, *Problème de l'église et de l'état*, p. 362. On the pride of place given Giles's *Contra exemptos* among the Augustinian Hermits, particularly by the contemporary Paris

professor Prosper de Regio Emilia, see Glorieux, "A propos de 'Vatic. Lat. 1086,' " p. 28 (on Prosper himself, see pp. 27, 38–39).

48. Valois, "Jacques de Thérines," pp. 193–209.

49. See, for example, Menache, *Clement V,* pp. 286 n. 49, 292–93 n. 90; Glorieux, *Répertoire des maîtres,* 2:262; Mahn, *Le Pape Benoît XII,* pp. 16–18, 22–23, 66; Buczek, "Medieval Taxation," p. 96; Peyrafort-Huin, *Bibliothèque médiévale de l'abbaye de Pontigny,* pp. 154–55. The exception is Müller, *Konzil von Vienne,* pp. 503–18. Schimmelpfennig, "Zisterzienser, Papsttum und Episkopat," p. 80, follows Müller.

50. Valois, "Jacques de Thérines," pp. 194–95, 203–4, 108–9.

51. Ibid., p. 194.

52. Ibid. p. 194 n. 8. Cf. Jacques de Thérines, *Quodlibets I et II,* 1.6, pp. 104–21: "Vtrum angelus intelligat alia a se per speciem."

53. Keck, *Angels and Angelology,* pp. 92–99. I am indebted to James Byrne, a Ph.D. candidate in History of Science at Princeton University, for bringing this book to my attention and for help in clarifying these issues.

54. On the active part played by students in the controversies, cf. Mowbray, "1277 and All That," pp. 217–38.

55. Valois, "Jacques de Thérines," p. 195 n. 3: "sicut fama communis fert." On the semantic field of *fama,* see Fenster and Smail, *Fama.*

56. Ibid., p. 195.

57. Ibid.

58. Cf. *GC,* 2:76–77.

59. Müller, *Konzil von Vienne,* p. 512 n. 65: "Accidit namque in Dioecesi Bituricensi cum ad quondam abbatiam Cisterciensis Ordinis, quae Locufregius [*recte*: Locusregius] nominatur, ipsemet declinasset, ubi nec procurationem habet de jure, nec de consuetudine, nec auctoritatem habet visitandi, cum ordo Cisterc. Per privilegia Apostolica a talibus sit immunis: Non fuit contentus cibis regularibus, quos illi de praedicta abbatia soliti erant liberaliter ministrare: sed volens ibidem comedere carnes, contra voluntatem religiosorum dicti loci et contra mandatum ac privilegium Sedis Apostolicae, sui proprii famuli violenter ibidem duos porcos rapuerunt et mactaverunt: Prioremque dicti loci contradicentem ac resistentem taliter tractaverunt et inhumaniter verberarunt, quod ex illa laesione amiserit oculum intra breve temporis intervallum." Valois, "Jacques de Thérines," pp. 195, 208–9. On Loroy, whose medieval history remains largely unexplored, a few facts have been brought together in Dufour, "Acte inédit de Louis VI," pp. 157–60, and Chochon-Plée, "Curiosité archéologique," pp. 479–96. Thirty-six original charters of the abbey dated 1141–1296 survive pasted and sewn into a codex, probably in the eighteenth century. This is now in the Bibliothèque Nationale Française: MS latin 9217, which I hope to discuss, in conjunction with a fuller reconstruction of the incidents narrated here, in a future publication.

60. Valois, "Jacques de Thérines," p. 195.

61. Müller, *Konzil von Vienne,* p. 514 n. 69.

62. Valois, "Jacques de Thérines," pp. 193–200; Müller, *Konzil von Vienne,* pp. 503–14.

63. Valois, "Jacques de Thérines," pp. 201–3. (Cf. Müller, *Konzil von Vienne,* pp. 514–17.) The rubric is at fol. 65v of BM, Dijon, MS 339 (248).

64. On the analogy, Valois, "Jacques de Thérines," p. 205. Although the treatise does repeat a great deal from the preceding works and makes ample references to those works, Valois's summary (pp. 203–6) does not do justice to it on one point. For scholars interested in how thinking about angels was transferred to ordinary problems of daily life, it is a treasure trove; Vienna, ÖNB, MS 4257, in the *Quaestio de exemptionibus,* fols. 127–47. Jacques's angelic material was also of little interest to his early modern editors, cf. *Annales ecclesiastici,* 23:579.

65. For the quotations, see BM, Dijon MS 339 (248), in the *Responsio,* fol. 81bis. Valois, "Jacques de Thérines," pp. 206–9; Müller, *Konzil von Vienne,* pp. 517–18.

66. Valois, "Jacques de Thérines," p. 196.

67. Ibid., pp. 196–97.

68. Dijon, BM, MS 339 (248), in the *Contra impugnatores,* fol. 48. *Annales ecclesiastici,* 23:571: "caput talis collegii aut habet aliquam jurisdictionem super ipsum, aut non: non potest dici quod non, quia tunc non esset caput"; further for his views of cathedral canons, 577. Valois, "Jacques de Thérines," p. 196.

69. Dijon, BM, MS 339 (248), in *Contra impugnatores,* fol. 3v. Valois, "Jacques de Thérines," pp. 197, 207.

70. Vienna, ÖNB, MS 4257, in the *Quaestio de exemptionibus,* fol. 140v. See also above, p. 48.

71. Valois, "Jacques de Thérines," p. 196.

72. Ibid., pp. 196–97.

73. Ibid., p. 202.

74. BM, Dijon, MS 339 (248), in the *Responsio,* fol. 81bis.

75. *Annales ecclesiastici,* 23:565: "illi praelati, qui solum quaestum temporalem quaerunt, de victualibus conquerentes, petentes procurationes, nihil seminantes, quod ad salutem pertineat animarum; et specialiter petentes esum carnium in ordine Cisterciensi contra indulta a sede Apostolica in favorem puritatis et asperitatis vitae, quae in eodem ordine vigere consuevit."

76. Valois, "Jacques de Thérines," pp. 196–97.

77. *Annales ecclesiastici,* 23:568.

78. Ibid., 565, and above, n. 75 for the quoted phrase. Dijon, BM, MS 339 (248), in the *Contra impugnatores,* fol. 5. Valois, "Jacques de Thérines," p. 197.

79. Dijon, BM, MS 339 (248), in the *Contra impugnatores,* fol. 3: "Imo de necessitate ad connexionem et convenienciam debitam et ad salutem christiani populi in regimine ecclesiastico requiruntur." Vienna, ÖNB, MS 4257, in the *Quaestio de exemptionibus,* fol. 132v: "exemptiones et privilegia religiosorum expediunt ad animarum salutem et tocius fidei christiane exaltationem declaro."

80. Dijon, BM, MS 339 (248), in the *Contra impugnatores,* fol. 5: "ad exaltationem fidei christiane et instructionem et illuminationem universalis ecclesie."

81. Müller, *Konzil von Vienne,* p. 516 n. 75. Valois, "Jacques de Thérines," pp. 197, 202, 208.

82. Vienna, ÖNB, MS 4257, in the *Quaestio de exemptionibus,* fol. 131: "de rege exeunte in exercitu adversarios debellandos qui pro custodia sui proprii corporis . . . milites strenuos et probatos." Valois, "Jacques de Thérines," p. 205.

83. Valois, "Jacques de Thérines," pp. 197–98.

84. *Annales ecclesiastici*, 23:567 (read *Karoliloci* for *Belliloci*). See also Müller, *Senlis*, p. 139; Valois, "Jacques de Thérines," p. 202; Rashdall, *Medieval Universities*, 1:318–19.

85. On Saint Guillaume de Donjeon, canonized in 1218, see *GC*, vol. 10, cols. 1509–10; Dimier, "Evêques cisterciens," pp. 530, 532.

86. For a sketch of the history of the polemics in Cistercian-episcopal relations from the establishment of the order until the late Middle Ages, and of Jacques's savage critique as more or less the culmination of that history, see Schimmelpfennig, "Zisterzienser, Papsttum und Episkopat," pp. 69–85.

87. Müller, *Konzil von Vienne*, p. 506 n. 56. Valois, "Jacques de Thérines," p. 197.

88. Dijon, BM, MS 339 (248), in the *Contra impugnatores*, fol. 11v: "et per malum et perversum consilium opprimunt subditos per avariciam super eos nimis tyrannice dominado querente magis questum quam animarum salutem"; and fol. 13: "loco ignis caritatis qui deberet in ipsis regnare habundat in eis ignis cupiditatis et avaricie."

89. Ibid., fol. 5: "Plures enim prelati unde dolendum est avaricie student a minimo usque ad maximum." Müller, *Konzil von Vienne*, p. 506 n. 56: "nec ipsimet Episcopi tale studium vel Collegium ordinarint. Imo magis impediunt quam promoueant." Valois, "Jacques de Thérines," pp. 197–98, 206.

90. *Annales ecclesiastici*, 23:573.

91. Ibid., 574. Valois, "Jacques de Thérines," p. 206.

92. Valois, "Jacques de Thérines," p. 198.

93. *Annales ecclesiastici*, 23:573; also "jurisdictio episcopi esset nociva."

94. Müller, *Konzil von Vienne*, p. 515 n. 73.

95. Valois, "Jacques de Thérines," p. 206.

96. Müller, *Konzil von Vienne*, p. 515 n. 73: "Nec supponitur, quod his diebus sunt episcopi majoris sanctitatis et perfectionis, nec majoris zeli pro divino cultu conservando et ampliando quam fuerunt tempore Beati Gregorii, qui eorum abusus et oppressiones praevidens, dictas exemptiones instituit et indulsit." Valois, "Jacques de Thérines," p. 206.

97. Cf. Menache, *Clement V*, pp. 292–93.

98. These developments are narrated with passion, but not too much nuance, in Mesle, *Histoire de Bourges*, p. 72.

99. Cf. Lawrence, *Friars*, pp. 14–15.

100. *Annales ecclesiastici*, 23:568: "jurisdictio ecclesiastica una est prima et suprema, scilicet jurisdictio Papae."

101. Ibid., p. 567; he mentions Giles by name, "quae scribit Ægydius in quodam tractatu contra exemptos" and adds, "suae rationes sunt in pluribus defectuosae."

102. Ibid., p. 568.

103. For example, in the *Quaestio de exemptionibus*, Vienna, ÖNB, MS 4257, fol. 132.

104. Dijon, BM, MS 339 (248), in the *Contra impugnatores*, fol. 6. Valois, "Jacques de Thérines," p. 202.

105. *Annales ecclesiastici*, 23:567.

106. Dijon, BM, MS 339 (248), in the *Contra impugnatores*, fol. 6v: "ad extirpationem scismaticorum et rebellium." Valois, "Jacques de Thérines," p. 202.

107. Dijon, BM, MS 339 (248), in the *Contra impugnatores*, fol. 6v: "Nam si nulli religiosi essent exempti citius et facilius possent prelati discedere et se subtrahere de facto a iurisdictione summi pontificis."

108. *Annales ecclesiastici*, 23:567: "quod revocatio seu detruncatio exemptionum esset damnosa multipliciter qua et suae potestatis plenitudinem non modicum obfuscaret, et sedi Apostolicae multipliciter derogaret." Valois, "Jacques de Thérines," pp. 200, 208.

109. Above, p. 46.

110. Dijon, BM, MS 339 (248), in the *Contra impugnatores*, fol. 10. Valois, "Jacques de Thérines," p. 197.

111. Dijon, BM, MS 339 (248), in the *Contra impugnatores*, fol. 47.

112. On the background of the *usus pauper* controversy and the material that I try so briefly to summarize in the next two paragraphs, see Burr, *Spiritual Franciscans*, pp. 33–65.

113. Ibid., p. 145.

114. Dijon, BM, MS 339 (248), fol. 47, in the *Contra impugnatores*, fol. 47, where he lists "beatus Franciscus" as one of the holy men of the exempt orders.

115. Burr, *Spiritual Franciscans*, p. 169.

116. Valois, "Jacques de Thérines," p. 205.

117. Further on his views of the mendicants, *Annales ecclesiastici*, 23:575–76.

118. On the commission, see Burr, *Spiritual Franciscans*, pp. 145–48.

119. For the list of commissioners (though not my theory as to Clement's motive), see Fussenegger, "Relatio commissionis," p. 158.

120. The text is edited in ibid., pp. 158–76. Six times the churchmen express their lack of unanimity on particular issues using the following phrases: "unus magistrorum contra sentit et alius dicit quod est preceptum absolute" (p. 160); "excepto uno magistro" (p. 160); "Unus vero magistrorum sentit quod non" (p. 161); "Dictorum autem magistrorum duo contrarium sentiunt, tertius vero dubitat" (p. 161); "excepto uno magistro" (p. 161); "duobus tantum magistrorum exceptis" (p. 161). Despite my best efforts I have not discovered whether any of these dissents came from Jacques de Thérines.

121. Burr, *Spiritual Franciscans*, pp. 145–48; Menache, *Clement V*, p. 295.

122. Cf. Nimmo, *Reform and Division*, pp. 121–22. The bull is printed in *Corpus Iuris Canonici*, vol. 2, cols. 1193–1200, and the *Regestum Clementis Papae V*, 7:342–50, no. 8873.

123. Above, chapter 5, pp. 88–90.

124. The issues summarized briefly in this paragraph are treated fully above, chapter 2, pp. 22–32.

125. *Annales ecclesiastici*, 23:580: "nam in diversis terris multi valde non exempti et non religiosi inveniuntur heretici, qui non essent: si exemptio esset causa illius mali, quia inveniuntur sine exemptione." Valois, "Jacques de Thérines," p. 200.

126. The portion of the *Contra impugnatores exemptionum* dealing with the Templars was excerpted and published separately in Müller, *Konzil von Vienne*, pp. 691–92. (It is on fols. 45 v–46 of Dijon, BM, MS 339 [248].) On Jacques's motivation for throwing doubt on the Templars' guilt, cf. Müller, p. 100, and Menache, *Clement V*, p. 236. See also Barber, *Trial of the Templars*, p. 230, for the quotation.

127. Müller, *Konzil von Vienne*, p. 691. Valois, "Jacques de Thérines," p. 198.

128. Müller, *Konzil von Vienne*, p. 691.

129. Ibid., pp. 691–92: "nobilibus et ignobilibus, diversorum generum et diversarum linguarum, educatis a legitimis parentibus, nutritis inter fidelissimos christianos." Valois, "Jacques de Thérines," pp. 198–99.

130. Valois, "Jacques de Thérines," p. 199.

131. Müller, *Konzil von Vienne*, p. 692.

132. Ibid. Valois, "Jacques de Thérines," p. 199.

133. Saporta and van der Kolk, "Psychological Consequences of Severe Trauma," p. 166. Demurger, *Vie et mort de l'ordre du Temple*, pp. 344–52, has some very useful words on the tortures.

134. If, Jacques argued, the charges were for every Templar who confessed (*Et si vera sunt universaliter*), then why did many recant in the face of the certainty of execution, "quomodo in Senonensis et Rhemensi cum aliis provinciis multi Templarii ex certa sententia permiserunt se comburi, a suis primis confessionibus recedentes: cum tamen scirent, se posse evadere, si redirent ad primitus confessata"; Müller, *Konzil von Vienne*, p. 692. Valois, "Jacques de Thérines," p. 199. See also, on the burnings per se, Barber, *Trial of the Templars*, p. 157.

135. Müller, *Konzil von Vienne*, p. 692.

136. Ibid., pp. 139–41; Menache, *Clement V*, p. 236.

137. Müller, *Konzil von Vienne*, p. 122; Valois, "Jacques de Thérines," p. 199. Subjecting the accused to torture ("questionibus et tormentis") was permitted and recommended for the process against the Templars everywhere (cf. *Regestum Clementis Papae V*, 6:104–5, 408–9, 439, 458, 463–64, nos. 6716, 7496–98, 7527, 7597, 7607, orders dated 18 and 30 March and 27 June 1311), but not always used; Barber, *Trial of the Templars*, pp. 114–16.

138. Müller, *Konzil von Vienne*, p. 692: "purissimus et ardentissimus zelus christianissimi et illustrissimi principis Regis Francorum."

139. Ibid. Valois, "Jacques de Thérines," pp. 199–200.

140. Müller, *Konzil von Vienne*, p. 692.

141. Valois, "Jacques de Thérines," pp. 199–200.

142. Even if "omnia essent vera, quae Templariis imponuntur, adhuc nihil per hoc rationabiliter concludi potest contra exemptos"; Müller, *Konzil von Vienne*, p. 692.

143. Ibid., pp. 518–33.

144. Valois, "Jacques de Thérines," pp. 209–10.

145. Ibid., pp. 210–11. See also Buczek, "Medieval Taxation," pp. 96–97.

146. Menache, *Clement V*, p. 238; Barber, *New Knighthood*, p. 304; idem, *Trial of the Templars*, pp. 228–29.

147. Barber, *New Knighthood*, p. 304.

148. Forey, *Fall of the Templars*, p. 228, points to the absence of evidence of Aragonese recruitment of former Templars, in contradistinction to the Portuguese case. Forey's treatment of the transition in Aragon, much more complicated than one might suppose, is masterful; pp. 156–209.

149. Barber, *New Knighthood*, p. 309.

150. Menache, *Clement V*, p. 239; Barber, *New Knighthood*, p. 304.

151. *Regestum Clementis Papae V*, 9:111–12, no. 10337: "ad id propter multiplicia et ardua negotia nobis incumbentia, quorum ad presens varietate distrahimur, personaliter intendere nequeamus."

152. Barber, *New Knighthood*, p. 314.

153. Cf. Beaune, "Rois maudits," pp. 21–24.

CHAPTER 4
AN UNEASY RELATIONSHIP: CHURCH AND STATE
AT THE CISTERCIAN ABBEY OF SAINTE-MARIE OF CHAALIS

1. Cf. Lawrence, *Medieval Monasticism*, p. 157.

2. For information on these various buildings, see Bruzelius, "Transept of the Abbey Church of Châalis," pp. 447–54 (drawing on and supplementing the work of Lefèvre-Pontalis); Dimier, "Abbaye de Châalis," p. 639; Müller, *Senlis*, p. 140; Gordière, "Chaalis," p. 110.

3. On lay brothers, see Kinder, *Cistercian Europe*, pp. 307–31; Lekai, *Cistercians*, pp. 334–46, and Lawrence, *Medieval Monasticism*, pp. 149–50. Cf. Cassidy-Welch, *Monastic Spaces*, pp. 167–93.

4. Lekai, *Cistercians*, p. 366.

5. On the requirement of prisons and the execution of this requirement, see Kinder, *Cistercian Europe*, pp. 359–61. On the supposed prison ruins at Chaalis, refer to Chatel, "Notice sur l'abbaye de Chaalis," p. 140. For evocative treatments of the maintenance of Cistercian prisons and parallel arrangements for the incarceration of dissident *conversi* and free-spirited and apostate choir monks beyond the monastic precincts, see Cassidy-Welch, "Incarceration and Liberation," pp. 23–42, and idem, *Monastic Spaces*, pp. 167, 196–216.

6. Kinder, *Cistercian Europe*, pp. 74–75. Information on these matters is also scattered through Lekai, *Cistercians*, in no very systematic way. See also Arbois de Jubainville, *Etudes*, pp. 156–66.

7. Le Goff, *Saint Louis*, p. 618.

8. Kinder, *Cistercian Europe*, pp. 365–66; Dimier, "Infirmeries cisterciennes," p. 805; idem, "Salle des morts," p. 836; Lekai, *Cistercians*, pp. 376–77. Cf. Cassidy-Welch, *Monastic Spaces*, pp. 226–28.

9. Carolus-Barré, *Procès de canonisation*, pp. 127–28.

10. Kinder, *Cistercian Europe*, p. 310; Lawrence, *Medieval Monasticism*, p. 149.

11. Cf. Lawrence, *Medieval Monasticism*, p. 150.

12. Cf. Lekai, *Cistercians*, pp. 340–41.

13. Above, p. 59.

14. For the migration, see *GC*, vol. 10, col. 1508. On the twelve-monk "rule," see Ribbe, "Wirtschaftstätigkeit der Zisterzienser im Mittelalter," p. 203.

15. Or, at least, this seems to have been the pattern for early twelfth-century Cistercian foundations, including Chaalis's mother house, Pontigny; cf. Kinder, "Toward Dating Construction of the Abbey Church of Pontigny," pp. 79, 84.

16. These officials are encountered time and again in the documentation: prior, sacristan, and, implicitly, *infirmarius* (Carolus-Barré, *Procès de canonisation*, p. 237); subprior (Müller, *Senlis*, p. 142); treasurer (Müller, "Vingt-Neuf chartes originales," p. 46); cellarer (Dimier, "Abbaye de Châalis," p. 639; idem, *Saint*

Louis et Cîteaux, p. 187 n. 332); scribes (chapter 3, pp. FE–FE). The phlebotomist can perhaps be inferred from the instructions Cistercians followed on the treatment of ill and aged monks (Dimier, "Infirmeries cisterciennes," p. 805; Lekai, *Cistercians*, p. 375; cf. Cassidy-Welch, *Monastic Spaces*, pp. 133–65). See also Kinder, *Cistercian Europe*, pp. 74–78, 361–64, and the older study by Arbois de Jubainville, *Etudes*, pp. 184–85, 196–205, 214–43 (summarized in Lambert, "Histoire de l'abbaye de Quincy," p. 223 n. 1).

17. Kinder, *Cistercian Europe*, pp. 74, 309; Lawrence, *Medieval Monasticism*, p. 149, and Lekai, *Cistercians*, p. 337.

18. Cf. Kinder, *Cistercian Europe*, p. 310. The ratio for a smaller monastery, with fewer or smaller estates, would probably be less. In the thirteenth century the Cistercian house at Meaux, Kinder notes, counted sixty choir monks and ninety *conversi*.

19. Kinder, *Cistercian Europe*, p. 309; Lekai, *Cistercians*, p. 337; Lawrence, *Medieval Monasticism*, p. 149.

20. On this form of registering, see above, p. 68.

21. *Actes du Parlement de Paris*, vol. 2, no. 5752.

22. Above, p. 70.

23. Above, pp. 60–61.

24. Above, pp. 59–60.

25. Lekai, *Cistercians*, pp. 65–76; Lawrence, *Medieval Monasticism*, p. 157; King, *Finances of the Cistercian Order*, p. 9.

26. This is because Pontigny monks first populated Chaalis; above, p. 57.

27. Useful information on the daughters is to be found in *GC*, 2:1356–59, and 10:1330–33, 1508. The cartulary and associated documents of Merci-Dieu were published in 1905 and reveal some aspects of the continuing relationship between mother and daughter houses, with various abbots of Chaalis serving as witnesses to Merci-Dieu's charters and benefiting, in one case, from an annual anniversary mass; "Cartulaire de l'abbaye de Notre-Dame de la Merci-Dieu," pp. 124–25, 153–54, 346–47, 359, 364.

28. King, *Finances of the Cistercian Order*, p. 61. None of Chaalis's accounts before about the year 1500 appears to have survived; cf. *Archives départementales de l'Oise: Répertoire numérique de la série H*, col. 145.

29. King, *Finances of the Cistercian Order*, p. 8.

30. Paris, BNF, MS latin 11003, fols. 224v–25.

31. Jordan, "Mortmain," pp. 488–89.

32. Carolus-Barré, *Procès de canonisation*, p. 133.

33. Strayer, *Reign of Philip the Fair*, p. 235. Of course, at difficult times in the reign he relented in his assault (cf. Strayer, pp. 256–58).

34. Paris, BNF, MS latin 11003, fol. 384v.

35. For the comparison, see Strayer, *Reign of Philip the Fair*, p. 129.

36. Paris, BNF, MS latin 11003, fol. 384v: "Et de hoc habemus litteram dicti magistri Petri [de Latilliaco] in titulo regio iunctam predicte littere regis sub hoc signo." See also above, chapter 5, p. 71.

37. Paris, BNF, MS latin 11003, fol. 225: "assecuratio hominum de terra quam fecerunt abbati et conventui karoli anno domini MᵒCCCᵒXVIIᵒ."

38. Valois, "Jacques de Thérines," p. 182 n. 2, refers to and summarizes this charter, on the basis of a description offered by the owner, a M. Longpérier-Grimoard. I have not been able to trace the original or identify an authentic copy.

39. Paris, BNF, MS latin 11003, fols. 136v–37. Fontaines appears in the Latin plural (*in territorio de Fontanis*) in early fourteenth-century documentation. In the modern period, the singular has become official.

40. Blary, *Domaine de Chaalis*, pp. 95–99.

41. Cf. Jordan, *Great Famine*, pp. 71, 75, 81, where it is shown that conversion to leasing was hardly a panacea.

42. Paris, BNF, MS latin 11003, fols. 212v–13v.

43. For what follows, see Strayer, *Reign of Philip the Fair*, p. 19.

44. Cuttler, *Law of Treason*, p. 118.

45. For an interesting comparative study with the nearly contemporary adultery scandal in England, involving Philip's own daughter, and its treatment by the affected parties and the chroniclers, see Wood, "Queens, Queans, and Kingship," pp. 385–400.

46. Strayer, *Reign of Philip the Fair*, pp. 9–10.

47. Favier, *Philippe le Bel*, p. 7.

48. Collard, "*In claustro venenum*," pp. 8–9, 13, 18; Strayer, *Reign of Philip the Fair*, pp. 300–313, and Favier, *Philippe le Bel*, pp. 456–61; Cuttler, *Law of Treason*, pp. 29, 75.

49. Lambert, *Medieval Heresy*, pp. 142–50.

50. Strayer, *Reign of Philip the Fair*, pp. 312–13.

51. Ibid., pp. 342–43.

52. Brown, "Reform and Resistance," p. 111.

53. Strayer, *Reign of Philip the Fair*, p. 343. For a comprehensive review of this maxim, see Brown, "*Cessante causa*," pp. 565–88.

54. Strayer, *Reign of Philip the Fair*, pp. 344–46; Cuttler, *Law of Treason*, pp. 95–96.

55. Brown, "Reform and Resistance," pp. 111–12.

56. Artonne, *Mouvement de 1314*, pp. 13–30; Favier, *Philippe le Bel*, pp. 517–19.

57. Strayer, *Reign of Philip the Fair*, p. 417. For my reasons for believing that he was unaware of his illness, see above, p. 64.

58. Baudon de Mony, "Mort et les funérailles de Philippe le Bel," p. 13. Further on Philip's concern for the shrine at Poissy, which was still unfinished, see Brown, "Royal Salvation," p. 372.

59. Baudon de Mony, "Mort et les funérailles de Philippe le Bel," p. 13; Brown, "Royal Salvation," p. 368.

60. Brown, "Royal Salvation," pp. 372–73; Strayer, *Reign of Philip the Fair*, p. 418.

61. Cf. Bande, "Philippe le Bel, le coeur et le sentiment dynastique," pp. 267–78. On the procedures in place for removing the heart in the period (the surgeons probably came up through the ventral viscera rather than through the thorax by slicing or cracking through the sternum), see Georges, "L'Exérèse du coeur dans l'embaumement médiéval," pp. 279–86.

62. *Steadman's Medical Dictionary*, s.v. "microcardia."

63. Baudon de Mony, "Mort et les funérailles de Philippe le Bel," p. 12.

64. Favier, *Philippe le Bel*, p. 528. Cf. Brown, "Kings like Semi-Gods," pp. 17 n. 44, 20.

65. Chroniclers, like Jean de Saint-Victor (*HF*, 21:661), rehearse the negotiations, which had begun in Philip IV's time, Louis's nearly adolescent eagerness and excitement at the prospect of the new bride (the display had disgusted his father), Clémence's ostentatious trip, and the marriage. See also Brown, "Kings like Semi-Gods," pp. 13–14, 19–21.

66. Artonne, *Mouvement de 1314*, pp. 43–69, 86–87, 90–101. See also Brown, "Reform and Resistance," pp. 119–28, for additional context and the outcomes of the opposition.

67. Artonne, *Mouvement de 1314*, pp. 31–42; Baudon de Mony, "Mort et les funérailles de Philippe le Bel," pp. 12–13.

68. Favier, *Conseiller de Philippe le Bel*, p. 217.

69. On Payot and the others, see ibid., pp. 213–14, 217.

70. Lehugeur, *Philippe le Long*, pp. 4–5, 20–22.

71. Artonne, *Mouvement de 1314*, pp. 38–39; Cuttler, *Law of Treason*, p. 28.

72. Artonne, *Mouvement de 1314*, p. 169, no. 7: "de gratis et concessionibus." Cf. Brown, "Reform and Resistance," pp. 136–37, appendix 9.

73. "Regum mansiones et itinera," *HF*, 21:465.

74. Jordan, *French Monarchy and the Jews*, p. 240.

75. Bloch, *Rois et serfs*, pp. 163–72.

76. Jordan, *French Monarchy and the Jews*, pp. 240–41.

77. Above, chapter 1, pp. 13–15.

78. Jordan, *French Monarchy and the Jews*, p. 241; Jordan, "Home Again," pp. 27–31.

79. Artonne, *Mouvement de 1314*, pp. 70–89.

80. On the grants from the Cistercians, see King, *Finances of the Cistercian Order*, p. 94. His references (to the *Comptes du Trésor*, nos. 551, 593) refer to contributions in 1316 (new style), but the lost account of 1315 would have recorded a similar subvention.

81. On the events narrated in the remainder of this paragraph, see Jordan, *Great Famine*, pp. 15–20.

82. Paris, BNF, MS latin 11003, fols. 275v–76 (dated 1316), 276 (dated 1317; numbered 1127 in a modern hand), and 321v–22v (dated 1316).

83. For example, Paris, BNF, MS latin 11003, fol. 276 (document numbered 1128 in a modern hand).

84. For the exchange, see Paris, BNF, MS latin 11003, fols. 321v–22v.

85. Above, chapter 5, p. 83.

86. Paris, BNF, MS latin 11003, fol. 322v: "quittavit ecclesie karoli omnem querelam quam moveret adversus eam."

87. Paris, BNF, MS latin 11003, fols. 320v–21v, transcribed in part and discussed in Valois, "Jacques de Thérines," pp. 181–82, esp. n. 3.

88. Marsy, "Droits de l'abbaye de Chaalis," pp. 13–16.

89. Paris, BNF, MS latin. 11003, fol. 320v: "Certa contentio verteretur inter ecclesiam karoli et communiam compendii."

90. On Chaalis's rights in Senlis, cf. Chatel, "Notice sur l'abbaye de Chaalis," p. 140; Müller, *Analyse du cartulaire*, p. 158, no. 273.

91. The reference to payment of this rent (*pro censu terre*) by the *prévôt* of Paris to Chaalis is in the royal accounts for All Saints 1285; *HF*, 22:642.

92. Blary, *Domaine de Chaalis*, pp. 327–36. The archaeological evidence is strongest for Senlis and Beauvais; the conclusion about the houses' privileged nature (freedom from tolls) is an extrapolation from the evidence for the Beauvais facility.

93. Paris, BNF, MS latin 11003, fol. 321v.

94. Lehugeur, *Philippe le Long*, pp. 73–74.

95. Ibid., p. 45.

96. Ibid., pp. 79–81.

97. For a full treatment of the Salic Law and its manipulation later in the century to exclude women from the French throne and quash their rights of transmission, see Giesey, *Juristic Basis of Dynastic Right*. (Cf. Favier, *Philippe le Bel*, p. 523.) Philip the Tall's failure to admit his niece's claim, though not based on the Salic Law, probably did help inspire jurists to seek a more fundamental justification for the exclusion of women; Jones, "Last Capetians," p. 394.

98. Collard, "Recherches sur le crime de poison," p. 100.

99. Wood, "Where Is John the Posthumous?" pp. 99–117; Lehugeur, *Philippe le Long*, pp. 75–78. Two quaint little books, the second virtually plagiarizing the first, also address these stories: Monmerqué, *Dissertation historique sur Jean Ier*, Cheney, *King of France Unnamed*.

100. Cf. Beaune, "Rois maudits," pp. 9–19.

101. Lehugeur, *Philippe le Long*, pp. 79–82.

102. Ibid., p. 80 n. 4.

103. Ibid., pp. 342–44.

104. Ibid., p. 346.

105. Paris, BNF, MS latin 11003, fols. 382–84 (Saint Louis's), 382v–84 (Philip III's).

106. Ibid., fol. 384.

107. Ibid., fol. 384–84v. See also Müller, "Vingt-Neuf chartes originales," pp. 46–47.

108. Above, pp. 59–60.

109. Three visits are documented: late June 1298, mid-May 1302, and January 1303 (NS). See "Regum mansiones et itinera," *HF*, 21:436, 439–41, Müller, *Analyse du cartulaire*, p. 168, no. 299.

110. Paris, BNF, MS latin 11003, fol. 384v.

111. *Comptes royaux*, vol. 1, no. 3859.

112. On Philip's itinerary, "Regum mansiones et itinera," *HF*, 21:457. For the council's sessions, see above, chapter 3, pp. 40–41.

113. Above, pp. 52–54.

114. Valois, "Jacques de Thérines," p. 182 n. 1. Cf. Paris, BNF, MS latin 11003, fol. 384 (dated 1317).

115. Valois, "Jacques de Thérines," p. 182 n. 1.

116. Ibid., n. 2; Lehugeur, *Philippe le Long*, p. 343.

117. Paris, BNF, MS latin 11003. For further information on the database for the reconstruction of the history of the abbey of Chaalis, see "Rapport de M. Desjardins," pp. 38–39; *Catalogue général des manuscrits des bibliothèques publiques*, pp. 363–66; and Blary, *Domaine de Chaalis*, p. 12.

118. Blary, *Domaine de Chaalis*, pp. 12, 14, etc. The note on fol. 3: "Cartulaire De Labbaye De Cháalis Redigé en Lan 1394 Sous le Regne de Charles Six."

119. The most recent record in the original hand is on fol. 213 and is dated 1318.

120. Cf. Delisle's hasty judgment, *Catalogue des actes de Philippe-Auguste*, p. 531.

121. The obvious comparison is with the exactly contemporary cartulary prepared for Pontigny, Paris, BNF, MS latin 5465. It has full transcripts rather than summaries of original charters (as in the Chaalis manuscript), but in places it lacks the large initials that were to introduce every charter (e.g., fol. 16). Yet this incompleteness has not led to any modern denigration, because, unlike the case of the Chaalis cartulary, very few additions were made to the Pontigny manuscript, so its pristine elegance was preserved.

122. The manuscript is divided into thirty-two sections. The first, ending at fol. 7–7v, differs from the twenty-eight topographically organized sections that follow in that it enrolls the earliest (foundation) records: "De concessione abbatie." After the twenty-eight topographical sections, there comes a section on "Carte reddituum que non habent proprietatem," fols. 378–79v. Then come the two concluding sections.

123. Fols. 371–76v.

124. Usually, the last record of each section is the most recent, although occasionally one has to go back a folio or two, because the scribe has explained one record with reference to another, earlier, that he then summarizes. Here are the folio numbers on which each section's final record, in the original hand, appears, accompanied by the date of the most recent record in the section in parentheses: fols. 8v (1138, foundation-related documents), 29 (1299), 37 (1296), 55v (1275), 61v (1289), 69 (1289), 76 (1280), 89 (1285), 92v (1242), 113 (1307), 137 (1314), 162 (1288), 176v (1296), 182v (1248), 187v (1227), 213 (1318), 225 (1317), 238 (1287), 246 (1286), 248v (1224), 252v (1297), 267 (1304), 276 (1317), 297v (1306), 322v (1316), 336 (1284), 343 (1297), 368 (1287), 376 (1279). For the last two sections, see below, nn. 127–30.

125. The evidence from the quodlibets is treated in chapter 2; that from his books, in chapter 3.

126. Fols. 382–84v (royal), 386–99 (papal).

127. Fol. 384v.

128. Cf. *Archives départementales de l'Oise: Répertoire numérique de la série H*, col. 144 (H 5190).

129. For Boniface's omnibus confirmation, fol. 398v. For the additional grants, fols. 398v–99.

130. Fol. 399: "Clemens V. Qui confirmat omnia privilegia nobis concessi tam a sede apostolica quam a regibus et principibus et personis aliis quibuscumque." Cf. *Regestum Clementis Papae V*, vol. 4, nos. 4419, 4421, 4435–36.

131. Above, chapter 5, pp. 86–88, 92–97.

CHAPTER 5
OLD FIGHTS AND NEW: FROM EXEMPTION TO *USUS PAUPER*

1. On the princely role, see Valois, "Jacques Duèse," pp. 404–5.

2. For brief assessments of his life and character, see Lambert, *Medieval Heresy*, pp. 200–203, and Heft, *John XXII*, pp. 1–13.

3. Heft, *John XXII*, p. 5.

4. The comprehensive study is Noël Valois's, "Jacques Duèse."

5. Heft, *John XXII*, p. 2.

6. Valois, "Jacques Duèse," pp. 520–28.

7. Mollat, *Papes d'Avignon*, p. 46; Heft, *John XXII*, p. 13; Valois, "Jacques Duèse," p. 407.

8. Mollat, *Papes d'Avignon*, pp. 46–47; Heft, *John XXII*, pp. 1, 11–13.

9. Cf. Given, *Inquisition and Medieval Society*, p. 14.

10. *Regestum Clementis Papae V*, 5:437–38, no. 6334. For other examples and pertinent references, but not involving the future pope, see, also from late 1310, 5:446–47, no. 6343; from May and June 1311, 6:120–21, 449–50, nos. 6771, 7575–76.

11. Schimmelpfennig, "Zisterzienser, Papsttum und Episkopat," p. 80.

12. Mahn, *Le Pape Benoît XII*, p. 7.

13. "Un Plaidoyer," p. 359.

14. On Abbot Simon, see *GC*, vol. 12, col. 448, and above, pp. 86–87.

15. "Un Plaidoyer," p. 359: "deliberatione prehabita, super his faceremus."

16. The edition: ibid., pp. 359–68. The two summaries: ibid., pp. 352–59 (with the quotation, "un petit chef-d'oeuvre," at 353), and Valois, "Jacques de Thérines," pp. 211–18. Mahn, *Le Pape Benoît XII*, p. 7, called the response to John XXII's questions "célèbre et adroite," a judgment that exaggerated its fame in Mahn's time, but not its quality (also pp. 8, 16). Valois ("Jacques de Thérines," p. 212) maintained that the report was "un souvenir précieux de l'éloquence de l'abbé de Chaalis." See also Buczek, "Medieval Taxation," pp. 98–99. King's judgment (*Finances of the Cistercian Order*, pp. 94–96) is somewhat more critical.

17. For an assessment of his character and the quotation, see Valois, "Jacques Duèse," pp. 406–7.

18. "Un Plaidoyer," p. 360: "inter potestates vero decentissime ordinates a Deo in ecclesiastica ierarchia, vobis sit concessa potestas in gradu altissimo et sublimissimo, quia in plenitudine potestatis."

19. Ibid.: "Cysterciensis autem Ordo vobis immediate subjacere noscitur."

20. Ibid.: "per vestram Sanctitatem juxta vestram oculatam prudenciam, que videt oculis linceis et viget facie aquilari." On medieval interpretations of the lynx, see Malaxecheverria, "Castor et lynx médiévaux," pp. 231–35.

21. "Un Plaidoyer," pp. 360–61.

22. Valois thought that the word *interdum* in the description of the frequency of the choir monks' manual labor, which he translated as *parfois* (sometimes) rather than as *entre-temps* (in the meantime), had to be taken as evidence that the Cistercians had fallen dangerously far away from their ideals, and that Jacques should have welcomed reformation of the sort the order underwent in the seventeenth century. Cf. Valois, "Jacques de Thérines," pp. 213, 218. This seems a forced interpretation. All the abbot intended to say was that in the intervals between prayer and celebrating the divine office, the monks worked. A twelfth-century Cistercian would have made precisely the same statement, even though twelfth-century choir monks spent more and longer intervals at manual labor.

23. "Un Plaidoyer," p. 361: "Et hec fuit una causa quare Gregorius decimus exemit per privilegium speciale Cysterciensem Ordinem ab omnibus exactionibus et decimis extraordinariis quibuscumque."

24. Ibid.

25. Ibid.

26. Ibid., pp. 362–64.

27. Ibid., p. 364: "Nec negamus quin in nostro Ordine, ut dictum est, sint aliqui defectus particulares."

28. Ibid.: "per quam [reformacionem] possent ad eternam beatitudinem felicius et efficacius pervenire."

29. Above, chapter 3, pp. 46–47.

30. "Un Plaidoyer," pp. 364–65.

31. Ibid., p. 365.

32. *Regestum Clementis Papae V*, vol. 4, no. 4423 (dated 4 September 1309).

33. "Un Plaidoyer," p. 365. For a superb analysis of the overall costs of this war to the French and English governments and the contributions of various groups to the war coffers, see Strayer, "Costs and Profits of War," pp. 269–91. The Cistercians' 60,000 l. contribution to the French cause was a drop in the bucket, less than 3.5 percent of the war's total cost, 1,735,000 l., for the French (p. 272). For the Crusade against Aragon that the French fought in 1285, as a basis of comparison, total expenditures on the French side were 1,228,666 l., of which 75,000, or nearly 6 percent, were assessed on the Cistercians; Strayer, "Crusade against Aragon," pp. 107–8, and Buczek, "Medieval Taxation," pp. 66–68.

34. Favier, *Philippe le Bel*, p. 194.

35. Above, chapter 1, p. 4.

36. "Un Plaidoyer," p. 365.

37. Ibid., p. 366.

38. Ibid.: "gentes Regis et principum aliorum accipiebant indifferenter per domos nostri ordinis equos, boves et oves, blada et vina, ita quod vix necessaria victui relinquebant; et plures abbatie in locis guerrarum funditus sunt destructe."

39. Ibid., p. 367.

40. Ibid., p. 365. On the services performed by the cardinal protectors at the Roman curia, see Lekai, *Cistercians*, p. 74.

41. "Un Plaidoyer," p. 365.

42. King, *Finances of the Cistercian Order*, pp. 95–96. Valois, "Jacques de Thérines," pp. 216–17 nn. 3–4, provides a summary of Cistercian tenths paid to the French crown.

43. King, *Finances of the Cistercian Order*, p. 96.

44. Jordan, *Great Famine*, pp. 19–21.

45. These matters were raised in the General Chapter as early as 1304, a meeting that Abbot Simon of Pontigny would have attended; cf. Valois, "Jacques de Thérines," p. 215 n. 4.

46. Jordan, *Great Famine*, pp. 79, 83–85.

47. Kusman, "Jean de Mirabello," pp. 919–20; Jordan, *Great Famine*, pp. 67–69, 85; Valois, "Jacques de Thérines," p. 217 n. 2. See also Goodrich, "White Ladies," p. 138.

48. Above, pp. 60–61.

49. Jordan, *Great Famine*, p. 75; Blachon, "Des Cisterciens aux seigneurs laïques," pp. 165–67.

50. "Un Plaidoyer," p. 366.

51. Jordan, *Great Famine*, pp. 15–19, 24–39.

52. King, *Finances of the Cistercian Order*, p. 96.

53. Jordan, *Great Famine*, pp. 70–71.

54. Ibid., pp. 65, 110.

55. Ibid., p. 73.

56. Courtenay, *Parisian Scholars*, p. 41 n. 28.

57. King, *Finances of the Cistercian Order*, p. 96.

58. See the list appended to ibid., pp. 207–25.

59. Cf. Buczek, "Medieval Taxation," pp. 66–68. On the number of nunneries, see Dimier, "Liste des abbayes cisterciennes féminines," pp. 591–94, who lists 138, of which 134 were in existence by 1300. Cf. King, *Finances of the Cistercian Order*, p. 146.

60. "Un Plaidoyer," p. 365.

61. Ibid.

62. Redoutey, "Note sur l'insertion de l'abbaye de Bellevaux," p. 733.

63. Mate, "Coping with Inflation," pp. 95–106 (summarized in Jordan, *Great Famine*, p. 77).

64. "Un Plaidoyer," p. 365: "Et nec imputetur malo regimini ministrorum."

65. Ibid., pp. 366–67.

66. Ibid., p. 366; Valois, "Jacques de Thérines," p. 216 n. 1.

67. "Un Plaidoyer," p. 368. The General Chapter expressed its displeasure with alienation; Valois, "Jacques de Thérines," p. 217 n. 4.

68. Cf. Jordan, *From Servitude to Freedom*, p. 32.

69. *Narrative and Legislative Texts from Early Cîteaux*, p. 463.

70. On John XXII's devotion to the Virgin, see Valois, "Jacques Duèse," pp. 530–31 (cf. p. 422).

71. "Un Plaidoyer," p. 368.

72. Ibid.

73. Ibid.

74. Mollat, *Papes d'Avignon*, pp. 77–78.

75. Valois, "Jacques Duèse," p. 406 (his tomb was opened in modern times and revealed the diminutive stature of the man).

76. *Lettres communes de Jean XXII*, vol. 2, nos. 5950 (the rapine of *nefandissimi*), 6111 (nuns seek former Templar property); Courtenay, *Parisian Scholars*, p. 41 n. 28 (masters' request); Jordan, *Great Famine*, pp. 67–69, 72 (examples of crushing indebtedness, alienation, and permission to offer annuities).

77. *GC*, vol. 12, col. 448: "Hîc tumulata patris pariter sunt ossaque matris / Simonis abbatis, quos jungas, Christe, beatis."

78. Cf. Lawrence, *Medieval Monasticism*, p. 157.

79. Cf. Peyrafort-Huin, *Bibliothèque médiévale de l'abbaye de Pontigny*, who, though hesitant as to why Jacques was chosen, notes the strong connection between the two abbeys (pp. 118 n. 10 and 168).

80. For most of the following information on the life and cult of Edmund, see Jordan, "Edmund of Abingdon, St."

81. Benoit, "Autour des tombeaux," p. 34.

82. Dimier, "Henri II, Thomas Becket et les cisterciens," pp. 733–36; idem, *Saint Louis et Cîteaux*, p. 114; Benoit, "Autour des tombeaux," pp. 34–38.

83. For a thematic treatment of Edmund's Marian devotions in relation to those of other *fideles*, see Elliott, *Fallen Bodies*, p. 114.

84. A remarkably fine study of Pontigny, given its date (1844), is Chaillou des Barres, "Pontigny," pp. 105–212.

85. King, *Finances of the Cistercian Order*, pp. 61, 210.

86. Bruzelius, "Transept of the Abbey Church of Châalis," pp. 447–54; Kinder, "Toward Dating Construction of the Abbey Church of Pontigny," pp. 77–88. See also Fontaine, *Pontigny*, pp. 58, 134.

87. Auxerre, AD: Yonne, H 1532, parchment document dated January 1295, with paper transcription of the seventeenth century.

88. Auxerre, AD: Yonne, H 1502, parchment document dated October 1287.

89. *Inventaire-Sommaire . . .: Yonne . . ., série H*, 3, pt. 2, pp. 329, 416.

90. In addition to those just cited, an impressive number of original charters and copies survive, including the cartulary of Pontigny, from which to piece together Simon's administration: see, for example, the array of documents in Auxerre, AD: Yonne, H 1532, and those inventoried in the *Inventaire-Sommaire . . .: Yonne . . ., série H*, 3, pt. 2, pp. 323–24, 326–27, 334, 339, 392, 395, 402, 416, 425–26. The original cartulary dated the year before Jacques de Thérines's accession to the headship of the abbey is Paris, BNF, MS latin 5465.

91. See, for example, Paris, BNF, MS latin 5465, fol. 94–94v, for the most recent of these (1317) before Jacques's abbacy. (Also, *Inventaire-Sommaire . . .: Yonne . . ., série H*, 3, pt. 2, pp. 323, 339, 395.)

92. Benoit, "Autour des tombeaux," pp. 33–70.

93. One has to make a distinction here between the monks who had charge of the relics and the men who saw to their display before the lay faithful, a distinction that Benoit (ibid., p. 54), is insufficiently clear about.

94. Ibid., n. 109.

95. Ibid., nn. 111 and 112: "cum . . . reportassent ad domum suam de consilio monachorum propter nimium frigus quod tunc erat," implying that it was the choir monks' decision, but it was the *custodes* who transmitted the advice to the faithful ("a custodibus reliquiarum est admonita").

96. On the *diffinitores*, whose establishment in the mid–thirteenth century was deeply resented by those favoring a more monarchical organization of the order, one emphasizing the abbot of Cîteaux's authority, see *Pour une histoire monumentale de l'abbaye de Cîteaux*, p. 154; Lekai, *Cistercians*, pp. 70–71; and Lawrence, *Medieval Monasticism*, pp. 159–60.

97. Lawrence, *Medieval Monasticism*, p. 157.

98. King, *Finances of the Cistercian Order*, p. 60.

99. I have somewhat simplified the description of this process. For a fuller treatment, see King, *Finances of the Cistercian Order*, pp. 60–62, 77.

100. Ibid., p. 8.

101. Ibid., pp. 11 (for the quotation), 62.

102. Ibid., pp. 210–11, lists the male monasteries in the filiation.

103. Above, chapter 3, p. 51.

104. Menache, *Clement V*, p. 295.

105. Nimmo, *Reform and Division*, pp. 123–34.

106. Burr, *Spiritual Franciscans*, p. 91; Nimmo, *Reform and Division*, pp. 137–38.

107. Nimmo, *Reform and Division*, pp. 100, 121; Burr, *Spiritual Franciscans*, p. 119. For the rather vague description of the habit in the Franciscan Rule of 1223, see *Regular Life*, p. 69.

108. Besides the habit, disputes involved the nature of the shoes worn, the proper amount of food eaten, size and ornateness of buildings, etc.; Burr, *Spiritual Franciscans*, pp. 116–26. Further on *usus pauper*, above, chapter 3, pp. 50–51.

109. Above, chapter 3, p. 51.

110. On the collapse of the Clementine settlement, see Burr, *Spiritual Franciscans*, pp. 159–77.

111. On John XXII's hostility, see Nimmo, *Reform and Division*, p. 135, and for a more comprehensive analysis of the context of John's views, Burr, *Spiritual Franciscans*, pp. 179–90.

112. Burr, *Spiritual Franciscans*, pp. 196–98.

113. "Unity," as in Nimmo, *Reform and Division*, p. 137, not "chastity."

114. Burr, *Spiritual Franciscans*, p. 197.

115. Ibid. On the command of obedience to the pontiff and Francis's successors in the Franciscan Rule, see *Regular Life*, p. 68.

116. Valois, "Jacques Duèse," pp. 432–33. The date, more precise than Valois's, is taken from Bihl, "Formulae et documentae," pp. 118–19, and is based on his careful collating of the terms of office of the commissioners, when these are ascertainable.

117. On John XXII's increasing frustration with the Spirituals' intransigence at this time, see Valois, "Jacques Duèse," pp. 426–33.

118. Burr, *Spiritual Franciscans*, p. 277.

119. For the commissioners, see *CUP*, 2:216–18, including the notes. Cf. Menache, *Clement V*, pp. 45 and 295 on Berengarius and Vitalis (Vidal).

120. Above, chapter 3, pp. 48–50.

121. Above, chapter 3, p. 51.

122. *CUP*, 2:215–16, no. 760. See also Burr, *Spiritual Franciscans*, pp. 197–98.

123. *CUP*, 2:216, no. 760.

124. Ibid., 216–17, no. 760.

125. Ibid., 217, no. 760.

126. Burr, *Spiritual Franciscans*, p. 204; Nimmo, *Reform and Division*, p. 138.

127. Burr, *Spiritual Franciscans*, p. 205.

128. Ibid., p. 206; Nimmo, *Reform and Division*, p. 138.

129. Lebeuf, *Mémoires*, 1:495–96, 4:162–63.

130. Ibid., 4:163.

131. Ibid.

132. Valois, "Jacques de Thérines," p. 183.

133. Since at least 1170 the oaths sworn included the words that offended Jacques de Thérines; Lebeuf, *Mémoires*, 1:496 n. 1.

134. For the locution "Nostre Dame de Saint Edme de Pontigny," see the various charters and transcriptions in Auxerre, AD: Yonne, H 1444.

135. Auxerre, AD: Yonne, H 1444, eighteenth-century paper copy of the document dated 1290.

136. Auxerre, AD: Yonne, H 1444, parchment original with paper transcription attached, with contemporary markings on reverse of the parchment beginning, "Instru[mentum] baillivi trec[ensis] quod prepositus sancti florentini ne piscaret. . . ."

137. The *liasse* in question is Auxerre, AD: Yonne, H 1444.

138. Lebeuf, *Mémoires*, 1:492–94.

139. Ibid., 4:163–64.

140. Ibid., 1:492–93, 4:164.

141. Ibid., 4:164. See also Moreau, "Abbaye Saint-Marien d'Auxerre," p. 125.

142. For this and the other information and quotations in this paragraph, see Lebeuf, *Mémoires*, 1:493, and 4:164. See also Valois, "Jacques de Thérines," p. 183.

143. Lebeuf, *Mémoires*, 4:163: "ubi principalius ejusdem sanctissimi pontificis [Amatoris] suffragia pia devotione fidelium implorari deberent."

144. So the notary signed along with the seals "dominorum Autissiodorensium episcoporum et abbatum predictorum"; Lebeuf, *Mémoires*, 4:165.

145. Ibid.: "ubique debent a Christi fidelibus venerari, ac etiam ad laudem et honorem Dei omnipotentis, B. Marie Virginis ac omnium sanctorum in dicta ecclesia [Autissiodorensi] exaltari."

146. Kinder, *Cistercian Europe*, pp. 51–55.

147. *Pour une histoire monumentale de l'abbaye de Cîteaux*, p. 154.

148. Cf. Lawrence, *Medieval Monasticism*, p. 159.

149. Auxerre, AD: Yonne, H 683, parchment manuscript dated 1319 with paper summary. The abbots of Prully, Vauluisant, Barbeau, La Colombe, and Varennes acquire a pied-à-terre in the Cistercian house in Dijon: "Notum facimus quod nos [Abbot Guillaume of Cîteaux] vendidisse et imperpetuum quitavisse eiusdem camere tempore capituli generalis in domo nostra divione." Abbot Guillaume added, "Et omnibus aliis quos sibi voluerint in dicta camera sociare pro quinquagenta libris tur. nobis a dictis venerabilibus coabbatibus nostris prenominatis iam solutis integraliter."

150. See Pope Clement V's excoriation in May 1312 of a group of Cistercian abbots in England, whose refusal to attend the costly meeting reached his ears (and so soon after he had upheld Jacques de Thérines's defense of exemption at Vienne); *Regestum Clementis Papae V*, 7:313–14, no. 8818.

151. Auxerre, AD: Yonne, H 1502, document dated 1320, marked on reverse in a fourteenth-century hand, "Transcriptum de venditione domus sancti Bernardi paris[iensis]."

152. The confirmation and these provisions are in the *vidimus* of the guard of the *prévôté* of Paris in Auxerre, AD: Yonne, H 1502, dated 1320, which has provided the information on the alienation.

EPILOGUE
UNCEASING STRIFE, UNENDING FEAR

1. Jordan, "Home Again," p. 32, and above, chapter 4, pp. 55–56.

2. Cf. Assis, "Juifs de France réfugiés," p. 310.

3. Jordan, "Home Again," pp. 32–33.

4. Ibid., p. 34; Lehugeur, *Philippe le Long*, pp. 381, 395–97.

5. Lehugeur, *Philippe le Long*, pp. 380–81, is rather more enthusiastic about the intent and implicitly the effect of Philip V's efforts to ameliorate the conditions of rural life, but he goes into little detail. The issues require further study for a definitive answer.

6. Jordan, "Home Again," p. 36.

7. Lehugeur, *Philippe le Long*, p. 417; Jordan, *Great Famine*, p. 170.

8. Cf. Lehugeur, *Philippe le Long*, pp. 194–99.

9. For a critique of cynical appraisals of Philip V's motives, see Tyerman, "Philip V," pp. 15–34.

10. Cf. Beaune, "Messianesimo regio e messianesimo popolare in Francia," pp. 114–36.

11. Barber, "Pastoureaux of 1320," pp. 165–66.

12. Cf. Kerov, *Narodnye vosstaniia*, p. 42.

13. Cf. the so-called *Chronicle of John Somer*, p. 272, a fourteenth-century compilation, a manuscript of which Somer, an English Franciscan, owned and annotated, and which was later redacted by other copyists; under 1320, "Collacio pastorum et ignobilium et dixerunt quod transmeaverunt et subito mutuarunt proprium et transcenderunt vias suas."

14. Challe, *Histoire de l'Auxerrois*, p. 280.

15. *Actes du Parlement de Paris*, 2:473, no. 6904.

16. Barber, "Pastoureaux of 1320," pp. 143–66, and Lehugeur, *Philippe le Long*, pp. 417–21. See also Jordan, "Home Again," p. 37.

17. Valois, "Jacques Duèse," pp. 421–25.

18. On the repression, see Jordan, *French Monarchy and the Jews*, p. 244, and Nirenberg, *Communities of Violence*, pp. 71–77.

19. Lehugeur, *Philippe le Long*, pp. 421–29.

20. Cf. Collard, "Recherches sur le crime de poison," pp. 107–8; cf. idem, "*Veneficiis vel maleficiis*," pp. 9–57.

21. Cf. Collard, "L'Empereur et le poison," pp. 113–32.

22. This is Lehugeur's paraphrase in *Philippe le Long*, pp. 422–23.

23. One of the best discussions of the interplay of fears of leprosy and lepers with political and social tensions may be found in Nirenberg, *Communities of Violence*, pp. 92–124. See also Jeanne, "Société rurale face à la lèpre," pp. 91–106. For more general and more comprehensive background on lepers, leprosy, and leper houses in France in the Middle Ages, see Bériou and Touati, *Voluntate Dei Leprosus*, and Bériac, *Histoire des lépreux*.

24. Jordan, *French Monarchy and the Jews*, p. 245. The author/annotator of the *Chronicle of John Somer*, p. 272, noted matter-of-factly that every leper in the southwestern part of the French kingdom was killed in 1321: "Omnes leprosi acquitainie fuerunt combusti."

25. In a testament of 1190 published in Quantin, *Cartulaire général*, 2:424–25, no. 420, reference is made to "viginti domibus leprosorum que sunt inter Trecas et Pontiniacum." (See also Bouvier, "Histoire de l'assistance publique," p. 240, although he provides an incorrect date.) A later testament, from 1276, reveals another concentration of these institutions in the region; Quantin, *Recueil*, pp. 348–49, no. 690.

26. See the record indicated in the *Inventaire-Sommaire des Archives de l'Hôpital de Sens*, vol. 5, no. 3759.

27. Nirenberg, *Communities of Violence*, p. 93.

28. Lehugeur, *Philippe le Long*, p. 425.

29. Moiset, "Ancienne maladrerie de Saint-Florentin," pp. 192, 194, but cf. idem, "Notice sur l'Hôtel-Dieu de Saint-Florentin," p. 4.

30. *Inventaire-sommaire . . .: Yonne . . ., série H, supplément*, 4:cxii.

31. *Actes du Parlement de Paris*, 2:420, no. 6661: "Mandamus vobis [Champenois *baillis*, among others] . . . quod confessiones leprosorum qui alios judeos super venenosis pocionibus aquarum et aliis criminibus . . . ut dicitur accusarunt."

32. Lehugeur, *Philippe le Long*, pp. 428–29.

33. Jordan, *French Monarchy and the Jews*, p. 246.

34. Jordan, "Home Again," p. 38.

35. Lehugeur, *Philippe le Long*, p. 428.

36. On Jacques's rejection of killing Jews, see above, chapter 1, p. 14.

37. I argued for 1322 in *French Monarchy and the Jews*, pp. 246–47, and it is the date provided by a near-contemporary Flemish chronicler (*Chronique de Jean de Hocsem*, pp. 169–70), though the editor of the text, for reasons that are unclear, questions the accuracy. The same chronicler is quite precise about the earlier expulsion of 1306 (p. 121). See also Mentgen, *Studien zur Geschichte*, p. 83 n. 38, and idem, "Vertreibungen der Juden," p. 50. Brown, "Philip V, Charles IV," pp. 294–329, has argued against any such expulsion's having taken place (at least until 1327).

38. Cf. above, chapter 1, pp. 15–16.

39. Valois, "Jacques de Thérines," p. 184.

40. Oudin, *Commentarius*, fol. 730: "Quem tenet hic fundus, Doctor fuit iste profundus, / Sanctus ut Edmundus fuit absque libidine mundus: / Istius Ecclesiae Pater et fons Theologiae / Vitae norma piae, fervens in amore Mariae. / *Cum duplex Jacobus sic fertur ad astra talentis.* / In testamentis praeclarus scriba duobus / Centum ter decies, septem ter, lumine Lucae. / Migrans ab hac luce: sit sibi, Christe, quies." Most authorities give this or a defective form of the epitaph without the simile on spiritual aspirations (italicized in the quotation); cf. Fabricius, *Bibliotheca latina*, 4:310. Only a fragment of the epitaph survives at Pontigny; Peyrafort-Huin, *Bibliothèque médiévale de l'abbaye de Pontigny*, p. 648.

41. "Regum mansiones et itinera," *HF*, 21:487.

42. Lehugeur, *Philippe le Long*, p. 466, and Brown, "Ceremonial of Royal Succession," p. 272.

43. Rouse and Rouse, "Publishing Watriquet's *Dits*," p. 152.

44. *GC*, vol. 10, col. 1512.

45. "Regum mansiones et itinera," *HF*, 21:487.

46. On the nature of King Charles's sojourn, see Longnon, *Documents relatifs au Comté de Champagne*, 2:526 n. 1.

47. Manuscript copies of various of his works may be found in Dijon, Heiligenkreuz, Lille, Paris, Troyes, the Vatican, Vienna, Wolfenbüttel, and Würzburg; Glorieux, *Répertoire des maîtres*, 2:262–63. Of course, the present distribution is only suggestive, at best. The Würzburg manuscript, for example, is of French provenance; Peyrafort-Huin, *Bibliothèque médiévale de l'abbaye de Pontigny*, p. 154.

BIBLIOGRAPHY

PRIMARY SOURCES

Manuscripts

AUXERRE

Archives Départementales (AD), H 321, 489, 683, 1444, 1502, 1532 (the individual manuscripts consulted in these bundles are fully identified in the notes).

DIJON

Bibliothèque Municipale (BM), MS 339 (248), Jacques de Thérines, *Contra impugnatores exemptionum, etc.*

PARIS

Bibliothèque Nationale Française (BNF), MS latin 5465, Cartulary of Pontigny.
BNF, MS latin 9217, *Cartae Dioec. Aurelian. Bituricen. Lemovicen.*
BNF, MS latin 11003, Cartulary of Chaalis.

VIENNA

Österreichische Nationalbibliothek (ÖNB), MS 4257, Albertus Magnus, *Liber de abundantia exemplorum*; . . . Jacobus de Thermis [*sic*: Therinis], *Tractatus de exemptionibus*; etc.

Printed

Actes du Parlement de Paris. Ed. Edgar Boutaric. 2 vols. Paris: Henri Plon, 1863–1867.
Annales ecclesiastici. Ed. Cesare Baronio and Théophile Raynaud. 38 vols. Lucca: Typis Leonardi Venturini, 1738–1759.
Aquinas, Thomas. *Opera Omnia*. Rome: Typographia Polyglotta S. C. de Propaganda Fide, 1882–.
———. *Quodlibetal Questions 1 and 2*. Trans. Sandra Edwards. Toronto: Pontifical Institute of Mediaeval Studies, 1983.
Barber, Malcolm, and Keith Bate, trans. *The Templars: Selected Sources Translated and Annotated*. Manchester: Manchester University Press, 2002.
Carolus-Barré, Louis, comp. *Le Procès de canonisation de saint Louis (1272–1297): Essai de reconstitution*. Rome: Ecole Française de Rome, 1994.
"Cartulaire de l'abbaye de Notre-Dame de la Merci-Dieu, autrement dite de Bécheron au diocèse de Poitiers." *Archives historiques du Poitou* 34 (1905): i–xxiv, 1–454.

Chartularium Universitatis Parisiensis. Ed. Heinrich (Henri) Denifle and Emile Chatelain. 4 vols. Paris: Delalain Frères, 1889–1894.

Chronicle of John Somer, OFM. Ed. Jeremy Catto and Linne Mooney. Camden Miscellany, 5th ser., 10:197–285.

Chronique de Jean de Hocsem. Ed. Godefroid Kurth. Brussels: Kiessling, 1927.

Comptes du trésor (1296, 1316, 1384, 1477). Ed. Robert Fawtier. Paris: Imprimerie nationale, 1930.

Comptes royaux. Ed. Robert Fawtier. 3 vols. Paris: Imprimerie Nationale, 1953–1956.

Corpus Iuris Canonici. Ed. Emil Friedberg. 2 vols. Graz: Akademische Druck- und Verlaganstalt, 1955.

CUP. See *Chartularium Universitatis Parisiensis.*

Dupuy, Pierre. *Histoire du differend d'entre le pape Boniface VIII. et Philippes le Bel, roy de France.* Paris, 1655. Reprint, Tucson, AZ: Audax Press, 1963.

Ebendorfer, Thomas. *Chronica pontificum romanorum.* Ed. Harald Zimmermann. Munich: Monumenta Germaniae Historica, 1994.

Fabricius, Johann, ed. *Bibliotheca latina mediae et infimae aetatis.* 6 vols. Florence: T. Baracchi et figlio, 1858–1859.

Field, Sean, ed. and trans. *The Writings of Agnes of Harcourt: The Life of Isabelle of France and the Letter on Louis IX and Longchamp.* Notre Dame, IN: University of Notre Dame Press, 2003.

Fussenegger, Geroldus, ed. "Relatio commissionis in concilio Viennensi institutae ad decretalem 'Exivi de paradiso' praeparandam." *Archivum franciscanum historicum* 50 (1957): 145–77.

Gallia christiana in provincias ecclesiasticas distributa. 16 vols. Paris: V. Palme, etc., 1856–1899.

GC. See *Gallia christiana.*

Giles of Rome (Aegidus Romanus). *On Ecclesiastical Power.* Trans. Arthur Monahan. Lewiston, ME: Edward Mellen Press, 1990.

———. *On Ecclesiastical Power.* Trans. Robert Dyson. Woodbridge, UK: Boydell Press, 1986.

———. *Opera Omnia.* Ed. Barbara Faes de Mottoni et al. Florence: Leo S. Olschki, 1985–.

HF. See *Recueil des historiens.*

Jacques de Thérines. *Quodlibets I et II.* Ed. Palémon Glorieux. Paris: J. Vrin, 1958.

Lettres communes de Jean XXII. Ed. G. Mollat et al. 17 vols. Paris: E. de Boccard, etc., 1904–1947.

Lettres de Jean XXII (1316–1334). Vol. 1, *1316–1324.* Ed. Arnold Fayen. Rome: M. Bretschneider, 1908.

Lizerand, Georges, trans. *Le Dossier de l'affaire des Templiers.* Bologna: Axiome Editions, 1999.

Longnon, Auguste, ed. *Document relatifs au Comté de Champagne et de Brie.* 3 vols. Paris: Imprimerie nationale, 1901–1914.

Narrative and Legislative Texts from Early Cîteaux. Ed. Chrysogonus Waddell. Nuits-Saint-Georges: Abbaye de Cîteaux, 1999.

Patrologiae cursus completus, series latina. Comp. Jacques-Paul Migne. 217 vols. Paris: [Ateliers Catholiques,] 1844–1864.

PL. See *Patrologiae cursus completus.*

"Un Plaidoyer du XIVe siècle en faveur des Cisterciens." Ed. Noël Valois. *Bibliothèque de l'Ecole de Chartes* 69 (1908): 352–68.

Porete, Marguerite. *Margareta Porete Speculum simplicium animarum.* Ed. Paul Verdeyen. Corpus Christianorum: Continuatio Medievalis, 69. Turnhout: Brepols, 1986.

———. *A Mirror for Simple Souls: The Mystical Work of Marguerite Porete.* Ed. and trans. Charles Crawford. New York: Crossroad, 1990.

———. *Mirror of Simple Souls.* Trans. Ellen Babinsky. New York and Mahwah, NJ: Paulist Press, 1993.

Porette [= Porete, variant spelling], Margaret. *Mirror of Simple Souls.* Trans. Edmund Colledge et al. Notre Dame, IN: University of Notre Dame Press, 1999.

Quantin, [Mathieu-]Maximilien, ed. *Cartulaire générale de l'Yonne.* 2 vols. Auxerre: Perriquet, 1854–1860.

———, ed. *Recueil de pièces pour faire suite au Cartulaire général de l'Yonne.* Auxerre: Société des Sciences Historiques et Naturelles de l'Yonne, 1873.

Recueil des historiens des Gaules et de la France. Ed. Martin Bouquet et al. 24 vols. Paris: V. Palmé, 1840–1904.

Regestum Clementis Papae V. 9 vols. and supplement. Rome: Bibliothèque de l'Ecoles françaises d'Athènes et de Rome, 1884–1892.

Regular Life: Monastic, Canonical, and Mendicant Rules. Ed. Douglas McMillan and Kathryn Fladenmuller. Kalamazoo, MI: Medieval Institute Publications, 1997.

Sanderus, Antoine [Antonius]. *Bibliotheca belgica manuscripta.* Lille, 1641–1644. Reprint, Brussels: Archives et Bibliothèques de Belgique, 1972.

Tierney, Brian, trans. *The Crisis of Church and State, 1050–1300.* Englewood Cliffs, NJ: Prentice-Hall, 1964.

Upton-Ward, J. M., trans. *The Rule of the Templars.* Woodbridge, UK: Boydell Press, 1992.

Weltchronik des mönchs Albert 1273/77–1454/56. Ed. Rolf Sprandel. Munich: Monumenta Germaniae Historica, 1994.

SECONDARY SOURCES (OFTEN WITH PRIMARY TEXTS INCLUDED)

Anheim, Etienne, et al. "Rome et les jubilés du XIVe siècle: Histoires immédiates." *Médiévales* 40 (2001): 53–82.

Arbois de Jubainville, Marie Henri d'. *Etudes sur l'état intérieur des abbayes cisterciennes et principalement de Clairvaux au XIIe et XIIIe siècles.* Paris: Auguste Durand, 1858.

Archives départementales de l'Oise: Répertoire numérique de la série H. Beauvais: Imprimerie Centrale Administrative, 1942.

Artonne, André. *Le Mouvement de 1314 et les chartes provincials de 1315.* Paris: Félix Alcan, 1912.

Assis, Yom Tov. "Les Juifs de France réfugiés en Aragon (XIIIe–XIVe siècles)." *Revue des études juives* 142 (1983): 284–322.

———. "Les Juifs de Montpellier sous la domination aragonaise." *Revue des études juives* 148 (1989): 5–16.

Baldwin, John. *The Government of Philip Augustus*. Berkeley and Los Angeles: University of California Press, 1986.

———. "Masters at Paris from 1179 to 1215: A Social Perspective." In *Renaissance and Renewal in the Twelfth Century*, ed. Robert Benson and Giles Constable, pp. 138–72. Cambridge: Harvard University Press, 1982.

Bande, Alexandre. "Philippe le Bel, le coeur et le sentiment dynastique." *Micrologus* 11 (2003): 267–78.

Barber, Malcolm. *The New Knighthood: A History of the Order of the Temple*. Cambridge: Cambridge University Press, 1994.

———. "The Pastoureaux of 1320." *Journal of Ecclesiastical History* 32 (1981): 143–66.

———. *The Trial of the Templars*. Cambridge: Cambridge University Press, 1978.

Barone, Giulia. "Le Clergé romain et le jubilé." *Médiévales* 40 (2001): 23–28.

Baudon de Mony, Charles. "La Mort et les funérailles de Philippe le Bel d'après un compte rendu à la cour de Majorque." *Bibliothèque de l'Ecole de Chartes* 58 (1897): 5–14.

Beaune, Colette. "Messianesimo regio e messianesimo popolare in Francia nel XIII secolo." In *Poteri carismatici e informali: Chiesa e società medioevali*, ed. Agostino Paravicini Baglioni and André Vauchez, pp. 114–36. Palermo: Sellerio, 1992.

———. *Naissance de la nation France*. Paris: Gallimard, 1985.

———. "Les Rois maudits." *Cahiers du Centre d'Etudes Médiévales* (Nice), no. 12 (1992): 2–24.

Benoit, Jean-Luc. "Autour des tombeaux de saint Edme à Pontigny au milieu du XIIIe siècle." *Bulletin de la Société des Sciences Historiques et Naturelles de l'Yonne* 133 (2001): 33–70.

Bériac, Françoise. *Histoire des lépreux au moyen âge: Une Société d'exclus*. Paris: Imago, 1988.

Bériou, Nicole, and François-Olivier Touati. *Voluntate Dei Leprosus: Les Léproux entre conversion et exclusion aux XIIème et XIIIème siècles*. Spoleto: Centro Italiano di Studi sull'Alto Medioevo, 1991.

Bianchi, Luca. *Censure et liberté intellectuelle à l'université de Paris (XIIIe–XIVe siècles)*. Paris: Les Belles Lettres, 1999.

Bihl, Michael. "Formulae et documentae e cancellaria Fr. Michaelis de Cesena, O.F.M., Ministri Generalis, 1316–1328." *Archivum franciscanum historicum* 23 (1930): 106–71.

Biller, Peter. *The Measure of Multitude: Population in Medieval Thought*. Oxford: Oxford University Press, 2000.

———. "Views of Jews from Paris around 1300: Christian or 'Scientific.'" In *Christianity and Judaism*, ed. Diana Wood, pp. 187–207. Oxford: Oxford University Press, 1992.

Blachon, Jérôme. "Des Cisterciens aux seigneurs laïques: Histoire de la ferme d'Ithe (XIIe–XVIIIe siècles)." *Paris et Ile-de-France: Mémoires* 49 (1998): 133–215.

Blary, François. *Le Domaine de Chaalis, XIIe–XIVe siècles*. Paris: Editions du C.T.H.S., 1989.

Bloch, Marc. *Rois et serfs: Un chapitre d'histoire capétienne*. Paris: E. Champion, 1920.

Boutaric, Edgar. *Clément V, Philippe le Bel et les Templiers*. Paris: Victor Palmé, 1874.

Bouvier, Henri. "Histoire de l'assistance publique dans le département de l'Yonne jusqu'en 1789." *Bulletin de la Société des Sciences Historiques et Naturelles de l'Yonne* 54 (1900): 235–318.

Brown, Elizabeth. "The Ceremonial of Royal Succession in Capetian France: The Funeral of Philip V." *Speculum* 55 (1980): 266–93.

————. "*Cessante causa* and the Taxes of the Last Capetians: The Political Applications of a Philosophical Maxim." *Studia Gratiana* 15 (1972): 565–88.

————. "Kings like Semi-Gods: The Case of Louis X of France." *Majestas* 1 (1993): 5–37.

————. "Philip V, Charles IV, and the Jews of France: The Alleged Expulsion of 1322." *Speculum* 66 (1991): 294–329.

————. "Reform and Resistance to Royal Authority in Fourteenth-Century France: The Leagues of 1314–1315." *Parliaments, Estates and Representation* 1 (1981): 109–37.

————. "Royal Salvation and Needs of State in Late Capetian France." In *Order and Innovation in the Middle Ages: Essays in Honor of Joseph R. Strayer*, ed. William Jordan, Bruce McNab, and Teofilo Ruiz, pp. 365–83, 541–61. Princeton: Princeton University Press, 1976.

Brundage, James. *Law, Sex, and Christian Society in Medieval Europe*. Chicago and London: University of Chicago Press, 1987.

Bruzelius, Caroline. "The Transept of the Abbey Church of Châalis and the Filiation of Pontigny." In *Mélanges à la mémoire du père Anselme Dimier*, 6:447–54. 6 vols. Arbois: Benoît Chauvin/Pupillin, 1982–1987.

Buczek, Daniel. "Medieval Taxation: The French Crown, the Papacy and the Cistercian Order, 1190–1320." *Analecta Cisterciensia* 25 (1969): 42–106.

————. " 'Pro defendis ordinis': The French Cistercians and Their Enemies." In *Studies in Medieval Cistercian History Presented to Jeremiah O'Sullivan*, pp. 88–109. Spencer, MA: Cistercian Publications, 1971.

Burr, David. *The Spiritual Franciscans: From Protest to Persecution in the Century after Saint Francis*. University Park: Pennsylvania State University Press, 2001.

Carolus-Barré, Louis. "Saint Louis et la translation des corps saints." In *Etudes d'histoire du droit canonique (dédiées à Gabriel Le Bras)*, 2:1087–1112. 2 vols. Paris: Sirey, 1965.

Cassidy-Welch, Megan. "Incarceration and Liberation: Prisons in the Cistercian Monastery." *Viator* 32 (2001): 23–42.

————. *Monastic Spaces and Their Meanings: Thirteenth-Century English Cistercian Monasteries*. Turnhout: Brepols, 2001.

Catalogue général des manuscrits des bibliothèques de France: Paris, Bibliothèques de l'Institut. Paris: Petits-Fils de Plon et Nourrit, 1928.

Catalogues général des manuscrits des bibliothèques publiques. Paris: Plon, 1886–.

Caudel, L. "Voie romaine de Senlis à Meaux (*Iter Fixtuinum*), 2e partie." *Comptes rendus et Mémoires du Comité archéologique de Senlis*, 2nd ser., 2 (1876): 19–23.

Chaillou des Barres, Claude-Etienne. "Pontigny." *Annuaire statistique du département de l'Yonne* 8 (1844): sec. 3, pp. 105–212.

Challe, Ambroise. *Histoire de l'Auxerrois: Son territoire, son diocèse, son comté, ses baronnies, son bailliage, et ses institutions coutumières et municipales.* Auxerre: Société des Sciences Historiques et Naturelles de l'Yonne, 1878.

Chatel, Eugène. "Notice sur l'abbaye de Chaalis (Caroli-Locus) près Senlis (Oise)." *Bulletin monumental* 8 (1842): 137–44.

Cheney, Charles. *A King of France Unnamed in History.* Chicago: Chicago Literary Club, 1902.

Chochon-Plée, Robert. "Une Curiosité archéologique: L'Eglise de l'abbaye de Loroy." In *Mélanges à la mémoire du père Anselme Dimier*, 6:479–96. 6 vols. Arbois: Benoît Chauvin/Pupillin, 1982–1987.

Collard, Franck. "L'Empereur et le poison: De la Rumeur au mythe. A propos du prétendu empoisonnement d'Henri VII en 1313." *Médiévales* 41 (2001): 113–32.

———. "*In claustro venenum*: Quelques réflexions sur l'usage du poison dans les communautés religieuses de l'Occident médiéval." *Revue de l'histoire de l'Eglise de France* 88 (2002): 5–12.

———. "Recherches sur le crime de poison au moyen âge." *Journal des savants*, January–June 1992, pp. 99–114.

———. "*Veneficiis vel maleficiis*: Réflexion sur les relations entre le crime de poison et la sorcellerie dans l'Occident médiéval." *Le Moyen Age* 109 (2003): 9–57.

Courtenay, William. "Between Pope and King: The Parisian Letters of Adhesion of 1303." *Speculum* 71 (1996): 577–605.

———. *Parisian Scholars in the Early Fourteenth Century: A Social Portrait.* Cambridge: Cambridge University Press, 1999.

Cuttler, S. H. *The Law of Treason and Treason Trials in Later Medieval France.* New York: Cambridge University Press, 1981.

Dahan, Gilbert. *Les Intellectuels chrétiens et les juifs au moyen âge.* Paris: Editions du Cerf, 1990.

Dautrey, Philippe. "L'Eglise de l'ancien Collège des Bernardins de Paris et son image." In *Mélanges à la mémoire du père Anselme Dimier*, 6:497–514. 6 vols. Arbois: Benoît Chauvin/Pupillin, 1982–1987.

D'Avray, David. *Death and the Prince: Memorial Preaching before 1350.* Oxford: Clarendon Press, 1994.

Delisle, Léopold. *Catalogue des actes de Philippe-Auguste.* Paris: A. Durand, 1856.

Demurger, Alain. *Vie et mort de l'ordre du Temple.* Paris: Editions du Seuil, 1989.

Denton, Jeffrey. *Philip the Fair and the Ecclesiastical Assemblies of 1294–1295.* Philadelphia: American Philosophical Society, 1991.

———. "Taxation and the Conflict between Philip the Fair and Boniface VIII." *French History* 11 (1997): 241–64.

Dickson, Gary. "The Crowd at the Feet of Pope Boniface VIII: Pilgrimage, Crusade and the First Roman Jubilee (1300)." *Journal of Medieval History* 25 (1999): 279–307.

Digard, Georges. *Philippe le Bel et le Saint-Siège de 1285–1304.* 2 vols. Paris: Librairie du Recueil Sirey, 1936.

Dimier, Anselme. "L'Abbaye de Châalis." In *Mélanges à la mémoire du père Anselme Dimier.* 2:639–40. 6 vols. Arbois: Benoît Chauvin/Pupillin, 1982–1987.

——. "Les Evêques cisterciens au XIIe siècle." In *Mélanges* (above), 2:529–32.

——. "Henri II, Thomas Becket et les cisterciens." In *Mélanges* (above), 2:733–36.

——. "Infirmeries cisterciennes." In *Mélanges* (above), 2:805–25.

——. "Liste des abbayes cisterciennes féminines de France au moyen-âge." In *Mélanges* (above), 2:591–94.

——. "L'Oise cistercienne." In *Mélanges* (above), 2:605–9.

——. *Saint Louis et Cîteaux.* Paris: Letouzey et Ané, 1954.

——. "La Salle des morts de l'abbaye d'Ourscamp." In *Mélanges* (above), 2:835–37.

Dufour, Jean. "Un Acte inédit de Louis VI pour l'abbaye cistercienne de Loroy (1129)." *Bibliothèque de l'Ecole de chartes* 153 (1995): 157–60.

Einbinder, Susan. *Beautiful Death: Jewish Poetry and Martyrdom in Medieval France.* Princeton: Princeton University Press, 2002.

Elliott, Dyan. *Fallen Bodies: Pollution, Sexuality, and Demonology in the Middle Ages.* Philadelphia: University of Pennsylvania Press, 1999.

Farmer, Sharon. *Surviving Poverty in Medieval Paris: Gender, Ideology, and the Daily Lives of the Poor.* Ithaca, NY: Cornell University Press, 2002.

Favier, Jean. *Un Conseiller de Philippe le Bel: Enguerran de Marigny.* Paris: Presses Universitaires de France, 1963.

——. *Philippe le Bel.* Rev. ed. Paris: Fayard, 1998.

Fenster, Thelma, and Daniel Smail, eds. *Fama: The Politics of Talk and Reputation in Medieval Europe.* Ithaca, NY, and London: Cornell University Press, 2003.

Flammermont, Jules. "Recherches sur les sources de l'histoire de l'abbaye de Chaalis." *Comptes rendus et Mémoires du Comité Archéologique de Senlis*, 2nd ser., 2 (1876): 35–38.

Fontaine, Georges. *Pontigny: Abbaye cistercienne.* Paris: Ernest Leroux, 1928.

Forey, Alan. *The Fall of the Templars in the Crown of Aragon.* Aldershot, UK: Ashgate, 2001.

——. "The Military Orders, 1120–1312." In *Oxford Illustrated History of the Crusades*, ed. Jonathan Riley-Smith, pp. 184–216. Oxford: Oxford University Press, 1997.

Froehlich, Karlfried. "Saint Peter, Papal Primacy, and the Exegetical Tradition, 1150–1300." In *The Religious Roles of the Papacy: Ideals and Realities, 1150–1300*, ed. Christopher Ryan, pp. 1–44. Toronto: Pontifical Institute of Mediaeval Studies, 1989.

Gams, Pius. *Series episcoporum Ecclesiae Catholicae.* Graz: Akademische Druck- und Verlagsanstalt, 1957.

Georges, Patrice. "L'Exérèse du coeur dans l'embaumement médiéval occidental." *Micrologus* 11 (2003): 279–86.

Giesey, Ralph. *The Juristic Basis of Dynastic Right to the French Throne.* Transactions of the American Philosophical Society, n.s., 51, no. 5. Philadelphia: American Philosophical Society, 1961.

Given, James. *Inquisition and Medieval Society: Power, Discipline, and Resistance in Languedoc.* Ithaca, NY, and London: Cornell University Press, 1997.

Glorieux, Palémon. "A propos de 'Vatic. Lat. 1086': Le Personnel enseignant de Paris vers 1311–14." *Recherches de théologie ancienne et médiévale* 5 (1933): 23–39.

Glorieux, Palémon. *Répertoire des maîtres en théologie de Paris au XIIIe siècle.* 2 vols. Paris: J. Vrin, 1933.

Goodrich, Margaret. "The White Ladies of Worcester: Their Place in Contemporary Medieval Life." *Transactions of the Worcestershire Archaeological Society,* 3rd ser., 14 (1994): 129–47.

Gordière, Louis-Alfred. "Chaalis." *Comptes rendus et mémoires du Comité archéologique de Senlis,* 2nd ser., 8 (1882–1883): 109–38.

Hanawalt, Barbara. "Whose Story Was This? Rape Narratives in Medieval English Courts." In *"Of Good and Ill Repute": Gender and Social Control in Medieval England,* pp. 124–41. New York and Oxford: Oxford University Press, 1998.

Heft, James. *John XXII and Papal Teaching Authority.* Lewiston, ME: Edwin Mellen Press, 1986.

Hood, John. *Aquinas and the Jews.* Philadelphia: University of Pennsylvania Press, 1995.

Hubert, Etienne, "Rome au XIVe siècle: Population et espace urbain." *Médiévales* 40 (2001): 43–52.

Inventaire-Sommaire des Archives Départementales antérieurs à 1790: Yonne, archives ecclésiastiques, série G. Ed. Mathieu-Maximilien Quantin. Auxerre: Albert Gallot, 1873.

——. *Yonne, archives ecclésiastiques, série H,* 3, pt. 2. Ed. Mathieu-Maximilien Quantin. Auxerre: Albert Gallot, 1888.

——. *Yonne, archives hospitalières, série H, supplément,* 4. Auxerre: Albert Gallot, 1897.

Inventaire-Sommaire des Archives de l'Hôpital de Sens (Yonne) antérieurs à 1790, série H, supplement, 5. Ed. Francis Molard and others. N.p.: N.d.

Jeanne, Damien. "La Société rurale face à la lèpre à travers le registre de l'Officialité de Cerisy de 1314 à 1377." *Annales de Normandie* 43 (1993): 91–106.

Jones, Michael. "The Last Capetians and Early Valois Kings, 1314–1364." In *The New Cambridge Medieval History,* vol. 6, *c. 1300-c.1415,* ed. Michael Jones, pp. 388–421. Cambridge: Cambridge University Press, 2000.

Jordan, William. "Archbishop Eudes Rigaud and the Jews of Normandy, 1248–1275." Forthcoming.

——. "The Capetians from the Death of Philip II to Philip IV." In *The New Cambridge Medieval History,* vol. 5, *c. 1198-c. 1300,* ed. David Abulafia. Cambridge: Cambridge University Press, 1999.

——. "The Cistercian Nunnery of La Cour Notre-Dame de Michery: A House That Failed." *Revue Bénédictine* 95 (1985): 311–20.

——. "Edmund of Abingdon, Saint." In *Dictionary of the Middle Ages: Supplement 1,* ed. William Jordan, pp. 175–76. New York: Charles Scribner's Sons, 2004.

——. *The French Monarchy and the Jews from Philip Augustus to the Last Capetians.* Philadelphia: University of Pennsylvania Press, 1989.

——. *From Servitude to Freedom: Manumission in the Sénonais in the Thirteenth Century.* Philadelphia: University of Pennsylvania Press, 1986.

——. *The Great Famine: Northern Europe in the Early Fourteenth Century.* Princeton: Princeton University Press, 1996.

————. "Home Again: The Jews in the Kingdom of France, 1315–1322." In *The Stranger in Medieval Society*, ed. F.R.P. Akehurst and Stephanie Cain Van D'Elden, pp. 27–45. Minneapolis and London: University of Minnesota Press, 1997.

————. "Jews, Regalian Rights, and the Constitution in Medieval France." *AJS Review* 23 (1998): 1–16.

————. *Louis IX and the Challenge of the Crusade: A Study in Rulership*. Princeton: Princeton University Press, 1979.

————. "Mortmain." In *Dictionary of the Middle Ages*, ed. Joseph Strayer, 8:488–89. 13 vols. New York: Charles Scribner's Sons, 1982–1989.

————. "Princely Identity and the Jews in Medieval France." In *From Witness to Witchcraft: Jews and Judaism in Medieval Christian Thought*, ed. Jeremy Cohen, pp. 257–73. Wiesbaden: Harrassowitz Verlag, 1999.

Keck, David. *Angels and Angelology in the Middle Ages*. New York and Oxford: Oxford University Press, 1998.

Kerov, Vsevolod. *Narodnye vosstaniia i ereticheskie dvizheniia vo Frantsii v kontse XIII–nachale XIV veka*. Moscow: Izdatel'stvo Universitety. Druzhby Narodov, 1986.

Kervyn de Lettenhove, le baron Henri. "Etudes sur l'histoire du XIII siècle: Recherches sur la part que l'Ordre de Cîteaux et le comte de Flandre prirent à la lutte de Boniface VIII et de Philippe le Bel." *Mémoires de l'Académie royale de Bruxelles* 27 (1853). Reprinted in *Patrologiae cursus completus, series latina*, comp. Jacques-Paul Migne, vol. 185, cols. 1833–1920. 217 vols. Paris: 1844–1864.

Kinder, Terryl. *Cistercian Europe: Architecture of Contemplation*. Grand Rapids, MI, and Cambridge: William B. Eerdman's, 2002.

————. "Toward Dating Construction of the Abbey Church of Pontigny." *Journal of the British Archaeological Association* 145 (1992): 79–88.

King, Peter. *The Finances of the Cistercian Order in the Fourteenth Century*. Kalamazoo, MI: Cistercian Publications, 1985.

Klaniczay, Gabor. *Holy Rulers and Blessed Princesses: Dynastic Cults in Medieval Central Europe*. Trans. Éva Pálma. Cambridge: Cambridge University Press, 2002.

Klepper, Deeana. "Jewish Expulsion and Jewish Exile in Scholastic Thought." Paper presented at the International Medieval Congress, Leeds, July 2002.

Kusman, David. "Jean de Mirabello dit van Haelen (ca. 1280–1333): Haute finance et Lombards en Brabant dans le premier tiers du XIVe siècle." *Revue belge de philologie et d'histoire* 77 (1999): 843–931.

LaCorte, Daniel. "Pope Innocent IV's Role in the Establishment and Early Success of the College of Saint Bernard in Paris." *Cîteaux* 46 (1995): 289–304.

Lajard, Félix. "Gilles de Rome: Religieux augustin, théologien." *Histoire littéraire de la France* 30 (1888): 421–566.

Lalou, Elisabeth. "Les Assemblées générales sous Philippe le Bel." In *Actes du 110e Congrès national des sociétés savantes: Histoire médiévale et philologie*, pp. 7–29. 1985.

Lambert, Eugène. "Histoire de l'abbaye de Quincy." *Annuaire statistique du département de l'Yonne* 27 (1863): sec. 3, pp. 189–224.

Lambert, Malcolm. *Medieval Heresy: Popular Movements from Bogomil to Hus.* New York: Holmes and Meier, 1976.

Langlois, Charles-Victor. "Marguerite Porete." *Revue Historique* 54 (1894): 295–99.

Lawrence, Clifford. *The Friars: The Impact of the Early Mendicant Movement on Western Society.* London and New York: Longman, 1994.

———. *Medieval Monasticism: Forms of Religious Life in Western Europe in the Middle Ages.* London and New York: Longman, 1984.

Lea, H. C. *History of the Inquisition of the Middle Ages.* 3 vols. New York: Harper and Brothers, 1888.

Lebeuf, Jean. *Mémoires concernant l'histoire civile et ecclésiastique d'Auxerre et de son ancien diocèse.* Rev. ed. 4 vols. Auxerre and Paris: Perriquet, 1848–1855.

Le Goff, Jacques. *Saint Louis.* Paris: Gallimard, 1996.

Lehugeur, Paul. *Histoire de Philippe le Long, roi de France (1316–1322).* Paris: Hachette, 1897.

Lekai, Louis. *The Cistercians: Ideals and Reality.* Kent, OH: Kent State University Press, 1977.

Lerner, Robert. "An 'Angel of Philadelphia' in the Reign of Philip the Fair: The Case of Guiard de Cressonessart." In *Order and Innovation in the Middle Ages: Essays in Honor of Joseph R. Strayer,* ed. William Jordan, Bruce McNab, and Teofilo Ruiz, pp. 343–64, 529–40. Princeton: Princeton University Press, 1976.

Lesne, Emile. *Les Ecoles de la fin du VIIIe siècle à la fin du XIIe siècle.* Lille: Facultés Catholiques, 1940.

Lewry, P. Osmund. "Papal Ideals and the University of Paris, 1170–1303." In *The Religious Roles of the Papacy: Ideals and Realities, 1150–1300,* ed. Christopher Ryan, pp. 363–88. Toronto: Pontifical Institute of Mediaeval Studies, 1989.

Lizerand, Georges. *Clément V et Philippe le Bel.* Paris: Librairie Hachette, 1911.

Longpérier, A. de. "Crosses de bronze doré de l'Abbaye de Chaalis." In *Oeuvres de A. de Longpérier,* ed. G. Schlumberger, 5:259–60. 7 vols. Paris: Ernest Leroux, 1883–1886.

Mahn, Jean-Berthold. *L'Ordre cistercien et son gouvernement des origins au milieu du XIIIe siècle (1098–1265).* Paris: E. de Bocard, 1945.

———. *Le Pape Benoît XII et les Cisterciens.* Paris: Edouard Champion, 1949.

Malaxecheverria, Ignacio. "Castor et lynx médiévaux." *Florilegium* 3 (1981): 228–38.

Marchandisse, Alain. "Entre defiance et amitié . . .: Des Relations politiques, diplomatiques et militaires tourmentées entre le roi de France et le prince-évêque de Liège au bas moyen âge (XIIIe–XVe s.)." *Académie Royale de Belgique: Bulletin de la Commission Royale d'Histoire* 164 (1998): 31–127.

Marmursztejn, Elsa. "Du Récit exemplaire au *casus* universitaire: Une Variation théologique sur le thème de la profanation d'hosties par les juifs (1290)." *Médiévales* 41 (2001): 37–64.

Marsy, Arthur, comte de. "Les Droits d l'abbaye de Chaalis dans la ville de Compiègne." *Comptes rendus et Mémoires du Comité archéologique de Senlis,* 2nd ser., 5 (1879): 13–16.

Martin, Hervé. *Mentalités médiévales XIe–XVe siècle.* Paris: Presses Universitaires de France, 1996.

Mate, Mavis. "Coping with Inflation: A Fourteenth-Century Example." *Journal of Medieval History* 4 (1978): 95–106.

McDonnell, Ernest. *The Beguines and Beghards in Medieval Culture, with Special Emphasis on the Belgian Scene*. New Brunswick, NJ: Rutgers University Press, 1954.

Menache, Sophia. *Clement V.* Cambridge: Cambridge University Press, 1998.

Mentgen, Gerd. *Studien zur Geschichte der Juden im mittelalterlichen Elsass.* Hanover: Verlag Hahnsche Buchhandlung, 1995.

———. "Die Vertreibungen der Juden aus England und Frankreich im Mittelalter." *Aschkenas: Zeitschrift für Geschichte und Kultur der Juden* 7 (1997): 11–53.

Mesle, Emile. *Histoire de Bourges.* Roanne: Edition Horvath, 1983.

Michaud-Quantin, Pierre. "La Politique monétaire royale à la Faculté de Théologie de Paris en 1265." *Le Moyen âge* 17 (1962): 137–51.

Moiset, Charles. "L'Ancienne maladrerie de Saint-Florentin." *Annuaire statistique du département de l'Yonne* 39 (1875): sec. 3, pp. 191–98.

———. "Notice sur l'Hôtel-Dieu de Saint-Florentin." *Annuaire statistique du département de l'Yonne* 42 (1878): sec. 3, pp. 3–10.

Mollat, Guillaume. *Les Papes d'Avignon (1305–1378).* 2nd ed. Paris: Letouzey and Ané, 1965.

Mongitore, Antonio. *Bibliotheca Sicula sive de scriptoribus siculis.* 2 vols. Palermo: Typographia Didaci Bua, 1708–1714.

Monmerqué, Louis. *Dissertation historique sur Jean Ier, roi de France et de Navarre.* Paris: Chez Tabary, 1844.

Moreau, Henri. "L'Abbaye Saint-Marien d'Auxerre." *Bulletin de la Société des Sciences Historiques et Naturelles de l'Yonne* 115 (1983): 121–41.

Mowbray, Malcolm de. "1277 and All That—Students and Disputations." *Traditio* 57 (2002): 217–38.

Müller, Eugène. *Analyse du cartulaire, des statuts, etc. de Notre-Dame de Senlis, 1041–1395.* Senlis: Imprimerie Eugène Dufresne, n.d.

———. *Senlis et ses environs.* Senlis: Th. Nouvian, 1896.

———. "Vingt-Neuf chartes originales concernant l'abbaye de Chaalis de 1155 à 1299." *Comptes-rendus et mémoires du Comité archéologique de Senlis*, 3rd ser., 6 (1891): 25–48.

Müller, Ewald. *Das Konzil von Vienne, 1311–1312: Seine Quellen und seine Geschichte.* Münster: Aschendorffsche Verlagsbuchhandlung, 1934.

Mundill, Robin. *England's Jewish Solution: Experiment and Expulsion, 1262–1290.* Cambridge: Cambridge University Press, 1998.

Nimmo, Duncan. *Reform and Division in the Medieval Franciscan Order: From Saint Francis to the Foundation of the Capuchins.* Rome: Capuchin Historical Institute, 1987.

Nirenberg, David. *Communities of Violence: Persecution of Minorities in the Middle Ages.* Princeton: Princeton University Press, 1996.

Obert-Piketty, Caroline. "La Promotion des études chez les cisterciens à travers le recrutement des étudiants du Collège Saint-Bernard de Paris au moyen âge." *Cîteaux* 39 (1988): 65–78.

Omont, Henri. "Recherches sur la bibliothèque de l'église cathédrale de Beauvais." *Mémoires de l'Institut National de France, Académie des Inscriptions et Belles-Lettres* 40 (1916): 1–93.

Oudin, Casimir. *Commentarius de scriptoribus ecclesiae antiquis.* Vol. 3. Frankfurt am Main: Weidmann, 1722.

Pegg, Mark. *The Corruption of Angels: The Great Inquisition of 1245–1246.* Princeton: Princeton University Press, 2001.

Pelikan, Jaroslav. *The Christian Tradition: A History of the Development of Doctrine.* Vol. 3, *The Growth of Medieval Theology (600–1300).* Chicago and London: University of Chicago Press, 1978.

Peyrafort-Huin, Monique. *La Bibliothèque médiévale de l'abbaye de Pontigny (XIIe–XIXe siècles): Histoire, inventaires anciens, manuscrits.* Paris: CNRS Editions, 2001.

Pour une histoire monumentale de l'abbaye de Cîteaux, 1098–1998. Ed. Martine Plouvier and Alain Saint-Denis. Vitreux: Revue Cîteaux, 1998.

Principe, Walter. "Monastic, Episcopal and Apologetic Theology of the Papacy, 1150–1250." In *The Religious Roles of the Papacy: Ideals and Realities, 1150–1300,* ed. Christopher Ryan, pp. 117–70. Toronto: Pontifical Institute of Mediaeval Studies, 1989.

———. "The School Theologians' Views of the Papacy, 1150–1250." In *Religious Roles* (above), pp. 45–116.

"Rapport de M. Desjardins sur une communication de M. Müller." *Bulletin historique et philologique,* 1891, pp. 38–39.

Rashdall, Hastings. *Medieval Universities.* Ed. Frederick Powicke and Alfred Emden. 3 vols. Oxford: Oxford University Press, 1936.

Redoutey, Jean-Pierre. "Note sur l'insertion de l'abbaye de Bellevaux dans la vie économique aux XIIe et XIIIe siècles." In *Mélanges à la mémoire du père Anselme Dimier.* 4:729–43. 6 vols. Arbois: Benoît Chauvin/Pupillin, 1982–1987.

Ribbe, Wolfgang. "Die Wirtschaftstätigkeit der Zisterzienser im Mittelalter: Agrarwirtschaft." In *Die Zisterzienser: Ordensleben zwischen Ideal und Wirklichkeit,* pp. 203–15. Cologne: Rheinland-Verlag, 1981.

Rivière, Jean. *Le Problème de l'église et de l'état au temps de Philippe le Bel: Etudes de théologie positive.* Paris and Louvain: Honoré Champion, etc., 1926.

Rouse, Richard, and Mary Rouse. "Publishing Watriquet's *Dits.*" *Viator* 32 (2001): 127–55.

Rubin, Miri. *Gentile Tales: The Narrative Assault on Late Medieval Jews.* New Haven, CT, and London: Yale University Press, 1999.

Saporta, José, and Bessel van der Kolk. "Psychological Consequences of Severe Trauma." In *Torture and Its Consequences: Current Treatment Approaches,* ed. Metin Başoğlu, pp. 151–81. Cambridge: Cambridge University Press, 1992.

Schimmelpfennig, Bernhard. "Zisterzienser, Papsttum und Episkopat im Mittelalter." In *Die Zisterzienser: Ordensleben zwischen Ideal und Wirklichkeit,* pp. 69–85. Cologne: Rheinland-Verlag, 1981.

Schmidt, Tilmann. *Der Bonifaz-Prozess: Verfahren der Papstanklage in der Zeit Bonifaz' VIII. Und Clemens' V.* Cologne and Vienna: Böhlau Verlag, 1989.

Scholz, Richard. *Die Publizistik zur Zeit Philipps des Schönen und Bonifaz' VIII.* Stuttgart: Ferdinand Enke, 1903.

Schulte, Johann von. *Die Geschichte der Quellen und Literatur des canonischen Rechts von Gratian bis auf die Gegenwart.* Vol. 2. Stuttgart: F. Enke, 1877.

Scordia, Lydwine. "Images de la servitude fiscale à la fin du moyen âge." *Mélanges de l'Ecole française de Rome: Moyen Age* 112 (2000): 609–31.

Shatzmiller, Joseph. *Shylock Reconsidered: Jews, Moneylending, and Medieval Society.* Berkeley and Los Angeles: University of California Press, 1990.

Spufford, Peter. "Monetary Practice and Monetary Theory in Europe (12th–15th Centuries)." In *Moneda y monedas en la Europa medieval (siglos XII–XV)*, pp. 53–86. Pamplona: Gobierno de Navarra, Departamento de Educación y Cultura, 2000.

Steadman's Medical Dictionary. 24th ed. Baltimore and London: Williams and Wilkins, 1982.

Stickel, Erwin. *Der Fall von Akkon: Untersuchungen zum Abklingen des Kreuzzugsgedankens am Ende des 13. Jahrhunderts.* Bern: Herbert Lang, 1975.

Strayer, Joseph. "The Costs and Profits of War: The Anglo-French Conflict of 1294–1303." In *The Medieval City*, ed. Harry Miskimin et al. New Haven: Yale University Press, 1977.

———. "The Crusade against Aragon." *Speculum* 28 (1953): 102–13.

———. *The Reign of Philip the Fair.* Princeton: Princeton University Press, 1980.

Thier, Ludger. *Kreuzzugsbemühungen unter Papst Clemens V (1305–1314).* Werl: Dietrich-Coelde-Verlag, 1973.

Thijssen, Johannes. *Censure and Heresy at the University of Paris, 1200–1400.* Philadelphia: University of Pennsylvania Press, 1998.

Tierney, Brian, and Sidney Painter. *Western Europe in the Middle Ages, 300–1475.* 3rd ed. New York: Alfred A. Knopf, 1978.

Töpfer, Bernhard. *Das kommende Reich des Friedens: Zur Entwicklung chiliastischer Zukunftshoffnungen im Hochmittelalter.* Berlin: Akademie-Verlag, 1964.

Tyerman, Christopher. "Philip V of France, the Assemblies of 1319–20 and the Crusade." *Bulletin of the Institute of Historical Research* 57 (1984): 15–34.

Valois, Noël. "Jacques de Thérines, Cistercien." *Histoire littéraire de la France* 34 (1914): 179–219.

———. "Jacques Duèse, pape sous le nom de Jean XXII." *Histoire littéraire de la France* 34 (1914): 391–630.

Verdeyen, Paul. "Le Procès d'Inquisition contre Marguerite Porete et Guiard de Cressonessart (1309–1310)." *Revue d'histoire ecclésiastique* 81 (1986): 47–94.

Visch, Carolus (= Charles or Karl) de. *Bibliotheca scriptorum sacri ordinis cisterciensis.* Cologne: Ioannes Busaeus, 1656.

Wood, Charles. "Queens, Queans, and Kingship: An Inquiry into Theories of Royal Legitimacy in Late Medieval England and France." In *Order and Innovation in the Middle Ages: Essays in Honor of Joseph R. Strayer*, ed. William Jordan, Bruce McNab, and Teofilo Ruiz, pp. 385–400, 562–66. Princeton: Princeton University Press, 1976.

———. "Where Is John the Posthumous? Mahaut of Artois Settles Her Royal Debts." In *Documenting the Past: Essays in Medieval History Presented to George Peddy Cuttino*, ed. Jeffrey Hamilton and Patricia Bradley, pp. 99–117. Wolfeboro, NH: Boydell Press, 1989.

INDEX